D0977129

PRAISE FOR

DO BETTER

"*Do Better* is a clear, powerful, direct, wise, and extremely helpful treatise on how to combat and heal from the ubiquitous violence of white supremacy. Using a voice that is both passionate and compassionate, Rachel Ricketts instructs where necessary and soothes when needed—but never flinches from the urgency of the mission at hand. These pages are meant not merely to be read, but to be studied, workshopped, and put into daily practice. I would recommend *Do Better* to anybody who wishes to live a life of higher consciousness and humanity. She has offered up an exceedingly valuable resource to a tired, troubled (and all too often delusional) world. This is a book we all need."

—Elizabeth Gilbert, *New York Times* bestselling author of *Eat Pray Love*

"Holy Healing! What Rachel Ricketts offers the world in *Do Better* is a healing balm for a society that has long needed a new perspective and approach to an ancient problem that has been ignored, denied, unaddressed, and unhealed. *Do Better* answers prayers that many have prayed. *Do Better* offers a bold possibility for change and healing. *Do Better* offers a deeply sacred choice that we must all make at such a time as this."

—Iyanla Vanzant, *New York Times* bestselling author and host of *Iyanla, Fix My Life*

"Through love, rage, and humor, Rachel Ricketts both challenges and inspires us all (but especially us white cis women) to turn anti-racist work into a daily practice; to sit in the discomfort of the violence we have perpetrated, and turn that discomfort into action. This book is absolutely essential reading."

—Zoe Lister-Jones, actress, producer, and director

"Rachel's book is a powerful and beautiful example of sharing herself from a deeply heart-centered place. . . . If you, like me, are ready to stop talking and start listening and really take the time to understand, this is the book you MUST read. Thank you Rachel for taking the time to write this incredible book. It was life changing to read."

—Rumer Willis, actress and singer

"*Do Better* is a much-needed addition to any spiritual person's anti-racism toolkit. This book not only opens the door to anti-racism work, but gives you the tools to walk through it. Rachel has created an engaging, inspiring, and practical resource that you will return to time and again."

—Jessica Lanyadoo, host of *Ghost of a Podcast* and author of *Astrology for Real Relationships*

"This is the book we've been waiting for. Wow . . . This is the book that will change lives, if you allow it. A must read and do!"

—Monique Melton, anti-racism educator

DO BETTER

SPIRITUAL ACTIVISM
for Fighting and Healing from
WHITE SUPREMACY

RACHEL RICKETTS

ATRIA BOOKS

NEW YORK LONDON TORONTO SYDNEY NEW DELHI

ATRIA BOOKS

An Imprint of Simon & Schuster, Inc.
1230 Avenue of the Americas
New York, NY 10020

First Atria Books hardcover edition February 2021

ATRIA BOOKS and colophon are trademarks of Simon & Schuster, Inc.

For information about special discounts for bulk purchases, please contact Simon & Schuster Special Sales at 1-866-506-1949 or business@simonandschuster.com.

The Simon & Schuster Speakers Bureau can bring authors to your live event. For more information or to book an event, contact the Simon & Schuster Speakers Bureau at 1-866-248-3049 or visit our website at www.simonspeakers.com.

Interior design by Suet Chong

Manufactured in the United States of America

1 3 5 7 9 10 8 6 4 2

Library of Congress Cataloging-in-Publication Data has been applied for.
ISBN 978-1-9821-5127-0
ISBN 978-1-9821-5129-4 (ebook)

This is for my mother, Suzette,
and Uncle Carlton.

For my ancestors,
who so often went unheard with hearts unhealed.

And for every Black girl+
who has ever felt they didn't belong.

May we all find freedom.

CONTENTS

PART II:
RING THE ALARM

My Love Includes Anger

> What I hope to do all the time is to be so
> completely myself... that my audiences
> and even people who meet me are
> confronted... with what I am inside and
> out, as honest as I can be. And this way they
> have to see things about themselves...
>
> —NINA SIMONE

We are living in entirely uncertain times. Our politics are increasingly divided with no reassuring route for recourse. As I write this the world is in a standstill to combat the worst global pandemic since 1918. Cities are on fire in all fifty states and folx of all races have taken to the streets around the globe in an uprising led by Black folx in the quest for Black, and thus collective, liberation. The systems of inequity that have persisted and been protected for centuries are being exacerbated, and the stillness forced by global quarantine has meant many are no longer able to turn away. White people have finally awakened to white supremacy and anti-Blackness in a way they refused to before. The things many of you were privileged enough to once take for granted are slipping from your fingers and shit is scary. Our personal and collective grief is palpable. Things are and will continue to be chaotic, and increasingly so. But amidst all this chaos and uncertainty is an opportunity. The oppressive systems and institutions as we once knew them are slowly beginning to crumble. Everything is being burned to the ground so that we as a collective can rise renewed. We are being summoned to the inner, spiritual work that revolution requires. Some are calling it the end of everything that never worked right in the first place—and it is. Though these systems were created to work exactly as designed, because they benefit their creators. Those with the most power and privilege. To overthrow them we must all take a long look in the mirror to deal with the hard shit. And this is a book *all* about the hard shit! White supremacy, heteropatriarchy, grief, oppression, and more. This is also a book about my inter-actions with the hard shit. I write what I know best, which is my experience—both personal and professional in equal measure.

My name is Rachel Ricketts (hayyy!), and my pronouns are she/her/hers. I am a Black, queer, cisgender, non-disabled, neu-rotypical, Canadian-born woman with ancestors of West Afri-can, Jamaican, Indian, Jewish, Portuguese, western European, and Taíno descent. I grew up Black and financially insecure in mostly white and wealthy spaces, and have spent a lifetime navigating intersecting systems of oppression. Though I am a trained racial justice educator, attorney, grief coach, and spiritual activist by profession, this work is personal. Because the most grief I have ever endured, and will continue to, is at the hands of white supremacy. This grief has rooted within me an overflowing reservoir of love and gratitude as well as an unwavering fire of righteous rage deep inside my bones and belly. Love *and* anger.

With good damn reason: white supremacy murdered my mother. It was after my mother's death that I rededicated my life to the work of fighting racial injustice. In her honor and mine.

Though I was born with my third eye open, my deep connection to Spirit intensified after helping my mother die, equipping me with the tools to help heal my heart and hold space for others to do the same. It led me to create my Spiritual Activism workshops—potent racial justice seminars that fuse spiritual-based soulcare with embodied anti-racism education so we can learn to tolerate the challenging emotions that arise when we address oppression. This book is an extension of my workshops blending my lifetime of personal experience navigating white supremacy with my soulful anti-racist teachings to create an accessible and relatable guide for all those ready to fight for a more equitable world in which everyone, most notably Black and Indigenous women+, can finally find freedom.

WHITE SUPREMACY HARMS US ALL

White supremacy is the status quo. It causes one of the greatest forms of systemic social trauma on the planet, inciting grief, guilt, loss, pain, anger, and shame. For everyone. Racism mires BI&PoC in emotional and physical violence, and, in order to perpetuate the oppression of others deemed "less than," it robs white folx of inner peace and meaningful connection to themselves and others.

For my fellow folx of the global majority, including the mixed-race folx and especially my fellow Black and Indigenous women+, addressing our internalized oppression is where we most get stuck. We've endured centuries of institutionalized discrimination. Of shittier housing, education, pay, job opportunities, health care, access to justice, etc., not to mention slavery, dehumxnization, intergenerational trauma, emotional violence, and constant reminders that we're "less than" because we don't belong to whiteness. We keep quiet and code switch in order to keep white people comfortable at the expense of our own well-being. Our anti-racist work is unplugging from whiteness and reclaiming *our* power.

For my white or white-passing friends, internalizing dominance and privilege results in a disconnection between head and heart. White supremacy requires you to cut yourself off from meaningful connection with yourself and others. The most pertinent thing you all can do to dismantle racist systems is first address your own personal racism (not just the racism "out there"), the ways you inherently perpetuate white supremacy, and the grief, loss, pain, and trauma that are creating obstacles for you to authentically do so. No small feat because, as we'll learn, when you start to become truthfully aware of who you are and the harms you've caused, your world turns upside down.

For mixed BI&PoC with white ancestry, you will likely find that your work is to address both your internalized oppression as well as your internalized dominance.

No matter your race, ethnicity, or mixture, racial justice begins with a sobering soak in your own reflection and all that lies beneath. To awaken to the ways in which white supremacy is playing out in your day-to-day, the ways you contribute to its prevalence, and the hurt it is causing us all. Here's the tea— racial justice starts with *you* and it starts *within*. There can be no genuine outer shift unless we get right with ourselves *first*—and racial justice requires a major collective upheaval. It necessitates an overhaul of every system we have ever known the world over. This is why I need you to tap into your heart space, connect to your righteous rage, and use it as fuel for systemic and collective change.

I wrote this for every hue-mxn ready, able, and willing to do the hard, vital, and urgent inner work required to dismantle white supremacy. So let me be clear, this ain't no cakewalk. Real talk. Learning about white supremacy and doing anti-racist work is *work*. This is not for those wishing to merely dip their toe. Oh no. Unpacking racism, oppression, and their impact is often triggering on a mental, spiritual, emotional, and at times physical level. Many elements of my story and teachings may flare up painful memories or traumas of your own. I cried a lot of tears writing this, and you are likely to shed tears reading it. Diving in takes courage, bravery, and resilience. You must acclimate your body to better withstand your discomfort and shower yourself in compassion so you have a hope in hell of bestowing that same compassion on others—particularly Black and Indigenous women+. When we come together to face oppression, we unearth potent personal and collective trauma. Moving through this book will be no different. It will expose your hurt, but my wish is that it will also inspire your hope. I am here to help you through and I do so from a space of deep love. For us all. Still, make no mistake—this is not a fluffy "love will change the world" manifesto. Love can change the world, but it is not a "send light and prayers" kinda love. The love needed to create radical racial justice includes daily, intentional, and informed action. On a global scale. It includes owning up to the emotional violence we have perpetuated on ourselves and others, both as individuals and as part of the collective, and most notably toward Black and Indigenous women+. It is a love embodied by truth and integrity. It runs the full spectrum of humxn emotions, including anger. Righteous rage has been a vital component in efforts to do better past and present. The collective shift racial justice demands requires this same fervor. I believe love and righteous anger are the precursors to the critical shift we desperately need to manifest in the world today. To doing better. Some call me the General of Loving Anger—you'll soon find out why!

I share my stories not to condemn the mistakes of others but to illuminate the ways we cause each other harm, often to those most oppressed. Harms that I too have inflicted as a perfectly imperfect person and oppressed oppressor. In these pages you will find carefully curated exercises to get into your body and enable you to better withstand the discomfort that inevitably arises as you partake in racial justice. I believe getting more comfortable with our discomfort first is the gateway to our collective salvation, to racial and social justice. It starts with compassionately connecting to yourself and filling up your soul so you can truly do the work and commit to collective change. A car can't drive on empty, am I right? Every chapter ends with a spiritual offering to tend to your soul and/or a tangible call to action to support you in tending to your heart and better holding space for yourself and the collective, all while prioritizing the most marginalized. From guided meditations and breathwork to reflection and visual exercises, you'll be armed with spiritual tools I've used time and again to support folx face their fears, confront challenges, and heal racial wounds. All of which is done in a culturally informed way, honoring the roots of the practices and the communities of color that cultivated them. Mindfulness and breathwork will serve as the pillars for returning to ourselves, navigating our discomfort, and actively doing better.

Part I takes you on a deep dive within to understand and address oppression at the inner level, and in Part II, I share more of my story enduring white supremacy and guidance for taking much-needed outer action. My goal is for you to finish the last page feeling enlightened, empowered, and ready to *act*. We need you. Especially the white folx because y'all. Are. *Late.*

WRITTEN TO, NOT FOR

Though this book is meant to inspire healing and change for all humxns, this book is directed primarily to, though not *for*, white women+. I did not want to write a book to white women+ (truly!), but white women+ have caused me the most racial harm so I feel compelled to address my first book to them directly. Especially cis women. Still, this book is for errybody. Every-body. I write for Black and Indigenous women+ first and foremost. Every facet of my work is for us and our healing. This book is written *to* white women+, but it is *for* us. Our well-being, our humxnity, and our liberation.

We are at a pivotal crossroads as a collective, one that has not been experienced since the civil rights movement of the 1960s. This is a global uprising. How we choose to harness the energy of the day—or not—will have lasting consequences on folx of all identities, worldwide, for centuries, perhaps lifetimes, to come. Especially in America. Though I am Canadian by birth, most of my immediate family lives in the United States. My grandfather was an indentured laborer in the States, and the impact of the violence he endured on American soil reverberates through my family's very being—and mine. I write about American issues as a foreigner, but a foreigner with blood, skin, and sinew at stake.

Around the world whiteness and white supremacy in all its forms cause BI&PoC harm every single day. Every hour. Every minute. Every second people are being hurt because of systems created by and for whiteness and the tangible, violent consequences of white supremacist ideology. And it is my duty, as assigned by Spirit, to help create a world where BI&PoC, being people of the global majority, and specifically Black and Indigenous women+, are no longer subjected to the racist, misogynist harms that I and so many others continue to endure. This is why I write, and the purpose of this book. Not to implore white people to recognize my or any other BI&PoC's humxnity, because I refuse and would die in vain waiting. But rather to illustrate the impact of their choices on us all. To examine why white and white-passing people have *chosen* to perpetuate white supremacy and ignore its impact, and thus *their* impact, on BI&PoC in the first place. Uncovering such choices is a critical part of how the hell we all get free. This is a good time to point out to the white folx reading that you're not going to like a lot of what I have to say. Not one bit. Your ego and white privilege will seethe. You'll be inclined to label me angry—classic!—and wonder who the fuck I think I am to speak to you this way (I am my ancestors' living legacy, for the record). You may feel I'm ruthless for spelling this out so publicly and unabashedly. It's all status quo, so if you feel you need to stay there, by all means—do you. But for those of y'all who truly give a shit, I hope this will give you pause and help you become empowered to show up for myself and other Black and Indigenous women+ in an authentic, active, and sustainable way.

> > < <

By virtue of being oppressed themselves, white women+ have a deeper capacity to understand and empathize with the oppression faced by BI&PoC. Still, despite having the capacity, white women+, especially cis women, have mostly failed to use it. As oppressed people who oppress people, no one has caused me more harm in my life than white women+. The fragility and victimhood mixed with pervasive bypassing, defense mechanisms, and emotional violence makes for a special sauce of racist venom. And yes, women+ perpetuate patriarchy too. This book in no way lets men+ off the hook—they have a major role to play in all of this without question; but right now, I need to talk to the folx who are most ready to listen, and then I need them to do their damn work and collect their people. I am here to share with white women+ a truth about themselves that is causing everybody, but no one more than queer and trans Black and Indigenous women and femmes, immense pain. Because white women+ don't know what they don't know (or stay refusing to learn).

BI&PoC, and the plethora of races, ethnicities, and experiences contained within and between us, have our work cut out for us as well. We must overcome centuries of systemic oppression, anti-Blackness, and colonization. Myself included. My objective is for BI&PoC to understand our specific roles in racial justice. I want us all to finally feel free, particularly Black and Indigenous women+. There is nowhere in the world where I as a Black woman can truly feel safe, and so until then I must write and I must write my absolute truth.

INVITATION TO BRAVE SPACE

I believe we are all limitless souls having a humxn experience and we all came to Earth at this exact time to learn, unlearn, and, ultimately, heal—ourselves and each other. I believe in the possibility for us to drop the old white supremacist scripts that have been holding us back and disconnecting us from ourselves and one another. And it is because of this belief that we can and must do better that I fight with so much fury. That I invoke Spiritual Activism and loving anger as my means of seeking and effecting change. That I tell it like it is, take no shit, and maintain wise compassion. It is how and why I channel my righteous rage into action and simultaneously recognize all of our struggles and humxnity, especially those who have been the most oppressed. In the quest for racial justice we all have work to do in different ways and to varying degrees. We all have shadows we need to illuminate and absolute truths we need to contend with, no one more than white folx. So, to the white folx joining me, welcome! I'm glad you're here now, but let's make no mistake, you are centuries late. For my fellow BI&PoC, especially Black and Indigenous women+, I acknowledge you, I affirm you, I honor you. Always and all ways.

No matter who you are, my teachings will make you uncomfortable. We spend so much of our lives evading challenging or conflicting emotions. Controversial topics like racial justice are ripe grounds for checking out, but I urge you to resist that temptation. If you want to create a world where all humxns can be free, then I need you to increase your tolerance for the hard shit— hard emotions, hard conversations, hard decisions. No matter how mindful I help you become, this book is not going to solve white supremacy (I wish!). It won't heal internalized oppression or make you an activist or an ally, though it will absolutely aid you in acting in allyship. It is simply a *start*. Even if you're decades in. I am arming you with heart-centered tools to put into your ever-expanding toolkit for doing this work, day in, day out, for the rest of your life. You will be stretched well past your comfort zone. But you'll be left feeling more supported and empowered in your journey to better show up for yourself and the collective in the ongoing war against white supremacy and, most important, in tangibly supporting BI&WoC worldwide. In doing so, you are helping to free the hearts, bodies, and minds of us all.

I'm not here to "tell" you anything but rather help guide you back to a truth you've always known. Back to yourself. Everything you need to do better already exists within you. What you read here will serve as guidance based primarily in my personal and professional experiences. Still, much like you, I am a learner still learning life's lessons. This is not work to get "perfect": I have not and cannot do it perfectly, nor can you. Perfection is an agent of oppression, so let us release ourselves from that expectation. There are undoubtedly elements of this book I'll later learn caused harm. I welcome learning more so I too can do better in the future. I invite you to do the same. You will still fuck up, as will I. You will continue to cause harm, but you will have tools empowering you to engage critically, see beyond the lens of whiteness, and minimize and rectify white supremacist violence from here on out. To continuously do and be better. Not perfect.

You may be scared, you likely have apprehensions, but racial justice requires each and every one of us. Lives and livelihoods are on the line; the earth as we know it is at stake. No matter where you are in your racial justice journey, you will find something here. A learning or unlearning. A sliver of hope and cementing of truth. I have poured my heart out onto the page for you to live and breathe these experiences alongside me. So you can witness me and, in doing so, better witness yourself. This is my personal invitation to a brave space. In the words of justice doula Micky ScottBey Jones, "we all carry scars and we have all caused wounds," so "there is no such thing as a 'safe space.'"[1] But here, as we move through this work together, I invite you to be brave. And vulnerable. To lean into compassion, to stretch past your discomfort, and to prioritize all those rarely prioritized elsewhere.

By guiding you through an internal exploration of your role

in perpetuating white supremacy, anti-Indigeneity, and anti-Blackness, and providing heart-centered tools to support you in moving through the grief that inherently arises as you do so, this book supports BI&WoC in healing from internalized oppression and racial trauma, white women+ in addressing their racism, and *all* women+ in rising up to free themselves and the collective from global systems of oppression.

This is a book to read and reread. To take at your own pace and digest as you need. It is a loving yet challenging call to action. A call to do the deep inner work that precipitates any external or collective shift. An active opportunity for you to acknowledge and accept yourself and your role in perpetuating white supremacy for what it is. An awakening that is urgently needed to unify a divided world and ensure the future of humxnity as a whole.

➢ ➢ ➢ ➢ ➢ ➢

I write this from a deep and profound well of love. For us all. My love includes anger. And this loving anger fuels my resolve for us all to both be and *do better.*

A NOTE FROM ME TO YOU

Any discussion of white supremacy is loaded and rife for mis-understanding, which is #notawesome, so before we dive in I hope to make clear a few key points unpacking my approach and perspective:

#1—There is a glossary of terms at the back of the book that I highly suggest acquainting yourself with now. Language is constantly (and quickly) evolving, so you may find some words or acronyms a bit overwhelming at first. That's okay! From here on out I've put an asterisk (*) next to each word from the glossary the first time it appears in the text to help you get better acquainted. Either way, when you come across something you don't understand, chances are it's in the glossary, but please do research them further on your own as well. The intention is always to foster your own critical engagement as you read, learn, and unlearn.

#2—I use the term "Spirit" throughout the book, which is interchangeable with Higher Power, Universe, Source, Sacred, and the Divine—though there are many other names. What I am referring to is the existence of and connection to something bigger than ourselves to which we all belong. There are folx* who call it God or Allah, some Indigenous tribes who call it the Great Mystery, others who prefer not to name it at all. I encourage you to insert whatever word best aligns for you.

#3—For the sake of clarity and space, I often use the umbrella term "Black, Indigenous, and people of color" (BI&PoC*) to refer to the diverse group of humxns* oppressed by white supremacy* as a result of being racialized as non-white (including multiracial folx). BI&PoC do not experience racism* identically or uniformly, particularly Black and Indigenous folx, which is why they are separately identified from PoC*. Still, I believe that BI&PoC can have sufficiently common experiences such that we resonate with the overarching oppression* caused by white supremacy, so long as we also acknowledge the key differences between our racialized experiences. I have referred to specific racial identities where it made sense to do so.

#4—I use African American Vernacular English (AAVE)* throughout the book (because, well, I'm Black!), and I honor and acknowledge the Black American, predominantly queer* and transgender*, communities that created it. My use of AAVE is not license for *any* non-Black person to do so and I implore you not to, as explained in the glossary and Chapter 10.

#5—I've done my best to use inclusive language as I understand it at the time of publication, though all words are subject to questioning in terms of their inclusivity and who finds them inclusive. For the sake of brevity I have used "women+"* to connote all women, whether cis* or trans, as well as femmes*, femme-passing folx, and those of any gender identity* who face misogyny like women with an understanding that these identities are in no way binary (peep the glossary for the full definition and the corresponding definition for men+*). I've used specific gender identities when referring to some but not all (i.e., women, femmes, etc.). Lastly, when I refer to "man," "woman," "male," or "female," I do so with the understanding that both sex* and gender identity are social constructs. We'll get into all this soon!

#6—I cannot and will not speak for all Black people (because we're not a monolith), nor will I hold myself to that standard. Neither should you.

#7—White supremacy is complex, entailing multiple forms of oppression. It is first and foremost a form of racial oppression including anti-Blackness* and anti-Indigeneity, but it also includes heteropatriarchy*, homophobia, transphobia, classism*, ableism*, ageism, fatphobia*, xenophobia, anti-Semitism, and all forms of oppression. As such, I believe racial justice* includes ending *all* forms of oppression. BI&PoC include all ages, abilities, ethnicities, classes, sizes, religions, cultures, etc., so we cannot advocate for the freedom of some without advocating for the freedom of all. Instead of naming each of these forms of oppression separately, they are included within my references to white supremacy, though, for clarity, I've made explicit references in some cases.

#8—I believe Black and Indigenous liberation is the key to collective freedom. My intention is to call out* harms against *all* BI&PoC of all identities, but I will focus on those *most* oppressed. Prioritizing Black, Indigenous, queer, trans, disabled*, fat*, poor*, dark-skinned, non-English-speaking, immigrant, elder, etc. women+ (i.e., those living at the most oppressed intersectional identities) is how we can best help create freedom for us all. We are certainly having separate experiences, but we are not actually separate.

Let's dive in!

PART ONE

GOIN' IN FOR DA WIN

Love and Justice are not two.
Without inner change, there can be
no outer change. Without collective
change, no change matters.

—REVEREND ANGEL KYODO WILLIAMS SENSEI

Getting Intentional

Before getting into this critical work, it is imperative to get clear on why you are here. This helps you to check if you're showing up for authentic reasons and serves as an anchor you can return to whenever shit gets hard (and trust me, it will!).

Read the affirmation below, and when you're ready, write or otherwise record your answer as a stream of consciousness.

Note whatever comes and then review, revise, and cut down as necessary until you have a clear, concise statement that you can return to as you move through this work.

I AM READY TO LEARN ABOUT SPIRITUAL ACTIVISM*, FIGHT WHITE SUPREMACY, AND DO BETTER BECAUSE:

_____

_____

_____

_____

_____.

> > > > > >

ONE

Me, Myself & I

I'm going to tell it like it is.
I hope you can take it like it is.

—MALCOLM X

For most of my life my biggest fear about addressing white supremacy was being rejected and abandoned for naming the realities of my oppressed experience as a queer Black woman, which has come to fruition more times than I care to recall. I have personally spent a lifetime feeling alone and misunderstood. I struggle to find places that accept me as my whole Black womanly self and people willing to listen and engage with my truth—one steeped in navigating a white supremacist world as the pervasive "other." From the tender age of four, I was aware of being treated differently due to my Blackness and girlhood. At day care, my white "caretakers" locked me outside in the pouring rain all alone. In kindergarten, my white teacher attempted to hold me back a year (from kindergarten!), explaining to my white-passing* mother, who the teacher erroneously assumed had adopted me, that my Black brain just wasn't as large as my white classmates'.

It was a sentiment derived from her teachers' manual, and in the year 1989 this educator deemed it solid ground from which to assume I lacked the intellect required to, I dunno, play with friends or say my name!? It was fucking despicable. And racist. Luckily, my mother was having none of it, and I was placed in a first-grade class after she threatened to sue the school board. Though I only knew about this incident after my mother shared it with me in adulthood, I distinctly recall knowing that I had to prove my intellect to others from first grade onward. That those around me—be it teachers, administrators, or friends—would assume that I was slow because I was a Black girl. I would look around my mostly white classroom and feel myself caged within four walls void of safe spaces, tangible or otherwise. Nobody looked like me and no one cared to understand me or my experience. I felt entirely alone, like an ugly duckling—deemed visibly undesirable and socially unsavory. Often remaining silent for fear of saying or doing anything to garner my Black body unwanted criticism, I disconnected from myself and my surroundings. Internalizing my heartbreak at being subjected to an onslaught of stereotypes, I vowed to excel and exceed all expectations of me whenever and however I could. I thought I could accomplish my way out of the Black box I had been placed in and became completely committed to controlling the narrative my white community had created for and about me. To try to achieve my way out of a form of discrimination I did not and could not yet grasp was deeply entrenched in the hearts, minds, and institutions of all those in my midst. Needless to say, I was continuously disappointed by the impact of my efforts, and with few resources to make sense of it all at just five years old, I assumed the oppression I faced was of my own making. That I was treated and perceived differently by all those in my community, including people I loved, because *I* was the problem. Growing up in Western Canada also meant being constantly compared with Black Americans. I was referred to as African American by non-Black folx for most of my upbringing—another way of being othered. But the truth is, the only place I felt truly free to be myself was visiting my auntie, uncle, and cousins in Washington State. A mere two-hour drive south presented an alternate universe full of Black love, Black food, and Black pride. I didn't know the extent at the time, but these glimmers of Black American joy were my salvation.

As a Black girl from a financially insecure, single-mom-led home, the culmination of my stereotypical existence with the racist rhetoric of white supremacist status quo* left me feeling incapable, unworthy, and undeserving. My Blackness made whiteness* uncomfortable, and I was treated as the culprit for white folx' discomfort—continuously made to feel too loud, too emotional, too boisterous. I learned to tone myself down. To keep quiet, play it safe, and never, ever speak my truth or prioritize my comfort or well-being above that of my white counterparts. In the rare moments I veered off course I was met with racialized harm in the form of emotional violence*, which rocked me like a kick to the head. Sticks and stones have never broken my bones, but words have really, really hurt me. I shrunk into the sliver of space deemed acceptable for a Black girl+* in a white world. It's a survival skill that stuck with me in all facets of my personal and professional life, and one I continue to process and unlearn three decades later. One of the many privileges afforded to white people by white supremacy is the ability to simply be who they are without preconceived negative stereotypes regarding intellect, ability, class, criminal history, language, origin, or otherwise thrust upon them strictly due to the color of their skin. From as far back as I can remember I have longed to walk into a room and be acknowledged for who, rather than what, I am. To simply be "Rachel" before being "a Black woman." But that is not my reality.

Reflecting on this now fills me with unimaginable anguish. I yearn to reach out to that little girl who felt alienated and isolated for nothing more than breathing while Black and femme. I want to hold her and let her know she is not wrong, but the system sure AF is. I want to shake my white teachers, friends, and friends' parents and demand that they address their misogynoir* and stop causing this Black child so much harm. Mostly, I want to tell my younger self that though she deserves better, this is how white supremacy works. It breaks young BI&WoC* down so early and efficiently that we often spend a lifetime swimming in a cesspool of trauma, self-hate, and internalized oppression*.

The racist assumptions and stereotypes like those I endured from toddlerdom are not abnormal, quite the opposite. They are, as white supremacy is, entirely run of the mill. White supremacy is not merely white men running around in white hoods in the woods. No, it is the air we all breathe, and more of us—more white people in particular—are finally taking note of its stench. It is intentional and, often, unintentional. Individual and collective, permeating every institution the world over, from health and education to military and politics, and the impact begins from youth. The Georgetown Law Center on Poverty and Inequality's 2017 report contains data showing that "adults view Black girls as *less innocent and more adult-like than their white peers*, especially in the age range of 5–14."[1] Black girls receive harsher punishment at school compared with their white peers and are further perceived as needing less nurturing, less protection, less support, and less comforting and as being more independent and knowledgeable of adult topics than white girls of the same age.[2] In sum, Black girls are not viewed as girls by society at all. In Canada, young Indigenous girls are twenty-one times more likely to die by suicide than their white counterparts, with several Indigenous communities declaring states of emergencies as a result of the ongoing suicide epidemic.[3]

Clearly, I'm not alone in enduring the pain of white supremacy from early childhood. Black and Indigenous girls+ are not getting the support they desperately need and deserve, and this is due in part, if not entirely, to systems of colonialism* and patriarchy* that have stripped us of our childhood and deemed us less worthy of care. Millions of melanated girls+ like myself have grown up ostracized and oppressed because of the color of our skin, and millions more still will unless we, as a collective, do something to change the oppressive systems as they currently exist.

The truth is that to be Black or Indigenous and a woman+ is to be in a state of constant grief* and rage. As James Baldwin said, "To be a [Black person] in this country and to be relatively conscious, is to be in a rage almost all the time."[4] Consciously and unconsciously, I'm infuriated over the reduced pay I earn for doing the same work as my male and white women and femme counterparts. I mourn the ability to express myself without being automatically discounted for being angry, to simply have my words received. I am traumatized by the frequent accusation of being overly dramatic when I name misogynoir. I'm enraged by a culture that still purports "all lives matter," and I grieve over the racist shit my well-intentioned white friends spew out all too often. This is not a pity party, for the record, it's just the facts of my life and the lives of so many other Black women+. Facts that are too often dismissed. Stop telling BI&PoC our experience is a damn illusion. It's not.

If I sound angry, rest assured it's because I am. As therapist and healer Dr. Jennifer Mullan stated, "When the exhausted, abused, traumatized, & the exploited are denied access after access; RAGE and all that goes with her energy are acceptable responses."[5] As they say, if you're not angered by the injustices in the world, you're not paying attention. Or perhaps you just don't care. But Black and Indigenous folx, young and old, are dying—emotionally, spiritually, and physically—every single day at the hands of white supremacy and all those perpetuating it. Not caring is a privilege we simply cannot afford.

ALONE ON AN ISLAND . . .

"White people [are] hypocrites. They're barbaric . . ."[6]

My guess is that you may have been met by a host of big emotions as you read that—am I right? I was too. It was August 2017 when I first watched the clip of a young Black man make this statement during a TV interview. I had just returned from a weekend away with my then (mostly white) friends. The same weekend of the now notorious Unite the Right rally in Charlottesville, Virginia. When I reviewed the news coverage of that fateful day, my heart was thrust into a state of all-consuming ache, and as I heard him utter "barbaric," I was met with a wave of wide-sweeping and conflicting emotions. First came affirmation. The Black Lives Matter protester had just called out the same group of people who, over the course of my lifetime and the lifetimes of my ancestors, treated us as less than solely for being Black. And he'd done so on live television. To a white person's face for all to witness. Then came the pang of deep and penetrating grief. Grief and loss from the omnipotent trauma of BI&PoC, specifically Black and Indigenous folx, who have been murdered, lynched, imprisoned, enslaved, assaulted, discriminated against, and spiritually, mentally, emotionally, and physically abused at the hands of white people for centuries. My face felt flush with righteous rage as I reflected on the pervasiveness of the problem. The widely held but frequently disguised racist beliefs held by those with power* and privilege* and their collective unwillingness to do a damn thing to truly change it. The very reason the events of Charlottesville were taking place to begin with. And then there was the fear. Fear for this young person's life and livelihood in that moment and for his foreseeable future. As well as the shame, anger, and emotional violence I knew would undoubtedly arise as a result of speaking his truth without apology and defiantly calling white supremacy out.

As I sat back in my chair, I released a long and labored exhale. I recounted all the times in which I had brought my truth to white people, when I had spoken up about the ways in which systems of white supremacy have hurt me and those like me, and all the times I was consequently rejected, ignored, and insulted—often by the white people closest to me. I found myself overcome with emotion—because of both the horrendously violent events that had taken place that weekend as well as the bravery of this young Black humxn and the way his words resonated so deeply within every bone of my being. Still, I was confused. I had just spent an entire weekend with white people. I was raised in a predominantly white community, most of my friends at that time were white, and I have white family members. Hell, 25 percent of my ancestry is white! Was it fair to name all white folx hypocrites and barbarians?!

As the Black uprising advocate in the news clip attempted to finish his first sentence, more grief ensued. The news anchor, through his white lens, lied and said the Black man wished to "kill all white people."[7] As commonly occurs, this dignified Black soul was made out to be a murderous enemy of the state. An angry thug on a mission to cause white people harm. *But that's not what he said.* He called white people barbaric, but he did not say they are all bad people, nor did he assert to wish any of them harm. Without so much as a thought, white supremacy translated this man's expression of pain—the collective pain shared by myself and many Black folx—as criminal, deviant, and dangerous. Just as enslavers the world over had done centuries before and just as American Jim Crow had upheld for decades afterward. It's an intentional, albeit often unconscious, defense mechanism white folx wield to guard against having to actually listen to or do anything about the truth: that no matter their intentions, *all* white people perpetuate a collective and institutionalized system of white supremacy created *by* white people, which benefits *all* white people to the detriment and oppression of *all* BI&PoC (particularly Black and Indigenous women+). And *that* is fucking barbaric. Periodt. In the same way cis men have a history of acting barbarically toward women, femmes, and feminine folx, hetero folx have behaved barbarically toward the LGBTTQIA+* community, non-disabled folx behave barbarically toward disabled folx, etc. We are all barbaric in some fashion, and part of our spiritual journey is being with that reality, processing the shitty feelings that arise when we confront the harm we've caused ourselves and others, and doing the work required to do and demand better.

What I believe this bereaved activist was saying, what Black folx are constantly having to say, is that, on the whole, white people hang us out to dry. Which, in fairness, is an improvement from when they hang us from trees . . . and they still do. White folx continuously demand we beg, plead, and fight for our humxnity to simply be recognized. When we audaciously assert the right to live and breathe with the same freedoms as white folx, we're denied, ignored, and attacked. This struggle is constant and the demand incessant, even when white folx are entirely unaware of the task they put before us. Yet again, a Black brother was put on the spot to do exactly that: plead for his right to simply exist. The only difference in this instance was that he wasn't having any of it. This righteous renegade was otherwise in the midst of a standard exchange with whiteness, one that silences Black struggles and prioritizes white comfort. It's an exchange I've endured time and time again, including that very same weekend.

> > < <

As thousands of alt-right white supremacists and Black Lives Matter protesters descended upon Charlottesville, I was at a friend's cabin—well, more like mansion—on an island near my birth town in Vancouver, BC. It was a typical weekend with wealthy, white folx. I was the only Black person in my friend group and often one of if not the only BI&PoC for miles. The weekend was full of reading and relaxing. That is, until I woke up on Sunday morning and checked the news. I saw a woman run over, murdered by a white supremacist in his car. I witnessed neo-Nazis violently assaulting and terrorizing Black men+ and women+. I heard the forty-fifth president of the United States proclaim, "There is blame on both sides."[8] I felt every cell in my body simultaneously howl in horror and retreat with remorse. Every tear, every bigoted remark, every hateful blow, was housed deep in my soul. I had not been there that frightening day in Charlottesville, and yet in so many ways, I had.

I made my way through the corridor of the island estate and descended the stairs to find the weekend crew lit and lively in the kitchen, going about their morning as though the world weren't on fire. But of course, it was. I knew people were in the hospital.

Black folx worldwide, especially Black Americans, were hurting on every level in every kind of way, and I was unsure how to process it all as I sat in the middle of a million-dollar "cabin" on a tiny, picturesque island surrounded by white folx who were entirely oblivious or, worse, unbothered by the situation down south and its implications for us all. The lack of awareness of those in my midst left me feeling isolated, angry, and disheartened. It was as though the trees lining the estate equally sheltered the home as well as its inhabitants. So, I did what had become my salvation in times like those, times when it felt like nobody around me understood my experience walking the world as a Black woman navigating white supremacy on the daily. I shared my pain publicly online with total strangers because it felt less agonizing than attempting to ask the white people in my immediate vicinity to give a fuck about racial violence and its impact on the Black woman right in front of them. That they honor and acknowledge my humxnity and the trauma that naturally arises in bearing witness to yet another example of white supremacist terrorism on Black people. *My* people.

The often unintentional but entirely harmful avoidance of race*-based issues by white folx results in my isolation and erasure of my experiences. It leaves me, and so many other BI&PoC, feeling as though white people don't understand our experience nor care to try, so what would be the point of us speaking up? In predominantly white spaces, I often feel as though it's me, myself, and I. Who is often the only person giving a damn about BI&PoC? *Me.* Where can I turn for support? *Myself.* Who bears the brunt of white silence*? *I.*

> >   < <

Sitting on the couch away from the crowd, I hit "post" on Instagram and went upstairs, where I sat on the bed and bawled. Alone and away from the callous community downstairs still whooping it up over eggs and bacon. I was on an island within an island. A world of pain that nobody in my presence would dare explore with or for me. Me. Myself and I. Was it possible they simply did not know? Obvi. But with the incessant media frenzy of our times, to be unaware is a choice. One made to prioritize white comfort at the exclusion and expense of all others. Later that day the hostess for the weekend, my closest friend there by far, saw my post and tried her best to acknowledge my pain in person. As she sat next to me on the couch and fumbled her way through something akin to consolation, I was appreciative of her attempt. Still, as typically occurs in exchanges with whiteness, I found myself exerting all the emotional labor*. I felt compelled to "induce or suppress [my feelings] in order to sustain the outward countenance that produces the proper state of mind"[9] in my white friend. Aka, I had to exert hella effort to make sure *she* felt safe during our chat about *my* race-based pain. And this wasn't the last time: less than a year later I spent a week consoling *her* after several of her close friends were racist *to me* during her bachelorette.

For BI&PoC, white supremacy regularly has us engaging in conversations about our oppression in a way that comforts our oppressor and/or upholds the oppressive status quo, which results in furthering our oppression. I left the interaction at the cabin both sad and exhausted. I did my best to enjoy the day, but my pain couldn't be contained. I cried standing along the water's edge, my salty tears falling to meet the salt water beneath me. All but one person took notice and, for a moment, stayed with me as I cried in an earnest effort to affirm the pain pent up in my chest. Other than that, my white friends did fuck all. Mostly avoided me, and thus the problem of racism and their implication in it, at all costs. And it hurt. We quickly returned to the sheltered structure of the cabin, and the sheltered lives of my well-to-do white friends marched on. And therein lay the crux of the issue: that white people, as a result of the privilege and protection afforded by whiteness and white supremacy, can and will continue to turn away from racism. To choose not to engage, which is an active choice not to care.

I believe many of the white people in my midst that day cared for me. But they cared about themselves and their comfort more. They were trained to. Just as I was trained to prioritize their needs and well-being above my own. White supremacy plays out in small and subtle ways just as potently as it does in large and grandiose actions. A group of young white folx in Western Canada wholly unmoved by racist acts of terrorism and who ignore their Black friend in distress is in no way disconnected to a group of right-wing extremists who parade and punch in the name of white pride. All of it is violent. All of it perpetuates the white supremacist status quo and causes BI&PoC harm and alienation. Further, as Dr. Shereen Masoud has shared, "the [Charlottesville] riots reified another fear that such blatant displays of racism and xenophobia would work to downplay or mask less apparent, more insidious racist attitudes and behaviors."[10]

          > >   < <

Charlottesville sent reverberations of racial unrest down the spines of people around the world, but there is little that is exceptional about anti-Black terrorism, as the double pandemic of COVID-19 and four hundred years of Black genocide has made clear. White supremacist violence has endured for centuries and it will continue to endure, unless and until we all, particularly white people who created and benefit from these systems, demand that it ends. Though there have been countless instances of racist rallies worldwide throughout history, and undoubtedly more to come, there have also been incalculable harms inflicted against Black folx, particularly queer and trans Black women+, by our well-meaning loved ones. Emotional violence can leave bigger bruises than physical acts of assault. Still, like many other Black people, I've spent much of my life failing to name these harms, as that brave young man did in Charlottesville, and for damn good reason—it was not and is not safe. Had I spoken my truth to the white people on that tiny white island, I have no doubt I would have been met with a regalia of racist resistance. I chose to be more or less silent about my pain, just as they chose to be silent about my oppression. It's no coincidence that many, if not most, Black anti-racist educators and activists were raised in predominantly white spaces. The immense harm we endured growing up in the throes of whiteness fired us up to not only fight against racial injustice but dedicate our lives to doing so.

I still frequently feel alone. I have yet to locate the mystical land of Wakanda where I can be my boldest, Blackest, and freest self, but I have come to realize that, for now, such a space must exist within. I can embody the freedom I wish to create in the world, and I believe it is my calling as bestowed upon me by Spirit and my ancestors to share my truth and the truth of so many Black women+, past, present, and future. To mobilize others to create a tangibly safe society for Black and Indigenous women+ worldwide. A space where our experiences will be welcomed. If there's any chance for equity* to actualize, people need to listen to the realities faced by the most oppressed. We all need to start sharing our stories with those different from ourselves while calling out oppression, actively listening, and questioning our perspectives even and especially when it makes us uncomfortable. I want to witness a world where white folx and non-Black PoC* are willing to risk their lives and livelihoods in support of Black liberation, in the same way Black women+ have been risking our lives and livelihoods for all of our collective freedoms. For centuries. A world where Black women+, especially queer and trans Black women, no longer have to lead the charge on the front lines of critical global change. I want Black women+ to be able to rest. And heal. The collective's liberation requires Black liberation, and Black liberation requires *all* of us. Particularly those currently possessing the most power and privilege.

Make no mistake, I still fear the harm I will undoubtedly endure for speaking my truth. My work, education, and training in racial justice do not and cannot inoculate me from feeling pain. I am in no way immune to the backlash that has already taken place and that is sure to ensue. Those who will blame me for speaking my truth, then drag my name through the mud in an effort to ruin me and my reputation. The many (mostly white) folx who no longer speak or associate with me, and all those to come. The death threats that will continue to fill my inboxes. All this and more is just another day of existing as a queer Black woman fighting racial injustice. The very act of writing this book is a form of activism and estrangement—to be an outspoken and unapologetic queer Black woman is to be a lightning rod for loathing. I have been slammed with every racist stereotype one can imagine—angry, uppity, divisive, too Black, not Black enough, too emotional, too loud, too much, too everything. Still, I must write and I must write my absolute truth. Indigenous lands continue to be stolen and destroyed. Black folx are still subjected to state-sanctioned slaughter in these global streets. Both Black and Indigenous folx are dying at the highest rates due to COVID-19 and anti-Black and anti-Indigenous pandemics. Governments are ruthlessly terrorizing those of us defying inequitable systems of power. And shit is only getting worse. There's too much at stake for us to stay quiet.

Naming Our Fears

Our first soulcare prompt creates space for you to illuminate your own apprehensions around racial justice. Find a quiet space to reflect and ask yourself this question: *What is my biggest fear or frustration about addressing white supremacy?*

Please close or lower your eyes.

Take note in your mind of any words, images, or emotions that emerge as you ponder this question. Maybe a memory arises. Perhaps you feel tension in your jaw.

Now open your eyes and jot down what came up for you below. If you are able to—for this exercise and those to come—try writing with your nondominant hand. This helps you to get out of your head and into your heart (and practice non-perfection, cuz it ain't pretty!).

MY BIGGEST FEAR OR FRUSTRATION ABOUT ADDRESSING WHITE SUPREMACY IS: _____

_____

_____.

WHERE DO I FEEL THIS IN MY BODY?_____

_____

_____

_____.

Naming our biggest fear and/or frustration lets us deflate some of its power and, in turn, create more space for us to hold space, show up, and do the work! Notice where this lives in your body and how/when it gets activated as you move through the book and this work.

> > > > > >

TWO

Where We Get Stuck

> Freedom is the difference
> between "justice" and healing.
>
> **—MCKENSIE MACK**

We are in a time of significant strife. Collective hurt. Personal pain. Psychic, emotional, mental, physical, and spiritual anguish. These are trying times, and learning how to navigate our way through the hot dumpster fire that has become our planet is no easy or small feat. In the midst of the COVID-19 pandemic my heart physically ached with grief in the same way it did after my mom died. I knew Black and Indigenous folx would be hit first and hardest, and then, of course, we were. Not to mention the four-hundred-year pandemic of anti-Blackness on top of it all.

Our lives are uncertain. We are overwhelmed by the 24/7 global news cycle highlighting violence, scarcity, and division. Climate change* has us living under a ticking time bomb, and future generations are unsure if they even *have* a future. Though my ancestors have been screaming from the rooftops for centuries, there is something distinctly different about the state of oppression and global disconnection at play today. I believe we are at a collective crossroads and the actions we take—or do not take—right now will change the future of our shared humxnity for all time. Shit is do or die.

The quest for racial justice is no different. Racial tensions have been increasingly high the past few years, particularly since the 2016 election of Donald Trump, but the floodgate is about to burst, and either we prepare ourselves to cultivate the energy of the day to truly dismantle systems of white supremacy, or we will *all* perish beneath it. Emotionally, mentally, and spiritually if not physically. We are all right here, right now, for good reason. We are at the threshold of an entirely new era. A new way of living, being, and connecting. The white supremacist systems that have governed the majority of the globe for centuries can finally be overthrown. But if there is ever to be a chance to change the world for the better, we gotta get it together. And we have to come together. Right now.

Many of us know this. We feel this. Hell, it's why you're reading this book! Still, we struggle with connecting our head with our heart. We struggle with knowing what to do and how to do it. And most important, we struggle with getting out of our own damn way. For all of these reasons it is imperative that we address the places we are prone to getting stuck. And after guiding thousands of folx through the work of racial justice I can tell you, there are some very specific areas where we repeatedly trip up. So we're going to unpack the six obstacles I repeatedly observe getting in the way of an authentic commitment to racial justice and how they play out for white women+ and BI&WoC, and of course, we're going to cover how we can best address the shit keeping us stuck so we can contribute to meaningful change! *Can I get a hell yes?!*

#1—The Need to Be Good & Right

The biggest obstacle that arises for women+, no matter their race, is when the need to be good and right supersedes the commitment to racial justice. In our heteropatriarchal world we are taught that being right is more important than being fair. And most, if not all, of us socialized as women or femmes are taught to be good from a young age. At all costs. We are told to be "good little girls." To please others. To follow instructions, do as we are told, and never rock the boat. We are taught to achieve for validation, so our self-esteem is often sourced from external achievements and perceptions. Consequently, as numerous studies on the gender* confidence gap have shown, we're afraid to fail, and when we do we are more likely to take it as an assault on our sense of worth.[1] In an internal report published by Hewlett-Packard, men were found to apply for a job or promotion if they met only 60 percent of the qualifications, while women applied only if they had 100 percent of the qualifications.[2]

As a recovering perfectionist myself, I can speak to this all damn day. I was obsessed with being right, doing things perfectly, and being perceived as good, worthy, and enough. I happen to be a Virgo and a Projector, so we tend to be annoyingly right about a lot of shit a lot of the time (just ask my husband); still, I can safely say my obsession with being good and right was not exactly fun for those in my midst (or for me). As a queer Black woman in a white world, I was always seeking validation and confirmation in a society constantly telling me I was wrong and less than. I also had a deep need to control, because it was a coping skill I learned to help keep me safe in response to childhood trauma. I still struggle with wanting to be right and a desire for control. But I understand that these behaviors no longer help, they hurt. Myself and those around me.

The need to be good and right is entirely counterproductive to racial justice. You *will* get it wrong, without question. And this deep, inner work of exposing and addressing the ways in which we have been harmed and caused harm to others does not feel good. If you're authentically anti-racist, you will fuck it up. And you will feel bad. In some way, shape, or form. I assure you. I have made many mistakes along the way. This book itself is an example of perfect imperfection—I can pretty much promise you I've fucked up somewhere. Somehow. That my imperfections will show their asses. But I strive to follow the lead of those most marginalized, do the best I can, rectify the harm I cause, and continue to learn to do better. My desire for perfection cannot become the enemy of progress. Had I let my perfectionism run the show, this book would never have come to fruition. When we are committed to being right as well as being perceived as good, to ourselves or others, we cannot get into the complicated, messy, and mistake-ridden work of addressing our privileges and minimizing our harm. For example, as a non-disabled*, cisgender, thin, light-skinned, Canadian, neurotypical*, traditionally attractive, financially secure, English-speaking, highly educated humxn in a hetero-passing relationship, I possess a lot of privilege. If I am obsessed with being good and right, then I have no capacity to understand the ways in which I am an oppressed oppressor, nor will I understand those whom I oppress and do what is required to cause less harm and dismantle systems of oppression. You cannot be committed to being good and right and be anti-racist. It just ain't gonna work, honey. We need to be open to humility, to fucking up, to getting it wrong. To receiving and learning things that rock us to our core. Racial justice requires resilience. It commands accountability, honesty, integrity, and action. All of which are undermined by perfectionism, people pleasing, and conflict aversion. These are present in most women and femmes in differing degrees and manifestations. And our brains literally get huge hits of dopamine when we *think* we're right, so we're working against our own physiology in a sense.[3]

White women+ stay all the way caught up in the need to be good and right, which is a form of white wildness*. They detect the words "racist" and "white supremacy" and immediately assume I am personally attacking them, their worthiness or their identity as a good person. But the truth is when we dive into this work, we come to realize that we're not as "good" as we likely thought we were. We've caused harm. Some of it major. And though we may not have done so intentionally, we have to reckon with the consequences all the same. Most white women+ endure an identity crisis when they undertake this work, and that is painful and hard and requires loads of self-compassion to move through, for sure, but it doesn't come close to what BI&-WoC have to endure at the hands of the white supremacy white women+ perpetuate. Since white women+ aren't used to having their identity or inherent goodness challenged in the way BI&-WoC often are, especially cis white women, they are less able to tolerate feeling bad or wrong; but it's a muscle white women+ are gonna have to flex if they want to be anti-racist. It shows up in all kinds of insidious ways, including the need for accolades simply for engaging in racial justice or anti-racism* (aka seeking "cookies"). To be clear, there will be no cookies here.

For BI&WoC, the need to be good and right often results in dimming our light. We minimize our voice and ensure the comfort of whiteness above all else, because to be considered "good and right" as a BI&WoC, especially a Black or Indigenous woman+, is to defer to white supremacy. For example, there were many times in my life when I wanted to name an action of a white friend or colleague as racist and anti-Black, but I also wanted to be accepted and "successful" (as much as it pains me to admit). Being good and right, according to white supremacy, meant ignoring the harms inflicted upon me. BI&WoC often can't call racist shit out for what it is because we'll be labeled angry, ostracized, and excluded. White women+ committed to being good and right are damn sure to inflict consequences when they are called out on their racism—be it emotional violence or otherwise.

So how do we untangle ourselves from this ugly-ass web? We gotta get like Rumi and cross "beyond ideas of wrongdoing and rightdoing."[4] Observe when your need to be good and right is at play. When you feel defensive or uncomfortable, get curious if and how it's arising. And when it is, know that this process of unlearning is a serious *fuck you* to the establishment. It is unplugging from the matrix. It is an act of deconditioning and deprogramming from the shit you've been taught by white supremacy from the get-go. And your mother before you and her mother before her. It is so ingrained in our way of being it may as well be part of our DNA. It's a cancerous growth and we need to cut it the fuck out. ASAP. So, have compassion for yourself and why these harmful behaviors exist *and* get your booty in gear to do what is required to change. At the end of the chapter I share some soulcare prompts to help you tune in and turn up the compassion to fuel this inner and outer shift.

#2—White Gaze*

As a Black woman I am used to having to overfunction, overexplain, and overdefend in almost every way, but especially when it comes to explaining my race-based oppression to white folx and to white women+ specifically. Growing up in a predominantly white and wealthy community meant the folx in my midst were unwilling to learn about, let alone engage with, race. When I engage in this discussion now, I often grapple with this inner conflict: How much do I need to explain? How can I best make my case to all the white folx who will disagree? It's an exhausting and demanding state of hypervigilance created by and for whiteness and the white gaze. Unsurprisingly, it reared its ugly head many times as I wrote this book.

The white gaze is a concept most notably articulated by Toni Morrison, who explained that most literature, no matter whom it is authored by, is written to and for a white audience.[5] And in doing so, as a non-white person, I am expected to cater my writing to white readers—to their comfort, experience, and understanding. For example, when you read "a young person rides their bicycle down the street," what race did you imagine that person to be? When I ask this in my workshops, the overwhelming response is: white. Irrespective of the participant's race. This expands far past the written page. The white gaze exists in nearly every book but also every home, school, church, relationship, and workplace. Be it through word, speech, or action, BI&PoC constantly live under and appease the white gaze. Whether we realize it, and so often we do not, we have all been socialized to consider white perspectives first and formulate our behaviors with the opinion of white people in mind. No matter your race, the white gaze is present right here right now. As I write, and as you read. It is one of the many insidious elements of whiteness that goes unnoticed and unaddressed. Much like the "male gaze" and the ways in which women+, consciously or unconsciously, operate within and consider the male perspective whether men are present or not.

As a Black woman educating about race, the presence of the white gaze means I am expected to explain white supremacy, through word and speech, in a way that will best be understood and received by white people so they do not feel attacked, upset, or uncomfortable. It means I am conditioned to reducing my argument to its most basic elements, to overjustifying each and every point because I fear, based on lived experience, that the white reader will discount and disbelieve me. This exercise requires constant internal evaluation and self-policing and, to be blunt, entirely fucks with my ability to write and teach. As Toni Morrison once said, "What happens to the writerly imagination of a [B]lack author who is at some level *always* conscious of representing one's race to, or in spite of, a race of readers that understands itself to be 'universal' or race-free?"[6] Let me remind you that we are all racialized people. Nothing is neutral. Including whiteness.

White supremacy is rooted in facts (of its own creation), figures, and left-brain analysis. As an attorney, I can do that all day. But it isn't how we can best learn. I am not here to "prove" anything to anyone, I am here to declare and share the reality of the oppression faced by myself and people of the global majority. Especially Black and Indigenous women. I refuse to defend my humxnity or argue with those committed to debating against it. When it comes to racial justice, appeasing the white gaze is to enable white violence*, and this means we'll never get where we need to be because BI&PoC often fear sharing their truth and white folx are too accustomed to avoiding their own discomfort (and silencing BI&PoC in order to do so). That shit will simply not fly here, my loves. We are diving deep. We are learning to tolerate our unease. Whether you're Black, white, or otherwise— watch for the ways in which the white gaze arises as you read. This is not an *if* but rather a *when*. White and non-Black folx aren't gonna like a lot of what I share, so y'all need to watch your ego because it *will* get defensive. Luckily you are not your ego, so you don't have to give in to that noise. No matter your hue, observe the moments you want to discount what I say. Be with the instances when you feel uncomfortable with the way I brazenly call out whiteness. Be with the big emotions you will likely feel at my audacity to do so. And notice when you feel the need for more "proof" and why.

#3—Disavowal

Next up we have disavowal, which can be described as a denial or repudiation of responsibility. In a word: gross! Disavowal occurs when we "split the ego" by recognizing the existence of something, even if only unconsciously, and simultaneously deny its existence or our role in it. Clear as mud, right? In racial justice it plays out like this: I name that I hold a racial privilege as a light-skinned (albeit Black) person—which I just did a few pages back—and in naming that, I am acknowledging that colorism is a thing that exists but I am also, mostly unintentionally, creating distance between myself and those light-skinned Black folx who don't name their light-skinned privilege. By naming the harm, I'm disavowing my role in the harm I am speaking to. More often than not, though, disavowal is perpetuated by white folx—no big surprise really since they have the most work to do to unlearn their white supremacy. The "anti-racist" practice of white people naming whiteness and their racism can actually reinforce white privilege*. Issa mindfuck, I know. Here's why: it creates a sense of the "good anti-racist" white person versus the "other" unconsciously racist white person, which does nothing to dismantle the systems of white supremacy but rather reinforces them. It's still about being good and right. Naming the oppression you cause is critical, but it does not actually eliminate that oppression. It's the beginning of the conversation, not the end. There is no "good white people versus bad white people." There is white people and white supremacy. Same holds true for all forms of oppression. Our naming it does not make us better or wiser or less harmful, and, ironically, believing it does, consciously or not, causes *more* harm. Not to mention that many white folx have now learned how to use anti-racist language without doing a damn thing to be anti-racist. As we learn about the ways in which we oppress others, let's get more comfy with calling ourselves out, but let's not confuse that with being anti-oppressive—there's much more to it than that.

#4—Lack of Meaningful Care

Another obstacle to racial justice is that we may not actually care as much as we think we do or would like to. We want *to want* to care, but do we actually possess the meaningful care required to commit to massive inner and outer change? And I mean massive change, folx, a little bit here and there isn't going to fucking fly anymore. We're past that. Like, way. So, if we don't sufficiently care about racial justice, we aren't going to do what is required to make it a reality. Periodt. Many folx want to care, and they know they should. They recognize racial justice is an increasingly important issue. They know individuals and institutions need to do better. And they're aware that they are perpetuating white supremacy and anti-Blackness somehow. The issue is that they don't want to have to change or give up *their* power and privilege—and that, my friends, means they frankly don't give a damn. Not *really*. If you care, like really and truly care, you act. You change behaviors. You do what is necessary to get shit done. Every person who comes to my workshops cares about racial justice. All of you reading this book, you care. Amen! My question to you is: Do you care *enough*? Are you ready, able, and willing to prioritize this work? Because people are dying day in and day out at the hands of white supremacy, and I ain't got time for you to try this half-assed. Get fully involved, or get the hell out the way.

#5—Inability to Face Our Shadow

This entire book is more or less based on this barrier, so of course, it's a biggie! Our inner child is that part of us that represents and yearns for play, innocence, wonder, awe, and curiosity. We all began this life as a child, and that child still resides within us. Many of us have not acknowledged our inner child, let alone the needs of that inner child or the wounds inflicted upon us as children that are still in dire need of care. In a white supremacist society, we are taught to deny the inner child and forgo our birthright to play and heal, leaving the inner child to kick, scream, and lash out on an unconscious level. This is where the shadow self is created. Our wounded inner child gets suppressed, and thus so do all the parts of ourselves we prefer not to address or own up to, like our stubbornness, sensitivity, or jealousy. Our shadow self is the often unconscious parts of ourselves we would rather hide. But our inner child and shadow are very much part of our identity. They are important and integral parts of who we are, and our healing must include owning up to and addressing these parts.

When we are unable to face our shadow self or tolerate the full spectrum of our humxn emotions or the emotions of others, then we are ill-equipped to authentically engage in anti-racism. In fact, we are likely causing more, rather than less, harm if we seek to do so without first facing our own selves. It leads to emotional violence like spiritual bypassing*, gaslighting*, white wildness, and so much more (all of which we will discuss!). When BI&WoC are too afraid to face our shadows, we cannot withstand the pain that arises from really realizing the harm we've endured, and when white women+ turn away from this work, they center themselves and inflict more harm on BI&WoC. Additionally, when white women+ do not face their shadow, they are unable to quell their fear—their fear of BI&WoC, especially Black women+, and our resilience, connection, and power. And most important, white women+ fear what all white folx fear, be it consciously or unconsciously: that Black and Indigenous folx will treat them the same way they have treated us (a truly terrifying thought!). As we'll explore, to face our shadow we must acknowledge that our shadow self exists. We must tend to our wounded inner child and continuously partake in the inner work, like challenging our inner white supremacist worldview.

#6—Getting Stuck in Our Feelings

The last major obstacle I frequently witness in this work is getting stuck in our feelings, most often grief. As an empath and highly sensitive person, I'm all in my feelings a lot of the time. But I'm aware that it ain't doing nobody no favors, and I'm doing major inner work to make modifications. When you get stuck in your feelings, you are getting stuck in your own self, and being stuck in your mind is not advancing anti-racism, it's settling into self-indulgence. Racial justice brings up big feelings. It is some of the deepest and hardest work you will ever do no matter your race or ethnicity*. You will feel the full range of emotions, from anger to guilt to grief, shame, and sadness. But feeling our feelings ain't the same as getting stuck in them. Way too often I witness (predominantly cis white) women+ get overwhelmed with emotions about how this work makes them feel, and that's where they stay. Stuck in a grief-ridden guilt trip. And that's not helping me, them, or anyone who has been harmed by them specifically or white supremacy on the whole. When you get stuck in your feelings you will inherently make anti-oppression work about *you* and not about those whom you have harmed, which is missing the point entirely. For BI&WoC, this most often shows up as a tendency to stagnate in grief, shame, or trauma. We often struggle to feel the fulsomeness of our feelings and tolerate the many mixed emotions that arise for us and the white folx we witness while doing this work. So I encourage everyone to feel *all* your feels, please! Let your feels flag fly. But let yourself truly feel those uncomfortable experiences, especially your personal and collective grief, to move up and out. To process to completion so you can transmute those feelings into supportive action. Fear not! I'll be helping you here. You ain't alone.

WORKING WITH WISE COMPASSION

The common thread in all the foregoing obstacles is that they can be combated with compassion, for ourselves and for others. "Compassion" means "to suffer together." It is the act of truly witnessing another person and their suffering *and* being motivated to help relieve it in some way. It is similar to empathy, but they ain't the same. Empathy is the ability to feel for another, but it misses the motivating factor to act on that feeling. In fact, neuroscientists have found that compassion is more beneficial than empathy, as it activates the areas of our brain affiliated with problem-solving, whereas empathy stimulates the areas of our brain affiliated with pain. In short, compassion feels good and leads to action. Empathy feels uncomfortable and leads to overwhelm. Compassion is the way to go, but many of us, especially women and femmes, were taught that compassion means supporting others even if it means ignoring our own needs. In Buddhist theory there is a concept of wise compassion, which is the notion that compassion must include *us*, not solely the subject we seek to support. It's the compassionate form of putting your oxygen mask on first, the reverse of which is unwise compassion. Caring for ourselves supports us in caring for others; after all, hurt people often hurt people.

When I started practicing wise compassion it shifted everything. Much of my identity had been wrapped up in serving others, from parents and partners to bosses and best friends. I didn't realize how undermining my own needs was creating less connection with people in my life, not more. I wasn't sharing the fullness of myself, nor was I focusing on myself and the work I needed to do in order to acknowledge where I needed to grow and take the necessary actions to water the seeds of change. I learned that caring for myself was not in fact selfish. It was necessary. I learned that racial justice and anti-oppression are revolutionary acts of collective healing, and that healing had to begin within *me*. There are many other institutional and systemic powers at play, but our personal power plays an important part. Practicing wise compassion and tending to our own heart spaces create connection with ourselves, our emotions, and the wounds that are a part of what prevents us from creating desperately needed personal and collective shifts. If we aren't able to face our shit, then we can't show up for ourselves to do this work and we definitely cannot contribute to healing the collective. We will fail at overcoming one of our first big obstacles to achieving anti-racism: ourselves. This requires us to slow down. To rest. To get off the capitalist patriarchal hamster wheel of constantly DOing rather than BEing. And feel so we can heal. In the words of Audre Lorde, "Within living structures defined by profit, by linear power, by institutional dehum[x]nization, our feelings were not meant to survive."[7] Under white supremacy, there is so much of ourselves that was never meant to survive—especially for queer and trans Black and Indigenous women+. Acknowledging where we get stuck in the quest for racial justice and showering ourselves in wise compassion in order to overcome those obstacles is how we ensure survival. Our own and each other's.

Spiritual Soulcare Offering

Heart Check-In

To lean into our wise compassion, you can use acts of soulcare to assist you in cultivating more connection with yourself and ultimately with others.

After my mother died, I needed to tangibly check in with myself so I could connect with my feelings and properly care for my heart. I created a daily phone alert that asks "How is your heart doing?" and six years later it still serves as a reminder to take a moment, pause, and actually check in with my heart. I've found it super helpful and maybe you will too. I suggest setting the alert for a time of day when you can pause to be with yourself rather than simply ignoring it. Maybe first thing in the morning, just before bed, or over lunch.

WHETHER YOU TRY THE PHONE ALERT OR NOT, SET AN
INTENTION TO CHECK IN WITH YOUR HEART EVERY DAY
FOR THE NEXT THREE TO FOUR DAYS, THEN REFLECT ON
THE FOLLOWING:

> How has my heart been feeling?

> Does my heart feel different from how I thought it might
  when I first checked in?

> What am I most afraid to feel? Why? How is this obstructing
  my anti-racist efforts?

> How can I better move toward that which I am not wanting
  to feel?

Call to Action

Getting Past "Good"

When you find yourself feeling defensive or fearful regarding
racial justice or anti-oppression, try the following:

1) Check in to see if your need to be good and right is running
   the show.

2) Pause, reflect, take a breath. Then ask yourself:

> Am I trying to feel or be perceived as "good" in this
  moment? Why? What am I afraid of?

> Am I trying to be "right" about this situation? Why?
  What do I believe I will gain from "being right"? Is that
  true?

> What might I lose from my need to "be right"? Whom
  might it harm? Why?

> How might my need to be (or be perceived as) good and right interfere with my need for connection? For understanding? For support?

3) For BI&PoC: Am I tempering myself (through silence, action, inaction, or otherwise) in order to be believed or accepted by whiteness?

4) For white/white-passing folx: Am I wielding my privilege in order to be, or be perceived as, "good" and/or "right"?

> > > > > >

THREE

White Supremacy Starts Within

Your willingness to look at your darkness
is what empowers you to change.

—IYANLA VANZANT

In 1851, Sojourner Truth gave what is known as the "Ain't I a Woman?" speech, a rallying decree calling on the white community to consider her doubly oppressed experience living at the intersection of being both Black and woman. Over 160 years later, BI&WoC around the world are still forced to ask this same. Damn. Question. We are still fighting for the right to be recognized, respected, and supported because white supremacy continues to censor us, to abuse us, and to attempt our complete eradication. Racial justice activists and anti-racism education have erupted in popular culture, particularly following the violent murders of George Floyd, Ahmaud Arbery, Nina Pop, Tony McDade, Breonna Taylor, and so many more Black folx, be it by police or vigilantes, as revealed during the COVID-19 pandemic. Still, we are enduring deepening racial inequities from a global health crisis, an influx of performative allyship from individuals and corporations alike, and the attempted white-washing* of the Black Lives Matter movement. We are mired in personal and collective race-based grief. Yet there is still an inability to create lasting, meaningful change despite "good intentions." So how do we acknowledge and address the white supremacist status quo? Where can we learn steps for creating lasting solutions? What tools are required for our collective healing? White supremacy creates grief and loss for all people, albeit in different ways. To address and process the oppression that we observe and experience out in the world, we need to first take a long, sobering exploration inside our own universe.

White supremacy is undoubtedly a systemic issue, but it *starts* in the hearts and minds of men+, women+, and children. Usually white ones. Often when we think of white supremacy and racism, we think of external, overt acts of harm. We picture Nazis in Germany, or the word "nigger" leaving someone's lips in disdain. We imagine tangible and egregious actions that we can point to and say, "*That* is racist." But as we'll learn, that ain't the way white supremacy usually works. White supremacy starts within because the broader social systems that create institutions of oppression started within. In the hearts and minds of white folx who disseminated this ideology across all races and gender identities. White supremacy is taught, learned, and absorbed from birth if not before. There are numerous doll test studies where both white and Black children as young as three years old affiliate white skin as prettier, cleaner, and/or better than dark skin. Both Black and white toddlers alike exhibit a strong internalized preference for whiteness, and this bias* remains in adulthood.[1]

Since white supremacy is part and parcel of the global status quo, it infiltrates every aspect of who we are and how we view the world and our place within it. Consciously and unconsciously.

Racism, internalized oppression, and white supremacy are a part of our collective genetic makeup and the thread composing the layered fabric of our global tapestry. They are insidious by design. So much so that we are often incapable of recognizing, let alone naming, them. Even, and often especially, when they exist within ourselves. And make no mistake here, beloveds, racism is housed within every white person on the planet. Internalized oppression afflicts all BI&PoC, and all white folx and non-Black PoC uphold anti-Blackness. All humxns are prone to perpetuating white supremacy because white supremacy is the status quo.

> > < <

There is a time and place for logic and academic analysis, but when it comes to healing the chasm that is the racial divide and creating understanding across ethnic, cultural, and racial lines, we must do so from our heart as well as our mind. Education alone is not enough. If it were, I wouldn't still need to repeat the same shit as Harriet Tubman, Marsha P. Johnson, or Malcolm X. We must learn to tolerate the challenging and conflicting emotions that arise when we address racism and white supremacy. Emotions like grief, guilt, anger, shame, hope, anxiety, relief, fear, and sadness, to name but a few. We must acclimate our body to withstand our own discomfort and shower ourselves in compassion so we have a shot at bestowing that same compassion on others—particularly queer and trans Black and Indigenous women+ who are most marginalized by race and gender identity oppression. Withstanding our discomfort also requires understanding that discomfort is a necessary and constant part of the work. Our goal is not to feel comfortable, because we won't. It is to better tolerate the discomfort that inherently arises. No matter your race, unless and until the violent and uncomfortable truths of white supremacy have resonated through your every cell, you will be unmotivated and ill-equipped to take the lifelong, daily, and demanding actions required to dismantle all systems of oppression as they exist within and outside of us, and create a world where all humxns can finally breathe easy.

White supremacy is one of the greatest forms of collective social trauma in the world. Failing to address the race-based grief faced by *all* humxns is a failure to heal our personal and collective pain. And our healing will be the revolution. Racism is an inside job. Because we cannot heal what we refuse to reveal.

WHERE WHITE WOMEN+ GET RACISM WRONG

Time and time again I encounter well-intentioned white women+ who want to commit to racial justice but have fooled themselves into believing that racism only exists outside of themselves and their direct and immediate control. Well, I'm here to call bullshit! The truth is that white supremacy starts within and therefore all anti-racism efforts must as well. At least any efforts that have a hope in hell of creating substantive change. It can be easy to think you are "doing the work" solely by addressing things outside of the four corners of your physical, spiritual, emotional, and mental being. But it's a lie. A ruse you have been sold by a capitalist system that wants you to stay busy and bothered so you do not and cannot recognize the larger system for what it is— racist, oppressive, and stacked against anyone who doesn't belong to the dominant groups.

First, it is vital that we address what "doing the work" in a racial justice context even means. To use a garden as a metaphor— and forgive me here, because I am nobody's gardener—is it pulling up your sleeves and getting your elbows dirty pulling out the weeds? Is it nourishing the seedlings you've planted so they have what they need to thrive? Or is it being with yourself so you better understand the ins and outs of how the garden actually functions, and how your personal experiences and ideologies are influencing every garden-related action and thus the well-being of the garden itself? I believe it's all of the above. But we can't effectively weed away the hate or nourish those who have been subjected to it without first understanding the intricacies of the ecosystem you're working in and how you contribute to its existence. Ya dig?

When I ask white women+ what they are doing to address racial injustice, be it in my workshops or on the interwebs, I routinely receive answers that allude to a racist world and ideology that exists entirely separate from them, their actions (or inactions), and their worldview. It's a tempting and intentional mirage created to other themselves from the white supremacist issue and the ills it causes the BI&PoC whom it was constructed to oppress. How convenient. But, in the words of Randy Jackson, it's a *no* from me, dawg. I don't have time for this self-aggrandizing line of fake reasoning. Too many Black folx are dying. When I receive common white answers in response to the "what are you doing?" query, like posting about anti-racism educators on Instagram, attending a rally, or donating to mutual aid, it can be hard to keep my cool. These are all important and appreciated acts, but they miss the most critical mark: *addressing the ways in which you as an individual perpetuate white supremacy day in and day out.* When you head out into the world in the hopes of taking tangible action to mitigate discrimination but have failed to first address the ways in which *you* have and continue to participate in the very oppression you are seeking to eradicate, you perpetuate more of the same. You operate from the oppressive systems socially encoded into your DNA and ignore your power, privilege, and the violence that ensues when you are ill prepared to illuminate and remedy your shadows. In sum, you cause harm. In no small measure. I am a queer Black woman and I face many oppressions as a result of that intersecting identity. And I also hold many privileges as a cisgender, light-skinned, multiracial, Canadian, English-speaking, highly educated, neurotypical, non-disabled, financially secure, thin, young(ish) person in a heterosexual-passing marriage. It is my work to unearth and address my own privileges so I can cause less harm to those whom I oppress. To acknowledge my status as an oppressed oppressor. White women+ need to do the same, but y'all are struggling.

White women+ and non-Black PoC are also prone to telling me how much they support me and my work while failing to engage in daily, personal racial justice or Black liberation education or efforts themselves. This itself is an act of white supremacy and anti-Blackness. Let me be real clear: it is utterly impossible to support me or any of the work I do when you aren't actively participating in racial justice and addressing anti-Blackness *yourself*. Full stop. How precisely are you supporting me or advancing racial justice when you can't even acknowledge that you are implicated in the oppressive systems of whiteness to which you belong and perpetuate simply by being white or benefitting from whiteness as a non-Black PoC? How can you help heal the collective divide when you refuse to heal your own race-based hurts as a means to hold compassionate space for the harms you and white supremacy have and continue to inflict on Black and Indigenous women+? The answer is simple: you can't. Any belief or intention to exclude your own actions or inactions is performative at best and deeply destructive at worst.

White supremacy shows its face in a myriad of ways, one of which is the belief that individual white people are miraculously outside the collective global structures of white supremacy. This is white exceptionalism*, and it's a farce. Straight up—it is impossible to address racism in an authentic way without addressing yourself, the harm you have caused, and the grief and loss that white supremacy inherently creates for all. If we want to burn the systems of white supremacy to the ground, and my hope is that's why you're here, we first have to examine ourselves. You need to explore the ways your racism, misogyny, transphobia, homophobia, classism, ableism, and/or internalized oppression are embedded in your body and how they infiltrate your every breath and relationship. Racial justice work mandates we address our own race and other oppression-based traumas and the traumas inflicted on humxns as a whole, especially queer and trans Black and Indigenous women+. It is a form of collective healing for our anger, our shame, and, most of all, our grief.

INVESTIGATING OUR INNER CHILD

Healing requires facing our shadow self and our wounded inner child. As we've discussed, all of us have endured some struggle, none of us were loved perfectly as children, and most of us still have childhood hurts and trauma in need of healing, all of which results in a wounded inner child. It is believed that a large part of our character is written in the first five years of our lives, and this plays an integral role in how we view and relate to the world.[2] Mix that with the fact that, as most neuroscientists agree, around 95 percent of our mind operates at an unconscious level (including those parts storing traumatic memories),[3] we come to understand that much of our worldview, including biases, are implicit and thus go unnoticed without intentional inquisition. This is precisely why we must do the inner work to acknowledge our wounded inner child and our shadow side. Our shadow self is very much present and often shows itself in inadvertent ways such as sarcasm, slips of the tongue, dreams, fantasies, oppressive worldviews, and/or projections characterized by immediate and intense emotional reactions. Our shadows contain our rage, jealousy, criticism, and ability to cause harm. We need not categorize the shadow as negative or in need of fixing; it is simply part of who we are. But issues arise when we refuse to acknowledge and accept those parts of ourselves so we can ensure they are addressed and expressed nonviolently. This becomes all the harder when we have not yet acknowledged or addressed our inner child, as our inner child is quick to behave like a toddler in a great tantrum. Our inner child is also always present and can provoke self-sabotaging, self-criticizing, passive-aggressive, or violent behaviors.[4] When we acknowledge the harms we endured as a child, and the childlike needs still present within us, it creates more compassion for the fullness of who we are, including if not especially our shadows. Then we can give ourselves the tender care we require to heal our hearts and thus help heal the hearts of others.

No matter who you are or where you come from, committing to authentic racial justice requires an upheaval and questioning of everything you once knew—be it about yourself, others, or the world. For white people and other oppressors, it often results in feeling as though the floor is falling out from beneath their feet—nothing is what they once believed it to be (whether that belief was a form of willful ignorance or not). When we engage in racial justice it is an investment in witnessing the world beyond the white supremacist status quo that has been carefully curated by those with the most power and privilege to keep them powerful and privileged, to the detriment and exclusion of all else. This requires a serious act of unlearning and relearning and, depending on your proximity to the oppressor, it can be an all-encompassing task. As I always say in my workshops, when we educate ourselves and begin to witness the world through an authentically anti-racist lens, we detach from the world as we've known it. For my fellow *Matrix* fans (hayyy!), it's akin to Neo popping that red pill from Morpheus, dissolving the state-sanctioned illusions he had bought into, and witnessing the world as it truly is. Committing to authentic anti-racism is unplugging from the matrix of white supremacy. It is an act of awakening our hearts and minds to the racial reality and confronting all the ways we have harmed and/or been harmed within it. As a Black woman, it is deeply painful to come to terms with the omnipresence of white supremacy and the ways it has resulted in my external and internal oppression. For white folx, the pain predominantly comes from realizing their racism and how they have been complicit in global systems of dominance. And all of us feel anguish in accepting the ways we have oppressed other BI&PoC, women+, and queer or trans folx as well as ourselves. This is why the inner work is the hardest work we can do. We must first face our actions, our privileges, our beliefs and emotions. We must first face and question *our-selves*. Fucking scary, right?!

I appreciate why pointing to external factors is so damn tempting. Self-growth and personal development are uncomfortable, messy, life-altering (and lifelong) commitments. Our desire to avoid pain, change, and the work necessitated by growth is *strong*. Our ego tries to convince us that we are in life-and-death situations—that a change to our worldview or self-identification is the same as facing a lion in the jungle. We get mired in flight, fight, freeze, or fawn. This shit is no joke! And this is precisely why we must commit to racial justice with all we've got—from the inside out. If we are not addressing the shadow self that resides within each of us, how can we expect to bring those facets of ourselves to the light for our personal and collective healing?

Doing the deep inner work to connect with our inner child, shadow self, and unconscious is imperative for addressing the inner harms that may be impairing our ability to show up for ourselves and others as well as illuminate the oppressive behaviors formed in early childhood. As Carl Jung said, "One does not become enlightened by imagining figures of light, but by making the darkness conscious [which we will!]. The latter procedure, however, is disagreeable and therefore not popular."[5]

White supremacy has us operating from the head over the heart, such that making the darkness conscious is an inconceivable task. We've been conditioned to fear ourselves. Our emotions. Our hearts. When we are unable to access our intuition or acknowledge our feelings, we cannot show ourselves kindness, let alone those with an experience entirely different from our own. We are rewarded when we move from the rational, logic-based, or scientific spaces and reprimanded when we operate from the intuitive, emotional, spiritual, or unknown. Leaning into our emotional intuition is deemed irrational, unworthy of trust. There is good reason why so many of us, especially women+, are terrified to reveal our own shit, tap into our intuitive knowledge, and heal our hearts—it can feel like emotional if not physical death. For many of our ancestors, it *has*. If you believe in past lives (I do), then perhaps you yourself have been oppressed or otherwise burned at the stake for embodying your emotions.

This is precisely why Spiritual Activism—invoking Spirit and partaking in culturally informed practices to help us face our shadow, better withstand our discomfort, and transmute our pain so we can fight racial oppression and contribute to raising the collective consciousness—is so damn vital. It gets to the root of our individual and shared evils. It is how we can personally and collectively get, and stay, free.

THE GRIEF INHERENT IN RACIAL JUSTICE

I define grief as the normal and natural humxn emotional response to a loss, change, or lack of change of any kind, usually exhibited by deep sadness and/or other conflicting feelings. This is a big, long, wordy definition (sorry not sorry), so let's slice it up into bite-size chunks, shall we? We shall.

First off, grief is entirely normal. Many of us were taught that grieving is some maladaptive, overdramatic reaction. It's not. It is a natural response to a change or lack of change of *any* kind. Any time we experience a change—like a move, breakup, job loss, miscarriage, end of a friendship, even happy shit like marriage, a job promotion, or becoming a parent—grief may arise. Grief can also come from a lack of change—for example, financial hardship, infertility, or four hundred years of violent oppression. Our grief presents itself as uniquely as the stars in the sky. We may feel sad, depressed, hopeless, guilty, or remorseful. But we may also feel a range of other emotions, be it before a triggering event, after, or all at once. Emotions like anger, relief, shame, resentment, hope, or joy. Grief is less of an emotion and more of an experience. When I hold space for people in my racial justice workshops, I am mostly holding space for their grief. The personal grief we each feel as a result of being the oppressed and/or oppressor. And the collective grief we endure at the hands of a hateful system that seeks to stamp out people who do not fall within the "correct" category of race, gender, identity, age, religion, citizenship, language, ability, sexual orientation, class, beauty standards, and the like. Somatic educator and intuitive Dr. Vanissar Tarakali states, "Oppression is a social trauma that traumatizes—although in very different ways—both the targets and the agents of oppression."[6] For targets of racial oppression this social trauma is continuous because it has existed for generations, and omnipresent because it is perpetuated by every system and institution around the globe. Racism traumatizes BI&PoC by restricting our social, civil, political, and other basic humxn needs required for survival. It also engages physical, emotional, mental, and/or spiritual violence as a tool, be it actual or potential.[7]

As a queer Black woman, white supremacy has caused me a lifetime of pain, from the loss of professional opportunities, love interests, and friendships, to constantly being deemed as less smart, pretty, worthy, or capable, to witnessing Black people murdered without repercussion solely because they're Black. As Claudia Rankine titled her *New York Times* article, "The Condition of Black Life Is One of Mourning." She goes on to share that "the unarmed, slain [B]lack bodies in public spaces turn grief into our everyday feeling that something is wrong everywhere and all the time, even if locally things appear normal."[8] This is exacerbated by our gender socialization, as Black women and femmes are most often the primary caretakers of our communities. As Audre Lorde said, "Black women traditionally have had compassion for everybody else except ourselves."[9]

The grief created by white supremacy is egregious for Black folx, both historically and present-day, but we are by no means alone. First Nations communities in Canada and the United States are forced to endure national celebrations of Indigenous genocide every Thanksgiving, not to mention continuous assaults on their land and identity. Latinx* children of a variety of races are dying in cages at the U.S.-Mexico border while detained migrant Black, Indigenous, and Latinx women+ are being sterilized without consent. Trans folx, especially Black trans women, are murdered at epidemic rates worldwide, and on it goes. The constant assault on my welfare and the welfare of BI&PoC worldwide is designed to keep us stuck, distracted, and fighting for our right to simply exist. There can be little if any thriving when the system is designed to keep us focused on merely surviving.

HOW WHITE SUPREMACY HARDENS OUR HEARTS

White supremacy creates and perpetuates grief for *all*, but no one more than Black and Indigenous women+. It is a system of oppression that includes and perpetuates heteropatriarchy, transphobia, homophobia, fatphobia, ableism, classism, ageism, anti-Semitism, colorism, xenophobia, and all forms of oppression. It requires oppressors such as men+, white folx, and cis straight folx to cut themselves off from themselves, their humxnity, their own worthiness and inner peace, in order to believe in the oppression of others based on race, gender identity, sexual orientation, or otherwise. As such, social trauma is continuous and omnipresent for oppressors as well as the oppressed. Transphobia harms cisgender folx by subscribing to a false gender binary and reprimanding those who don't fit within subscribed "male" or "female" gender identity roles. Patriarchy harms men+ by causing them to feel shame for having basic humxn needs like vulnerability. The result of internalizing dominance is deep disconnect.

White supremacy requires all oppressors, especially white folx, to deny, dissociate, and defend. It robs oppressors of their inner peace and the ability to fully arrive in their heart space or genuinely connect with those they oppress, especially Black and Indigenous women+. In the words of white queer feminist Mab Segrest, "The pain of dominance is always qualitatively different from the pain of subordination. But there is a pain, a psychic wound, to inhabiting and maintaining domination."[10] There is a lot of inner, unconscious work required for oppressors to subjugate others based solely on race, gender identity, sexual orientation, or the like.

White supremacy requires all oppressors, most notably white folx, to internalize dominance. As Dr. Tarakali states, dominance requires:

> numbness
> obliviousness to the oppression and those they oppress generally
> denial and defensiveness
> avoiding, attacking, and blaming those they oppress
> refusal to take responsibility for oppression
> self-absorption[11]

What all of this adds up to, whether you are Black or white, man+ or woman+, gender conforming or not, oppressor or oppressed, is a whole lot of grief. Now, straight up, the grief white supremacy causes white people pales in comparison to what BI&PoC endure at the shit end of the discrimination stick. BI&PoC, especially queer and trans Black and Indigenous women+, have little choice but to contend with multiple systems of oppression that seek to exterminate us because of our race, gender identity, and other marginalized identities. Alternatively, the race-based grief experienced by white people is often so subtle it goes unnoticed, to themselves and the collective alike. Still, learning about the ways in which they have undoubtedly oppressed others, caused harm, and perpetuated white supremacy is tough! I know because I witness it in my work every day. To deny the existence of grief endured by all humxns is doing racial justice a serious disservice. Harm is cyclical. And the extent to which white people are unable or unwilling to address their grief and trauma is the extent to which we can rest assured a world free from the systems of white supremacy *they* created, perpetuate, and benefit from will never come to pass. Like, ever. The same holds true for anyone attempting to address the oppression they perpetuate on other grounds.

It is imperative to make space and honor all of our grief, both personally and collectively, so that we can heal our hearts and do the work required to create a just and free world for all and particularly for those who have been the most marginalized. Listen, I know this shit is hard. Unpacking white supremacy and its impact is triggering on a mental, spiritual, emotional, and physical level. It takes courage, bravery, and resilience. It is daily, lifelong work. It is hard AF. And—it must be done. You'll be learning how to do that inner work in these here pages.

Facing our shadow and committing to authentic, as opposed to performative or superficial, racial justice is some of the hardest work you will ever do. White supremacy has intentionally conditioned us *not* to do this work. Because our healing will set us free from the prison created by the most powerful and privileged, and a liberated society will overthrow oppressive systems and stakeholders. This revolution, led by queer and trans Black and Indigenous folx, has already begun.

Trust me when I tell you that embracing my shadow side and facing the racial reality are not things that just fell into my lap. Shit took work. When I began to confront my shadow self and address the ways in which I perpetuated white supremacy and other forms of oppression, it was physically and psychically painful. I had to acknowledge the ways I had favored white people in my relationships. How I had toned myself down in order to appease whiteness, ensure I did not make white people uncomfortable, and, in a word, survive. I got real honest about the ways I had participated in colorism and the ways I had oppressed other BI&PoC and queer or trans folx through thought, speech, action, or inaction. I'm not proud to admit that I laughed along with my white high school friends when we partied on the Musqueam First Nation reserve. It sickens me to recall when I believed bisexuality* wasn't real. And it aches to think back on my four-year-old self and the ways she felt she had to stifle her truth and conform to whiteness in order to be accepted. Still, facing my truth has allowed me to accept and transform it. I still feel all the feelings because I am humxn, but I'm no longer stuck in grief, anger, fear, or shame. Instead, I am devoted to and have the capacity for healing—mine and others. This is why committing to racial justice requires working toward healing our own pain in order to get to the vital work of creating a world where the most oppressed can find freedom.

SOULCARE VERSUS SELF-CARE

Spiritual Activism requires us to do the deep inner anti-racist work required for collective external shifts, and that inner work starts with and is sustained by a spiritual self-care I call "soulcare." This is a care that tends to our hearts, helps process our pain, and nourishes our souls. Though the term "self-care" has partial roots in Black feminist activist circles (like those of Audre Lorde), it has become an overused and white-washed capitalistic term void of meaning. I've witnessed far too many white women+ (especially cis women) tell me they are not engaging in politics or watching the news as a form of self-care when they never engaged with it in the first place. That may seem caring for *you*, but your inaction is also perpetuating white supremacy and the oppression of others. I've witnessed ignorance, denial, spiritual bypassing, tone-policing, and gaslighting—all forms of emotional violence—justified under the guise of self-care. Under white supremacy, self-care is often equivalent to self-indulgence and selfishness. Prioritizing ourselves is not the problem, but the issue arises when our self-care is not about care at all but indulgence that causes harm. All of which is in fact the least caring act you can take.

Soulcare addresses such harm. It is the actions or inactions we undertake in order to best care for our soul and highest selves as opposed to our ego or skin regimen. It may be messy and hard and uncomfortable—indeed it often is. Soulcare is part of communal care and understands that we must care for one another, as well as ourselves, in order for any of us to truly be well. It says, "My well-being is intrinsically tied to the well-being of others, so I will undertake actions that help me be whole, happy, and healthy, even when it's hard, so I can fulfill my purpose and contribute to fighting for the collective." It is about giving ourselves what we need in order to nourish our beings so that we can get into the world and demand a more equal and more just planet for *all*. It is a form of ancestral care.

Self-care often manifests as getting a mani-pedi, removing yourself from challenging convos, or consistently ignoring the consequences of white supremacist systems because they make you feel sad. It can be rooted in racist, classist, ableist, and patriarchal ideology. Soulcare manifests as setting healthy boundaries, tending to your inner child, declaring your needs, going to therapy, letting go of people, places, and things that oppress you or others, and healing your heart from your personal pain so you have capacity to support those most in need. As such, it is often based in spiritual offerings that support us in best supporting ourselves. For the record, I'm not knocking getting your nails did; I get mine done on the regz. What I'm saying is that soulcare isn't about treating ourselves. It's more like brushing your teeth—not something we necessarily love to do (I loathe it) but required for optimal health. Soulcare also appreciates that the people who are doing my nails often do not possess class, race, and gender privilege and that my need to feel good ought not supersede their access to basic humxn rights. Soulcare is about caring for ourselves in a deep and meaningful manner that arms us to better withstand our discomfort, face our shit, and ultimately care for the collective.

What is deemed self-care versus soulcare is also dependent on the person in question. As a Black woman who is plagued by trauma porn of Black men+, women+, and children being murdered on the regular, my choice to pass on mass media from time to time is an act of soulcare. For example, I have many Black girlfriends who couldn't bring themselves to watch the docuseries about the exonerated Central Park Five or R. Kelly's sexual attacks because they're too close to the trauma of our lived experience. And to that I say—soulcare on, my sistas! For Black women+, the pursuit of our joy can be a form of Spirit-led resistance. However, for a white or non-Black woman+ to claim it is too hard to endure watching such shows is quite another thing. Assuming there aren't other trauma triggers involved, it is not their lived experience so it is uncomfortable at best, not triggering. Making the choice not to enlighten themselves about the anti-Black realities faced by so many is purely a play of privilege. Soulcare for white and non-Black folx in that instance would be making a point to watch those shows and doing so with an intentional plan to care for their hearts before, during, and after.

Racial justice is an act of remembering and recalibrating. It demands a comprehensive internal review. This is why I've included a soulcare prompt at the end of every chapter, to support you in supporting yourself through this daily and never-ending journey of addressing your wounds in order to help heal the wounds of the world. Spiritual Activism requires us to address our hurts and biases from the inside out, and it necessitates surrender. None of which are easy. I was recently learning how to float in the ocean (at thirty-five years young), and as I did, I noticed how hard it was to relax. No matter how much I wanted to float, no matter how many other body parts I softened, until I relaxed every inch and trusted I wouldn't drown, floating simply wasn't possible. As soon as I surrendered, my body followed suit and showed up to support me entirely. I floated to the surface—because that's what the body wants to do. It is its natural response. But I was so stuck in my fight and fear I didn't trust what was possible. Doing the inner work is a lot like learning to float. Your shadow will fight you and you'll feel like you're going to drown. Most of you may be on board, but your inner child won't fucking relax and so the whole thing goes to shit, because every last ounce of you, your whole self, needs to relinquish in order to commit to racial justice. White supremacy starts within, and until we address what's going on in our hearts as well as our minds, there's no hope in hell of effectively eradicating oppression.

The journey you're about to take will not be easy. You will feel all the feels. Sometimes you will feel all those feels toward yourself and at times you will feel a lot of feelings about *me*. No matter how it manifests, it is vital that the inner work for the outer shift gets done. It starts here. It starts now. It starts with *you*.

Dancing with Your Inner Child

This soulcare prompt is an opportunity to get into your body, connect with your inner child, and start addressing any unconscious hurts that may be obstructing your capacity to address how white supremacy exists within you and how you engage in racial justice. When we aren't showing love to our shadow side and inner child, we can't dive into our inner realms to unearth all that needs baring and caring for in order to show up for ourselves and others. So, let's get connected!

Find a quiet space alone where you can turn on your fave tune (or just one you love dancing to). After you hit "play," turn it up, close your eyes, and move your body in whatever way you are able to and feels good, or simply envision yourself moving in your mind's eye. No matter how silly you may feel or think you appear. This is a time to shake shit up and out. If you feel stuck, shake your hands or feet or nod your head if you're able. Sing along in your mind or out loud. Let yourself take up space. As you move, envision your inner child is there dancing alongside you and cheering you on.

However your inner child shows up is perfectly fine—maybe they appear like you did when you were little, maybe it's a ball of light or just a feeling. Keep dancing and focus your energy on calling in your inner child. Listen for any messages or words of affirmation your inner child wants to share with you. Dance for the duration of the song (or longer if that feels good!). When you're done, reflect on the following:

> How did it feel to get into my body?

> What, if anything, did my inner child share with me (words, images, emotions)?

> What has caused my inner child pain? How is that pain obstructing my ability to care for myself and others, especially Black and Indigenous women+?

> How can I better acknowledge the ways white supremacy has impacted my shadow self?

> In what ways has white supremacy caused me to deny, dissociate, and/or defend the truth of who I am?

> What does my inner child need more of? Perhaps play, rest, joy, support, etc.

Take a few moments to journal these responses—or if you're still in the mood to play, draw a picture or make up a dance or song to reflect each answer.

If you find yourself feeling anxious or overwhelmed as you move through the book or beyond, come back to your inner child. Pause, check in, and ask what your inner child most needs.

For more support moving through personal and collective grief, peep my curated grief resources list at www.rachelricketts.com/grief-resources.

> > > > > >

FOUR

White Supremacy Runs the World

> I have never lived, nor have any of us, in a
> world in which race did not matter. Such a
> world, one free of racial hierarchy, is usually
> imagined or described as dreamscape—
> Edenesque, utopian, so remote are the
> possibilities of its achievement.
>
> **—TONI MORRISON, "HOME,"**
>
> ***THE HOUSE THAT RACE BUILT***

There isn't a single safe space on the planet for Black women or femmes. I love singing along to Queen B's "Run the World" anthem as much as anybody, but the hard truth is that girls do *not* run this world. Especially not Black and Indigenous women+ or girls+. All too often we discuss race solely in an American context when in reality white supremacy and anti-Blackness are rampant *worldwide*. The modern hierarchal construct of race originated in Europe, though the United States really ran with it in a diabolical way. Yes, America has a specifically dire state of race relations built upon centuries of kidnapping, enslaving, and lynching Black people and committing genocide against Native Americans. But America was not the first nation to partake in racist acts, and it is certainly not alone in upholding and perpetuating systems of white supremacy today. To assert otherwise creates a false paradigm where non-American states and citizens refuse to acknowledge that racism, anti-Indigeneity, and anti-Blackness exist within their nation's borders because it is an "American issue."

Over my years of living and traveling throughout the globe I've faced oppression on every single continent. During the year I lived in Scandinavia, often hailed as the most liberal and progressive region in the world, I was regularly subjected to anti-Blackness. My first night in Copenhagen was marked by a local leaning a few inches from my face to tell me how happy he was that his company didn't have to hire any Black people. In Sweden, I witnessed numerous acts of aggression against Afro-Swedes by white cops and security guards. When I got married in Morocco a group of local teens screamed "nigger bitch" after me, and growing up steeped in the insidious and "polite" anti-Blackness of Canada was nothing short of traumatizing. These are but a few of the countless incidents that have served to remind me that I am othered, ostracized, and unsafe no matter where in the world I may be. The constant exotification and emphasis on being deemed different wherever I roam is exhausting and pervasive. For trans Black women+, even more so.

Analyzing global white supremacy is a whole book in and of itself (whew, *chile!*), so we won't get into the nitty gritty here. Still, learning the framework underpinning racial oppression is part of the spiritual work. We cannot genuinely dismantle systems we don't fully understand.

RACE AIN'T ACTUALLY REAL

Fun fact: Race. Ain't. Real! Not scientifically. The Human Genome Project (HGP) published its findings in 2003 breaking down the genetic blueprint for humxns and concluding that we are 99.9 percent genetically alike.[1] The HGP researchers found that there was no support for the classification of humxns into distinguishable races. They also concluded that humxns share similar genetic makeup with bananas—so in case you needed a humbling moment today, there it is!

Despite race being a genetic, scientific, and biological fallacy, the impacts of race are very real and monumental in significance. Access to housing, health care, education, justice, immigration, upward mobility, equal pay, social supports, and the like are all directly influenced by the concept of race. I would happily do away with the concept of race. Who counts as what race, and when, can be incredibly arbitrary (as many multiracial folx will tell you). And we all descended from the womb of an African woman in the first place![2] But white supremacy has made damn sure that all BI&PoC are oppressed because of race, so white supremacy is the reason it must be taken into account.

Race is now pervasively accepted as a social construct, something created by and agreed upon within society. But what does it really mean when we say race is a social construct? Race did not pop up by happenstance. It is a concept that was intentionally created by white folx, to ensure they retained power and privilege to the detriment and exclusion of everybody else— being those who were not classified as "white." It was and remains a source of evil.

WHAT IS RACISM REALLY?

The modern concept of race was created by and for the empowerment of those who qualify as white, and this is the heart of what racism is and how it operates. Contrary to dictionary definitions created by white people to maintain white innocence*, racism is a global system of race-based hierarchy, oppression, and discrimination created by and for the benefit of white people (read that again). Racism is the culmination of prejudice*, privilege (a subset of power), and power as only held by white or, at times, white-passing individuals. What does that mean? Let's break it down.

Prejudice

Prejudice, based on prejudgment, is a feeling toward a person or group member based solely on that person's group membership. All humxns hold prejudices about others for a vast variety of reasons, not all of which are negative. Race-based prejudices include things like assuming Black people are criminal or Indigenous folx are alcoholics. Gender-based prejudices include believing all women and femmes are overly emotional, and a heteronormative* prejudice is believing trans women aren't women.

Privilege

A privilege is a special right, advantage, or immunity granted or available only to a particular person or group of people. We observe a lot about white privilege, and in the context of race it is certainly the most important, but there are many privileges pertaining to lots of things in addition to race, for example gender identity, sexual orientation, ability, class, citizenship, skin color, ethnicity, body type, and more. Any person of any race can hold a privilege; for example, I am cisgender, non-disabled, neurotypical, and financially secure. All of these are privileges because I and others who fall within the dominant group for the category in question inherently (meaning without intention or action) hold a special right or advantage simply by virtue of belonging to that group.

As International Ambassador for Black Lives Matter Janaya Future Khan states, "Privilege isn't about what you've gone through; it's about what you haven't had to go through."[3] Privilege permits us to disregard the impact of issues simply because they do not impact us personally. In the context of race, holding white privilege does not mean your life has been easy, but it does mean your life has been easier as a result of never having to endure racial oppression—whether you're aware of that advantage or not (and you're usually not). Examples of white privilege include regularly witnessing people who are the same as you portrayed in media, not having your community relegated to a reserve, not having to contend with the ongoing trauma that comes from generations of enslaved ancestors, and getting hired without others assuming you got the job because of your race, though in many ways, due to the insidious benefits created by white privilege, you likely did #thankyouwhiteness.

Power

Power in the global sense can be described as the legitimate or legal ability to access or directly control or influence all institutions sanctioned by the state. Unlike prejudice and privilege, power belongs solely to whiteness. As we saw with the classification of race, white folx have intentionally orchestrated global systems to ensure they maintain power and privilege, meaning in most cases economic and political power. Part of power is knowing that no matter where you are in the world, you can call state authorities to uphold your legal rights because both the global hierarchy of laws as well as those put in place to enforce it were created to ensure *your* safety and success. In America, this manifests as white people calling the cops, who originated as Southern slave patrols, any time they feel unsafe. And power is knowing the cops will believe you. This access to control extends past Western borders into predominantly BI&PoC territories as well.

In daily life, these racial power dynamics play out nonstop. For example, if I run a shop in London and I refuse to sell my goods to white folx, that's an act of racial prejudice. But, as a Black woman, I lack power. I do not have the ability to create unbridled harm against white people as a result of that prejudice. Black people neither created nor operate the British judicial, health, or political systems such as to have a detrimental impact on the lives and livelihood of white people. They will always find a store to serve them. My prejudice may serve as a temporary annoyance, but that's it. In fact, it is likely that *I* will face the most repercussions for my prejudice, because white folx hold the most financial power (so my customer base decreases) and their access to the state means they are likely to successfully persecute me for my prejudiced behavior, which is not the case when white or white-passing folx act prejudicially toward non-whites, even when we are murdered by white agents of the state.

What I'm driving home is that racism is a system of white supremacy that can only be exerted by white and, when perceived as white, white-passing folx, and them alone. *Only* white and white-passing people are racist because racism is about power. Any assertion that non-white-passing BI&PoC can be racist is misguided and dangerous. Racism was created by white people, is operated by white and white-passing people, and benefits white and white-passing people. *All* white and white-passing people. Be it tangibly or intangibly, financially, emotionally, physically, and/or psychically. Be it rich or poor, straight or queer, North American or European, cisgender or not.

And *all* white people are racist. Yes, all. Of. Y'all (even you, Linda). Whether you like it or not or intend to be or not. Simply by virtue of belonging to whiteness all white people perpetuate and benefit from the global system of white supremacy—on an individual and collective level. As do white-passing people in the situations they are considered white-passing. Take a moment right now and let that really sink in. Racism can be individual, institutional*, or systemic*, but it can only be perpetuated by white folx. Racism and white supremacy are in no way exceptional. They constitute the normal everyday status quo of societies around the world. To be white is to be racist. Just as being heterosexual is to be transphobic and being non-disabled is to be ableist. It is not an *if* but rather a *how*.

This isn't easy to receive, but I assure you, it's way harder to endure. So let's press "pause." Take a long, deep breath and note what's coming up. You may feel sad or mad. You might have some raw and real emotions. Whatever you feel: observe. Get curious about what your feelings want you to know. Keep breathing and let's keep at it.

RACE VERSUS ETHNICITY

The construct of race is often erroneously confused with another social construct: ethnicity. Ethnicity can be defined as a group of people who identify with one another based on common ancestral, social, cultural, or national experiences. Ethnicities based on ancestral or cultural experiences include Latinx, Hispanic*, and Jewish; ethnicities based on national and cultural experiences include African American.

Ethnicity is not the same as race and using them interchangeably glosses over important nuances. Latinx and Hispanic ethnicities each comprise a vast range of races—like Indigenous Latinx or Afro-Latinx—so using them to describe one race is inaccurate. If you are white and Hispanic, you're still white (not white-passing). Confusing ethnicity with the construct of race creates the false belief that white people who belong to marginalized ethnicities cannot be racist, especially to others within their ethnic group. A 2019 Pew report found dark-skinned Hispanics viewed as non-white face more discrimination than Hispanics viewed as white (64 percent versus 50 percent).[4] When we talk about ethnicities we need to be more specific as to whom we're actually talking about, because these groups are not a monolith and treating them as such only furthers and serves white supremacy.

Before some of you pop off, this does not take away from the fact that Latinx, Hispanic, Jewish, and other ethnic communities are, as a whole, oppressed in serious historical, global, and systemic ways. They absolutely are and that oppression needs to be condemned. Immediately. But ethnic-based oppression is not founded on race, and attempting to conflate the two erases the very real experiences of those living at the intersection of both racial *and* ethnic discrimination (like Afro-Indigenous folx). Racism is a very specific form of oppression. We cannot undo these systems of oppression without getting clear about the specific and complex ways in which they operate, both within and outside our various social groupings. Still with me? Good, let's continue.

WHITE SUPREMACY SPELLED OUT

Racism is a pervasive global system of white supremacy, but they are not one and the same. White supremacy is the common, status quo, globally held, and often unconscious belief that white people, and thus white ideas, beliefs, actions, and ideologies, are in some way superior to non-whites. It is the conscious and unconscious collective, institutional, and systemic belief that white people are and deserve better than other races, are rightfully entitled to hold the global majority of power, privilege, and all the benefits that go with them, and earned such power and privilege in a manner that did not take advantage, abuse, and oppress BI&PoC in order to do so. White supremacy is present in all facets of our daily lives. It shows its ass in science, health care, education, housing, justice (or a lack thereof), politics, government, the military, social welfare, banking, religion, nonprofits, and every single institution or system you can think of. Anyone of any race can perpetuate white supremacy, but in the end, only white or white-passing people benefit. *All* white people. Whether they intend to or not. Whether they're rich or poor, Jewish or Christian, straight or queer, cis or trans. Denying this fact is simply perpetuating further oppression and leading to more violence inflicted on BI&PoC. Now, let me be clear: I'm not saying all white people are bad or evil. What I *am* saying is that all white people belong to whiteness and perpetuate a system of white supremacy that has and continues to harm BI&PoC, especially Black and Indigenous women+, day in and day out. Often without intention. White supremacy is the normal state of being and it needs to stop. Like, now. All white people are responsible for the system of whiteness and its inherent white supremacy, and nothing is going to change until white people own and acknowledge their role and commit to dismantling the brutish systems they have created. Periodt. And BI&PoC need to make our own commitments and hold ourselves and one another accountable. For example, white supremacy shows up for me when I assume someone who is talking about a lawyer or doctor is talking about a white person, when I succumb to writing for the white gaze or otherwise prioritize the comfort of white people to the detriment of my own.

There are many ways white supremacy plays out, ranging from normalization to genocide, but its "softest" form is, according to

Fig 1—The Pyramid of White Supremacy by Scarlett Thorby-Lister, visual designer at the Equality Institute (as adapted from the Safehouse Progressive Alliance for Nonviolence)

the Equality Institute, indifference.[5] Let's go back to my getaway during the Charlottesville protests for a hot second: my white friends did not seek to know or much care about the brutal race-based assaults that had taken place that weekend. Indifference is like nourishing water to the grand oak tree of white supremacy. As set out in the Pyramid of White Supremacy on the previous page, indifference to racism leads to its minimization, minimization leads to veiled racism, veiled racism to discrimination, which morphs into calls for violence and ultimately mass murder.[6]

Racist violence and genocide grow not from the manure spewed by a few egocentric villains, but rather from the tiny seeds planted day in and day out by and through the indifference of everyday global citizens. You get to decide what kind of citizen *you* will be.

WTF IS WHITENESS?

Whiteness and what it means to be white often go entirely un-discussed. The focus of discussions of white supremacy is almost always solely framed around BI&PoC, which is another way white supremacy works (she sneaky)! It makes whiteness neutral, standard, and invisible. As though there aren't qualities or characteristics attributable to whiteness. But of course, there are. Whiteness can be described as an ideology rooted in belonging to a socially constructed "race" of humxns possessing the most power and privilege of any other race and believing in that race's superiority. It is the state of both being white (or white-passing) and perpetuating white supremacy.

Whiteness is a constantly shifting boundary separating those who are entitled to have certain privileges from those whose exploitation and vulnerability to violence is justified by their not being considered white. I say shifting because who qualifies as "white" is not fixed. White-passing multiracial folx may receive all the benefits of white privilege in some or all spaces whether they wish to or not, or may even identify as white. Irish and Italians were once excluded from the category but very much qualify today. Sometimes racially white Jews are considered white and sometimes not (def not to those rockin' white cloaks). Under the U.S. Census, South Asians were classified as "white" for one year in 1970,[7] and all North Africans are still classified as "white" today.[8] This all speaks to the socially constructed nature of whiteness, which is at its core rooted in anti-Blackness and defined by being everything Blackness is not. The construct of what is deemed white was simultaneously created through white slave traders' construction of what is Black. The practical reality is that "whiteness" is a fallacy just as "Blackness" is—each encompasses a broad range of folx from diverse places, cultures, languages, ethnicities, and nationalities. Whiteness requires white people to forgo their diverse cultures, traditions, and ancestry in order to belong to and benefit from it. Elements of whiteness include:

> perception of normalcy and inherent belonging—all others are foreign and exotic
> invisibility and unconsciousness—white people are generally unaware of their whiteness
> an imagined monolithic "white" race and culture
> perception of neutrality, which requires no contemplation or explanation of ethnicity or family origin

> definition by negation and the relational—whiteness *is* what Blackness and Indigeneity are *not* (i.e., savage, criminal, dumb, ugly, lazy, etc.)

> appropriation and domination of BI&PoC cultures and identities[9]

Being white means you belong to the system of whiteness and white supremacy like bread to whiteness's butter, but that doesn't mean all white peeps are pricks. As comedian and activist Amanda Seales shares, there are "white people" and then there are "people who happen to be white."[10] What's the diff? People who happen to be white understand that they benefit from and perpetuate white supremacy simply by virtue of being white. They appreciate the power and privilege that white supremacy has granted them, and they not only own and acknowledge that privilege but actively work to shift the power imbalance and create opportunities for oppressed folx every damn day. They are aware of their whiteness but actively negate it and the construct that belies it.

Then there are "white people," which is, unfortunately, the majority of white folx—and they be trippin'. They wander through life unaware of their whiteness and the ways in which they benefit from and perpetuate white supremacy on the daily, resulting in chronic acts of unintentional violence toward BI&PoC. But here's the thing: in this day and age, not knowing is often an intentional act. We live in a world where access to information is easier than ever. Google processes more than forty thousand searches every *second* (let alone other search engines)![11] BI&PoC have been making the same arguments for centuries. Nothing that I am saying, nothing that any modern racial justice activist is saying, is new. So y'all should have been knowing. A long-ass time ago. But your privilege-cloaked whiteness protected you from bringing this information into your consciousness. From needing to know.

As a matter of survival, BI&PoC have had no choice but to study, understand, and, to the extent possible, adhere to the ideology of whiteness. For this reason we understand it better than white people ever could themselves. In studying white supremacy for our own welfare, we have had to absorb its toxicity. In the words of James Baldwin, "I have spent most of my life . . . watching white people and outwitting them, so that I might survive."[12]

WHITE SUPREMACIST CULTURE*

One of my oldest memories from my predominantly white law school, with my all-white professors, was my first day in first-year property law. I remember my blond-haired, blue-eyed professor explaining that the majority of land in Canada was owned by the government, making the Canadian government one of the largest landowners in the world, entirely disregarding that the land was stolen from Indigenous people. I surveyed my classroom in disbelief, like, are we all just gonna pretend land fell from the sky into the laps of some lucky white guys? Oh, we are. Okay, cool.

When I showed up to my first criminal law class it was more of the same. I learned about the standard of the "reasonable person." Again, I looked around the room at my white professor and mostly white classmates like, for. Fucking. Real?! Who is this "reasonable person," though? Do they look like me? Are they navigating a world that is constantly using legal, social, and political willpower to stamp them out? Nah, didn't think so. The rest of my law school experience was precisely like this. Shocked and appalled at the extent to which the white-washing of the world was legally enshrined.

I was still naive back then, but all of this is precisely how white supremacy works.

In addition to being an ideology to which the majority of the world subscribes, consciously or not, white supremacy is also a culture. It is an ethos of values and characteristics that helps to perpetuate a paradigm of race-based and other oppressions. As Tema Okun outlines, white supremacist cultural characteristics include:

> individualism and perfectionism
> belief in objectivity
> power hoarding
> either/or thinking (right versus wrong)
> worship of the written word
> defensiveness
> paternalism and urgency
> quantity over quality
> fear of open conflict and right to comfort[13]

I would also add:

> binaries (including gender)
> entitlement to ownership and wealth accrual (aka capitalism)
> heteropatriarchy, fatphobia, ableism, homophobia, transphobia, colorism, and pretty much every form of oppression as it currently exists (most of which originated as a means to define "whiteness" as separate and superior to Blackness)

The grand revisionist history I was bombarded with in law school, an institution literally made by and for the encoding of white supremacist values, was very much par for the course. White supremacist culture is responsible for the capitalist culture of extraction and exploitation that created the climate crisis threatening the future of all life on Earth. It leads to the bullshit belief in an "American dream" (where anyone, no matter their access to power and privilege, can work their way to billions), overworking and pervasive burnout, and a culture where money allows you to cause harm with impunity.

BLACK & INDIGENOUS LIBERATION

As a result of misogyny, slavery, and colonization, Black and Indigenous women+ have the most intimate, violent, and long-standing relationships with white supremacy while also being subjected to global anti-Blackness and anti-Indigeneity from all races, ethnicities, and gender identities. Race impacts every humxn on the planet, but it is critical to be clear that it was created by white enslavers, for the purpose of justifying the enslavement of Africans, labeled "Black," as well as the slaughter of other Indigenous folx worldwide. Why? To ensure the wealth, power, and privilege of those presumed white. It is for this reason I highlight the dichotomy between white and Black and white and Indigenous (and particularly Black Indigenous). Since so much of the racial hierarchy was born from the oppression of these two groups, the resulting harms faced by Black and Indigenous folx have grand consequences for *all* who face race-based marginalization. Eradicating the system of racial harms endured by Black and Indigenous people will also lead to eradicating such harms toward non-Black and non-Indigenous PoC.

ANTI-BLACKNESS

When I was in grade seven, I was part of the class that put on an annual play, and in my year the chosen play was *Snow White*. At twelve years old I was the sole Black person in my entire school, so I was well aware of my otherness in a lot of ways—but still unaware of others. I lived to sing and dance, but my mom couldn't afford to put me in lessons, so this play was my big break. To say I was excited is like saying Aretha Franklin can sort of sing, aka a serious understatement. I did what any young girl who loves the center stage would do: I auditioned for the lead role. Uh-huh. I was ready to rock out as the most sensational Snow White and I didn't know of any reason why I wouldn't win the role. I could sing, I could act, I loved to dance. I had it in the bag. Except, I didn't. My white teachers cut me in the final round and I was devastated. I wasn't given any good explanation, and I could tell my teacher felt like she had done something wrong, but I couldn't tell why. It was only decades later in retrospect I realized I never had a chance for the role because, well, I'm Black! When I got hip to this in my early twenties I felt like a fool for even auditioning. But a friend reminded me that the teachers didn't have to choose a play that centered around whiteness that year (or ever). And actually, they still could have selected me for the role. It would have required some nuance, but hey, anything's possible. At the time the teacher wanted to make it up to me, though she wouldn't say why, so she gave me an alternate role of distinction. I was put on the playbill as, drumroll please: the lead dancer and witch's black cat! I wish I could ask my mom about this now, because I'm sure she had a stern word with the school administration, yet again.

Anti-Blackness highlights the specific racial oppression Black people face globally by all humxns at the hands of white supremacy. Every race, culture, and ethnicity oppresses those of Black-African descent, including the Black community. "Anti-Blackness" is used to name this expansive form of oppression against those of Black descent as perpetuated by any- and everybody.

To be clear, non-Black PoC certainly face prejudice from other races and racism from whites. That is an unquestionable fact. But the impact of anti-Blackness is particularly pervasive and brutal and results in discrimination against Blacks in all cultures the world over. For example:

> The most prominent form of hate crime in America is anti-Black hate crime, with 2,428 reported victims in 2018 alone.[14]
> Brazilians who appear Black or mixed-Black make up 76 percent of the bottom tenth of income earners.[15]
> Adult Black Americans are the most incarcerated population in the world, with one in twenty Black men between the ages of thirty-five and thirty-nine in state or federal prison.[16]
> Statistics Canada concluded that irrespective of class "the overriding factor determining vulnerability to household food insecurity [in Canada] is [being Black]."[17]
> Black Caribbean kids are permanently expelled from school three times more than the national UK average.[18]
> Black women+ are the most likely to suffer pregnancy-related death in the Western world, with Black Brits dying at a rate 5 times the national average[19] and

Black American women+ being 3.3 times more likely
to die from causes relating to pregnancy than white
Americans, irrespective of class or education.[20]

Clearly, privilege and oppression are not equally distributed
among communities of color, and unless we acknowledge and
address the inequitable experiences between us, we can never
unite against white supremacy. White supremacy by whites is
the worst oppression of all, but anti-Blackness by non-Black PoC
perpetuates a similarly toxic sludge. For example, Black Africans
were not only enslaved en masse to create unparalleled genera-
tional wealth for white western Europeans and North and South
Americans, but also Arabs. Over hundreds of years my Black
ancestors, mostly women, were kidnapped by Arabs to work as
laborers and concubines in India and the Persian Gulf. Capitalism literally relies on anti-Blackness, which is why capitalism is
part and parcel of white supremacy. As anthropologist Dr. Dori
Tunstall shares, "No other race's oppression is so intimately tied
to the global economic system as it currently exists."[21]

Black folx worldwide have been racially repressed by whites
and non-Black PoC, with Black women+ bearing the brunt of
both anti-Blackness and misogyny from all races and gender
identities. As Angela Davis said, non-Black PoC perpetuating
anti-Blackness often do so believing that they are enacting original ideas and beliefs that emerge from their own experiences;
in reality, they are carrying out the established anti-Black ideology of the state as created by and for white supremacy. And
it sucks. When BI&PoC tear each other down, we are distracted from tearing down the system. Anti-Blackness shows
up among BI&PoC and ethnic minorities in a number of ways,
including:

- Non-Black PoC using AAVE and otherwise stealing from Black culture for monetary and other gains.
- Choctaw, Creek, Chickasaw, and Cherokee nations enslaving Blacks as an assimilation tactic.[22]
- Black Ethiopian Jews being ostracized from the greater (white) Jewish community for centuries (and present day).[23]
- The undermining of the vital contributions of Black American leaders, many of whom were murdered or persecuted, to advance racial equity, LGBTTQIA+ rights, women+'s rights, etc. for *all* Americans.
- Black men+ who refuse to date Black women+ or only dating light-skinned Black women+.
- The resentment of the Black Lives Matter movement by non-Black PoC and the invalidation of the specifically violent race-based harms Black people face worldwide.

Moreover, pervasive forms of oppression like fatphobia and colorism are steeped in anti-Blackness, since whiteness created the white, thin, Eurocentric ideal of beauty specifically as a means to differentiate from and subjugate Blackness.[24]

Much like everyone else I have participated in anti-Blackness. I spent a lot of my life trying to be whiter in speech and spirit and was afraid to date Black men+ for fear of how Black love was judged by the white gaze. But we need to do better. Particularly white and other non-Black folx. We need to honor the ways all races and ethnicities are complicit in oppressing Black people (no one more than whites of course). In the words of the Combahee River Collective Statement, "If Black women were free, it would mean that everyone else would have to be free since our freedom would necessitate the destruction of all the systems of oppression."[25] We need to accept anti-Blackness as the most evil and widespread racial terrorism on the planet and consequently recognize how addressing anti-Blackness supports the liberation of *all*. To assert otherwise is to perpetuate the white supremacist system that treats all non-whites, and thus our experiences, as equivalent and invariable. And, as with anti-Blackness, we need to honor the ways Indigenous folx face extreme racial oppression through their erasure.

ANTI-INDIGENEITY AND DECOLONIZATION*

I grew up as an uninvited guest on unceded Musqueam territory, lands that were stolen by settlers who dispossessed the rightful stewards—the Musqueam peoples—removing them from their homes and hunting and fishing grounds, ripping them from their land and thus their identity. The atrocities of such state-sanctioned terrorism were never mentioned in my nineteen years of education on those stolen lands. Indigenous people were rarely thought of let alone spoken about, except as the brunt of some joke. Most of the identifiably Indigenous folx I saw growing up were living on Vancouver's Downtown Eastside, one of the most impoverished and addicted communities in North America. Every non-Indigenous person in the Americas, whether your family arrived as a slave, settler, migrant, or refugee, lives on stolen Indigenous land and consequently possess some form of settler privilege. White supremacy seeks to erode, deny, and ignore Indigenous peoples, perpetuating Indigenous invisibility whereby the majority of non-Indigenous folx know little, if anything, of Indigenous culture or even what Indigenous folx look like. All BI&PoC are indigenous to the lands we originate from—be it

Kenya, the Philippines, or Peru. All folx living in the Americas who are not indigenous to the lands we live upon, myself included, perpetuate and benefit from anti-Indigeneity and colonial land theft. All white people in the Americas are settlers and must acknowledge their settler privilege, and many non-Indigenous PoC in the Americas perpetuate settler privileges. As Potawatomi professor Dr. Kyle Powys Whyte states, "Having settler privilege means that some combination of one's economic security, . . . citizenship, sense of relationship to the land, mental and physical health, . . . career aspirations, and spiritual lives are not possible—literally!—without the territorial dispossession of Indigenous peoples."[26] The result is a long list of horrors for Indigenous peoples worldwide, with current consequences, including:

> European colonizers committing genocide against Indigenous groups worldwide, including my ancestors, the Taíno of Jamaica, who were essentially decimated by the Spanish.[27]

> Portuguese Jesuits in South America leading missions to hunt, enslave, and evangelize Indigenous people.[28]

> The Māori of New Zealand were frequently refused service throughout the '50s and '60s, with many hotels, bars, and other establishments displaying "European only" signs.[29]

> The traumatizing legacy of violent residential schools throughout the United States and Canada, which sought to "assimilate the Indian" and the last of which closed in 1996.[30]

Today, the culmination of these and so many more white supremacist atrocities have resulted in an Indigenous mental health epidemic, with suicide and self-harm constituting the leading cause of death in Indigenous Americans and Canadians up to age forty-four. Decolonization is beginning to get more traction, but non-Indigenous folx are still co-opting the Indigenous narrative and, to be blunt, fucking it up.

Decolonization is "a long-term process involving the bureaucratic, cultural, linguistic, and psychological divesting of colonial power," as defined by Māori professor and author Linda Tuhiwai Smith.[31] It is a specific intellectual and deeply spiritual act of not only divesting colonial power but also promoting Indigenization. As Indigenous scholars Eve Tuck and K. Wayne Yang assert, treating decolonization as a metaphor for general social justice efforts is yet another act of colonizing Indigenous theory and thought, which "kills the very possibility of decolonization" by recentering whiteness and settler innocence.[32] Decolonization certainly falls under the umbrella of racial justice, but it asks for something different, which is to imagine and create an existence outside of the settler nation. It differs from reconciliation, which is motivated by moves toward settler innocence and seeks to "rescue settler normalcy." Decolonization necessarily upsets the status quo in a confrontational—not to be confused with violent—way.

To decolonize is to withdraw from white supremacy in a way that tangibly counters anti-Indigeneity and promotes Indigeneity. It is to follow Indigenous peoples' lead without expecting them to do all the work to decolonize. It is to acknowledge the specific horrors faced by Indigenous peoples worldwide, past and present; challenge settler privilege; and renounce settler innocence—no matter your race or ethnicity.

INTERSECTIONALITY* & STANDPOINT THEORY*

What is vital in the conversation about oppression is intersectionality—an often misused term coined by Black law professor Kimberlé Williams Crenshaw in the 1980s. Intersectionality is, in Crenshaw's words, "a metaphor for understanding the ways that multiple forms of inequality or disadvantage sometimes compound themselves, and they create obstacles that often are not understood within conventional ways of thinking about anti-racism or feminism* or whatever social justice advocacy structures we have."[33] To dismantle white supremacy requires dismantling heteropatriarchy (and vice versa) alongside ableism, classism, ageism, capitalism, fatphobia, transphobia, homophobia, and the like. Given the global and pervasive state of white supremacy and its disproportionate impact on Black folx, Indigenous folx, women+, and LGBTTQIA+ folx, unsurprisingly queer and trans Black and Indigenous women+, living at the intersection of those most marginalized by white supremacy, are the most equipped to understand how to dismantle it. According to standpoint theory, a feminist theory arguing that knowledge derives from social position, those who share political struggles based in oppression are the best candidates to define and explain important social and natural problems. The theory maintains that those dominating social hierarchies (aka holding the most power and privilege) are out of touch with social reality and humxn connection and, as a result, can't view or frame their intellectual contributions objectively or soundly. Kinda like whiteness being invisible to white folx.

In order to survive, queer and trans Black and Indigenous women+ have to immerse themselves in the racist, sexist, cisgender, and heteronormative power structures and have no choice but to bear the brunt of those oppressive power structures, even if they aren't consciously aware of it (though methinks that would be hard). As a result, they understand systems of power and privilege the most and are best suited to educate and lead the collective as to how to dismantle them. Everyone else, especially cis hetero white folx, need to learn how the fuck to follow.

The most disrespected people on this *planet* are Black and Indigenous women+, especially Black-Indigenous women and femmes. We *all* need to address our anti-Blackness, promote decolonization, and uplift, support, learn from, check in on, pay, and follow Black and Indigenous women+ educators and activists (ideally queer and trans ones). Our collective well-being depends on it.

GLOBAL RACE RELATIONS

Now we have a clearer sense of the pervasive nature of white supremacy, anti-Blackness, and anti-Indigeneity. We understand that they're global systems that have existed for centuries and continue to play out on the international stage in a myriad of ways. White supremacy has conceived of Blackness and Indigeneity in very specific ways to ensure white power. This is why folx have been considered wholly Black under the "one drop rule" (to increase the number of enslaved workers), while Indigenous Americans had to prove their status based on blood quantum (to ensure their erasure and the freehold of stolen lands). If we acknowledge the bigger picture, we can recognize that race relations are fraught and fragile worldwide. We are in the midst of a racial crisis, most notably targeting Black and Indigenous people, and it is not new. Though it may be to *you*. Let's take a gander:

> America, the most notorious enslaver, was built on Indigenous murder and Black slave labor, cementing white wealth today. According to the Institute for Policy Studies, by 2050 the median white family will have $174,000 of wealth, but median Black wealth will be $600.[34] A 2018 U.S. Census found Native Americans have the highest poverty rate of any racialized group at 25.4 percent.[35]

> In 2019, the Canadian National Inquiry into Missing and Murdered Indigenous Women and Girls found the ongoing pattern of violence against Indigenous peoples, especially girls+, women+, and LGBTTQIA+, constitutes "Canadian genocide."[36]

> Sweden's racist legacy began with profiting from the transatlantic slave trade for nearly one hundred years as a major supplier of ships and chains, as well as owning a Caribbean slave colony.[37] In 2018, the Sweden Democrats, founded by Nazi supporters, became the country's third-largest political party.[38]

> In the UK, an OG enslaving nation, Black folx are forty times more likely than whites to be stopped by cops, while other visible PoC are four times more likely.[39] The UK's anti-Black ecosystem is so bad that Prince Harry and Meghan Markle, the first openly biracial member of the British monarchy, essentially left the royal family—and she's white-passing![40]

> In 2019, Brazil, the last country in the Americas to give up slavery and the largest enslaver, kidnapping nearly five million Africans (ten times more than the United States),[41] elected the "Trump of the Tropics," Jair Bolsonaro, who has permitted open siege on

Indigenous tribes, resulting in murders and the intentional burning of the Amazon rainforest.[42] What the actual fuck.

I could go on for days and we'd barely scratch the surface. Racism, anti-Blackness, anti-Indigeneity, and white supremacy are universal social constructs with unrivaled historical and present-day impacts. They are rampant and rule every corner of the globe, and we need to acknowledge that shit. We need to breathe it the fuck in and really and truly be with the truth of the consequences so we can get to dismantling these inhumxne global systems and overthrowing the power dynamics that created them (white folx especially). And that effort, my loves, starts with *you*. None of us live outside of these systems, and the only way we can disassemble the toxic structure from the inside is by first searching inside ourselves. We all have a role to play and specific gifts to contribute.

Exploring Our Anti-Blackness

Before we begin, for my Black loves, please take good care as you move through this exercise, as it can be triggering.

PAUSE, CLOSE YOUR EYES FOR TWENTY SECONDS, AND BRING INTO YOUR MIND'S EYE THE WORD "BLACK." WHEN YOU ARE DONE, OPEN YOUR EYES AND NOTE OR WRITE THE MAJOR IMAGES, WORDS, EMOTIONS, OR SOUNDS ASSOCIATED WITH THE WORD "BLACK" THAT AROSE FOR YOU (DO NOT READ ANY FURTHER YET!).

_____

_____

_____

_____

_____

NOW, CLOSE YOUR EYES FOR ANOTHER TWENTY SECONDS AND BRING INTO YOUR MIND'S EYE THE WORD "WHITE." WHEN YOU ARE DONE, OPEN YOUR EYES AND NOTE OR WRITE THE MAJOR IMAGES, WORDS, EMOTIONS, OR SOUNDS ASSOCIATED WITH THE WORD "WHITE" THAT AROSE FOR YOU (AGAIN, DON'T READ ANY FURTHER YET!).

When you've finished, review your two lists. Were your associations more positive or negative for a particular word? If so, which one and why? In my workshops, most folx come to discern how anti-Blackness is so deeply ingrained it rules our innermost thoughts and language.

Irrespective of our skin color, most of us have more negative associations when we think of the word "black" (criminal, dirty, immoral, ghetto) than "white" (pure, innocent, angelic), which is part of centuries-long social conditioning designed to prioritize whiteness and the white race as supreme and denigrate Blackness and Black people. If you genuinely didn't (good on you!), you're doing powerful work to counter status quo narratives. Either way, if it's available to you, hop online and check a thesaurus to confirm the status quo affiliations for each word.

REFLECTIONS:

> How did this exercise feel? What did you learn?
> How will you use this information to help counter your inherent anti-Blackness moving forward?

When you finish, practice this exercise or simply check the thesaurus for the following word pairings (again, for the oppressed group in question, take good care as you do so): "Indigenous" and "white"; "man" and "woman" (binary terms intentionally used here); "straight" and "queer"; "thin" and "fat"; "disabled" and "non-disabled"; "cisgender" and "transgender"; "rich" and "poor"; and any others you'd like to address. Explore what arises and use that as information to support your inner anti-oppression work.

> > > > > >

FIVE

Inheriting Mama Trauma

Pain is important: how we evade it,
how we succumb to it, how we deal
with it, how we transcend it.

—AUDRE LORDE

Our ancestry impacts everything we do whether we're aware of it or not. We bring our ancestors with us into every room we enter. Every conversation we have and every relationship we're in is somehow impacted by those who came before us, particularly those from our ancestral line. Most BI&WoC are aware of this fact, as we are forced to endure daily racist misogyny and the legacy it has created, much like our ancestors did. White women+, on the other hand, have the privilege of reaping the benefits of their ancestors' actions without much thought or attribution to how those benefits came to be or the fact that they are benefits at all. As history professor Kevin Gannon said in the documentary *13th*, "We are the products of the history that our ancestors chose, if we're white. If we are [B]lack, we are products of the history that our ancestors most likely did not choose."[1]

The key to escaping the consequences of our ancestors' choices, or lack thereof, is to unearth and address not only their existence but their impact. The trauma created by our ancestors and the ways that trauma gets passed down ancestral lines, causing grief, harm, and ongoing cycles of oppression. For us all. Past and present. White, Asian, whatever, but particularly for Black and Indigenous women+.

It is estimated that between 75 and 90 percent of all visits to primary care practitioners in America are stress-related.[2] This is magnified for those subjected to systemic oppression and all the more for those whose ancestors were as well. Enduring the brunt of white supremacy day in and day out takes its toll on Black and Indigenous women+ spiritually, mentally, emotionally, and physically. My mom's struggle with a lifetime of race- and gender-based violence, which led her to betray her own needs, voice, and dignity, is a prime example. She was unable to share her truth, especially her anger, and these repressed emotions and oppressive traumas manifested as physical suffering. The impact of my mom's trauma began well before I was born and resulted in her spending decades unable to move while writhing in unfathomable pain. Decades of my being a primary caregiver rather than a child in need of caregiving. My mom's physical pain creating personal pain of my own. Her lifetime of trauma, partly resulting from her mom's lifetime of trauma before her, being passed down the family line like an heirloom. In the end, the pain from all this trauma was so great, dying became her only option for the reprieve she desperately desired and deserved.

Before we get into it, please prepare yourself emotionally and otherwise for the following content containing medical racism, ableism, misogynoir, physical and sexual abuse, and death.

A LIFETIME OF PAIN

My mother was forced to starve herself to death. It was the fall of 2015, and she had been battling primary progressive multiple sclerosis, battling her own body, for nearly twenty years. That's two decades of tripping and falling, hopes and dreams slipping to the wayside, helplessness and isolation. Multiple sclerosis, also known as MS, had ravaged her nerves and organs, leaving her stuck in unbearable chronic pain. Once a decorated interior designer, hostess with the mostess, and role model to single moms everywhere, at just sixty-five years young, she was left with the sole ability to control nothing more than her eyes and mouth, with bones poking through skin and nerve endings that screamed merely at the touch . . . and that ain't no way to live.

My mom loved entertaining, and our home was a hub of social gatherings and celebrations. Christmas, Thanksgiving, and especially Easter were holidays to be cherished, and she went all out with table settings, four-course meals, and exquisite decor. To attend one of her dinner parties was an experience of the senses—every part of you left warmer and wiser. And really freakin' full! My mom celebrated everything. When I went off to college, I would regularly receive handwritten cards for all occasions, but her dis-ease stole her ability to partake in the things she most loved, like writing, cooking, and hosting.

Prior to her diagnosis, my mom had been one of the first female stockbrokers in Canada, working at a Toronto firm by eighteen. Though she started as a receptionist, she was bright and the partners picked up on her electricity right away. Not only was my mom a young Jamaican, she was "yella," considered neither Black nor white, but rather a racial mixture disregarded and unaccepted by both. She would tell me tales of walking the streets and getting spit on. By everyone. Her culmination of Black, South Asian, and white ancestry not quite making the cultural cut of 1960s racial politics. The isolation and ongoing oppression causing her great grief. There was an Italian guy she had wanted to marry, but his family wouldn't allow him to be with a "colored" girl. She was heartbroken. Tired of the misogynoir, my mom moved back to her hometown in Kingston. Unfortunately, she also moved back to a country in crisis.

When my mom returned in the mid-'70s, Jamaica was in the midst of its most violent political conflict to date. On more than one occasion she was chased and shot at by random men for no reason. After the second such occurrence, where the police refused to believe or assist her, she became depressed, hopeless, and suicidal. A psychiatrist diagnosed her with phobic "hysteria." It was the '70s after all, so medicalized misogyny was alive and well! My mom was scared and stressed. The whole experience was so disturbing she left Jamaica never to return, and never spoke of what happened.

After her second departure from Jamaica, my mom worked for another securities firm out west, but when the big stock market crash of 1987 hit, she lost everything. Her white male counterparts protected one another to save their estates while throwing her under the bus. In the midst of that crash, she met and married my father, a Jamaican survivor of physical and other abuses himself. She wound up badly beaten and locked in closets at my father's hand, all while pregnant with me. Meaning I have experienced abuse from the womb. When my father laid his hands on me, my mom left with nothing but the clothes on her back and baby Rachel in her arms.

In addition to enduring the impact of white supremacy through intimate partners, capitalist greed, and postcolonial disarray, my mother also suffered severe psychic pain resulting from sexual violence. In the course of writing this book, I discovered that she was sexually abused as a child, not only by a family friend but likely also by her own mother, my grandmother, an alcoholic hypochondriac who inflicted emotional, verbal, and sexual violence on several members of my family. Learning this was painful beyond words, and I hold a lot of anger at my grandmother for her horrendous acts, but I also acknowledge she was a survivor of abuse herself.

I, like my mother, like her mother before her, inherited traumas passed down the ancestral line from environmental and genetic influences alike. As Iyanla Vanzant says, "In the womb, we marinate in the energy that becomes the foundation of our beginnings, our sense of self."[3]

INHERITED TRAUMA

An emerging science has found links between the traumas our ancestors endured and impacts on our physical, mental, and emotional well-being. Epigenetics, also known as inherited trauma, is much debated by modern white-washed science, but the premise is that the expression of a gene is altered or modified in some way by an environmental factor, for example childhood abuse or a lifetime of enslavement, without changing the DNA code itself. Several mice studies have shown how trauma can pass down the familial line. One study found that mice who were repeatedly shocked while smelling cherry blossom developed a flinch (i.e., trauma response) when exposed to the scent on its own. The mice began to equate cherry blossom with pain. Nothing "shocking" about that (pardon my pun!), but scientists also found that the offspring of those mice exhibited a similar trauma response when exposed to the scent of cherry blossom. And it gets *more* wild! The grandbabies of the mice who were shocked also exhibited a heightened sensitivity to the cherry blossom scent. The trauma was subtly altered between the three generations, but it was there. It was inherited.[4] In humxns, a small study found that the descendants of Holocaust survivors had epigenetic changes to a gene linked to their stress hormone, resulting in higher states of stress for the survivors' offspring. Even if the trauma is altered and lessened in later generations, the impact of inheriting our ancestors' trauma can be massive. Particularly for Black and Indigenous women+ whose ancestors have faced kidnapping, enslavement, genocide, and all-out oppression for hundreds of years. Harvard bioethicist LeManuel "Lee" Bitsoi argues, "Native healers, medicine people, and elders have always known this and it is common knowledge in Native oral traditions."[5] It is what Bonnie Duran, associate professor at the University of Washington School of Public Health, calls a "colonial health deficit."[6]

POST-TRAUMATIC SLAVE SYNDROME

Not only do we inherit ancestral trauma through our genes but also from our environment, referred to as historical, multigenerational, or intergenerational trauma. Within the Black American context, Dr. Joy DeGruy has coined this phenomenon "Post-Traumatic Slave Syndrome," or PTSS.[7] Her research concluded that PTSS is the set of intergenerational maladaptive behaviors, beliefs, and actions originating as our ancestors' survival strategies to cope with the extreme stress caused by enslavement, systemic racism, and anti-Blackness, including lynching, Jim Crow laws, sterilization, and mass incarceration.[8] As Dr. DeGruy asserts, "We're talking about multiple traumas over lifetimes and generations. . . . Living in Black skin is a whole other level of stress."[9] Be it America, Canada, or the Caribbean, the impact of the enslavement of Africans worldwide has left a wake of inner and outer turmoil across the Black diaspora. In my case, inherited and intergenerational trauma has contributed to and/or manifested as cycles of abuse, addiction, and chronic illnesses throughout my ancestry. My Black American family members, with the strongest and longest legacy of enslavement, have suffered the most harms. Still, we didn't just inherit trauma, we inherited resilience too. Black folx are some of the most adaptable people on the planet, because we were forced to be. Though white folx benefit greatly from the oppression of all BI&PoC, we have a stronger hold on community and survival. Our oppressors harm themselves by harming us.

INHERITING DOMINANCE

There are adverse impacts to being the dominator as well as being the dominated. Those who carry out the oppression of others deprive themselves of our must humxn need: connection. As Dr. Tarakali shares, dominant group members face a disruption of their understanding of or felt sense of interconnectedness with those members of the group they are oppressing. In addition, children in dominant groups fear losing connection with and acceptance from their dominant caregivers and/or community in the event they do not fulfil the societal, implied, often unconscious expectations of the dominant group.[10] In this way, domination is very much inherited from our environment and upbringing and it creates grave harm for all. For white or white-passing folx, many, if not most, of whom have ancestors who committed unspeakable harms toward communities of color, the intergenerational trauma that derives from being descendants of people who could commit such atrocious acts, be it on a communal or personal scale, is not something we ought to take lightly. Harming others also harms you. And the shame and guilt and all the repressed emotions that go along with them live on across generations. As does the harm of having to erase one's culture to belong to whiteness.

Those who oppress others are in their own world of pain. When I witness white men+ out in the woods with hoods, not only do I observe violent aggressors, I observe people in pain. People who are hurt, scared, disconnected, and in need of somewhere to place the anger that arises as a result of a desire not to feel their deep feelings. I witness people who absorbed the pain of their ancestors and, as was also often passed down their familial line, choose to inflict their pain on BI&PoC. As Bessel van der Kolk, author of *The Body Keeps the Score*, has said, "Our capacity to destroy one another is matched by our capacity to heal one another. Restoring relationships and community is central to restoring well-being."[11] Trauma begets trauma and the cycle has and will continue unless white folx and other dominators actively seek to stamp it out in themselves. Only then can we stamp out the impacts those traumas have on the most marginalized.

THE MINDBODY

As an only child, I hung on my mother's every word. Plus, she said everything with such conviction it was hard not to! But, as her MS progressed and traumas became more evident, I began to understand where she was stuck. Stuck in stories, in shame, and in serious suffering. My commitment to my personal growth (and a shit ton of therapy) had illuminated the codependent nature of our relationship and the areas I needed to address in order for us to heal. I had always put my mom and her needs first, even as a child, but after decades as her primary caregiver it was time for me to begin to care for myself too. By the summer of 2015 we were no longer speaking every day as we had for my lifetime before. But she phoned me while I was at work, and in that discussion, she again told me atrocities that made me leave my body. It was yet another account of being abandoned by the caregiver she depended on and her hands being unable to dial her modified phone to let me, or anyone else, know. Of being left in soiled, feces-filled diapers for fourteen hours at a time. Of occupational therapists undermining her Black pain and social workers misconstruing her Black anger. An ongoing tragic tale of how the government refused to give her the money she needed for sufficient care and was once again trying to fuck her out of essential items. I was used to these stories by now. But the impact of these accounts never ceased to soften. I could never adequately brace for the impact of the violent acts committed toward her or the pathology of her predicament. So, in order to prevent myself from completely falling apart, I peaced from my body. Dissociated from my physical self and compartmentalized this egregious information until I was able to get there to help remedy another terrible situation. My mom also lived in a near-permanent dissociated state in order to merely survive her day. As her hardships became increasingly acute, my ability to handle it all became increasingly dysfunctional. I was burned the fuck out and, to be honest, was tired of dealing with it. I didn't want to play mom anymore. To be "Miss Fix-It." Lawyering myself up and preparing for battle against oppressive people and institutions alike. I was just tired. As I would later learn, these are also classic symptoms of trauma.

> >   < <

Trauma can manifest as fatigue, dissociation, a reduced ability to deal with stress, feeling helpless, anxiety, hypervigilance, etc. We often feel trauma is reserved solely for the most egregious of occurrences, but studies have shown it's not all that extraordinary. Any experience that is distressing or emotionally painful, that overwhelms your ability to cope and leaves you feeling powerless, can result in some spectrum of trauma. Especially if it occurs during childhood, which happens more than we may think. Studies have shown that on average 61 percent of adults have experienced at least one type of Adverse Childhood Experience (ACE) before turning eighteen, and one in six people have experienced four or more types (myself included). These include abuse, divorce, or witnessing violence in our home or community, all of which can result in trauma, even if we are unaware of it.[12]

As Dr. Gabor Maté, author of *When the Body Says No*, shares, "The essence of trauma is disconnection from ourselves," it is the separation of our mind from our emotions.[13] But our mind is not separate from the body; in fact leading experts refer to it as "the mindbody" to encapsulate their inherent interconnectedness—a foundational concept in traditional Chinese and other Eastern medicines.[14] Basically, anything that promotes a repression of our emotional state, especially challenging emotions like anger and grief, can adversely impact our health. Things like being oppressed because of your race or gender identity, feeling overwhelmed at the state of the world, or being abandoned by a caretaker as a child. When it becomes too painful for us to stay connected, we disconnect as a defense. For me, the disconnect came from a culmination of navigating white supremacy in my own life while also working tirelessly to help care for my mom, who was not only suffering as a result of a lifetime of trauma stemming partially from systemic oppression, but mired in a medical and social institution founded and steeped in racism, sexism, and ableism. Like many other Black women+, my mother and I were forced to deal with the compounding impact of white supremacy from both the ancestral trauma and the tangible daily oppression it created.

Because the mindbody are one and the same, our emotional trauma can manifest into physical disease, or the body's response to a lack of inner peace. It is unsurprising that my mom, who never felt sufficiently safe to share and thus heal her traumas, wound up stuck in her own body. Debilitated and unable to move. Paralyzed by fears of white supremacy's creation. The stress, trauma, and repressed rage transmuted into chronic illness, as though my enslaved ancestors' shackles were replaced by mental ones. The cause of MS remains elusive to this day, though it is known that there is a genetic and environmental element, with many believing stress plays a significant factor. This is in no way to blame my mom for her illness, at all, but as Dr. Maté explains, when we repress our emotions we relegate them to the unconscious realm, which, to be blunt, totally fucks with our body's defenses.[15] This can lead to those defenses turning against us rather than offering protection. Impacts of mindbody disconnect are most often found in folx with a long history of trauma and emotional repression, which creates stress on the body and usually manifests as chronic illnesses like cancer, Alzheimer's, or autoimmune disorders like . . . MS!

HOW TO KILL YOUR MOTHER

It was a midsummer's day when I got the call. I was rushing out the door when she called to tell me of yet another traumatic incident. She had suffered more abuse by caretakers' hands. Her pain was constant and immeasurable, and though she needed 24/7 care, it wasn't financially feasible. As an attorney and daughter, I had done all I could to fight for and defend her. But we were at a loss. I told her how much I loved her but that I couldn't keep being her only source of support. "Mom, I think it's time we find you a therapist so we can get you the emotional support you deserve," I said. For the first time in a long time she broke down. "I know, honey," she said, "I can't do this anymore and it's only getting worse. I think it's time for me to die."

Those words were utterly heartbreaking, but deep inside I also felt something like relief. After decades of supporting her as her only child and primary caregiver, constantly fighting with the racist systems that strived to keep her stuck, I wasn't sure how I was going to survive decades to come of being her primary source of support. In fact, I often wondered if I would be the one who died first trying to manage it all. The truth is there was no place that would sufficiently support my mom. Nowhere for a neurotypical quadriplegic Black woman in chronic, untouchable pain to try to have a life. That's not to say it's not possible; it is to say that a racist, ableist, sexist, and capitalist society did not prioritize caring for her or those like her in order to make it so. Folx of all abilities live thriving, joyful lives, but my mother was and could not. Her days were confined to ensuring basic survival. And survival was no easy thing within the white supremacist institution charged with her care and the impacts of trauma from a lifetime of various injustices. Her immense suffering manifested as physical pain but also hopelessness, anxiety, loneliness, and loss of meaning. In short, it consumed her entire existence. No matter how hard we tried, with our limited resources, the oppressive obstacles, and the magnitude of her repressed traumas, it just wasn't in the stars. White supremacist capitalism wants us to live as long as possible so we can produce as much as possible, without any care for our well-being, or lack thereof, while the institutionalized fear of death makes many a rich white man richer. Sure, my mom could live, as in inhale oxygen, but she couldn't have any kind of *life*. Dying while she still had some semblance of dignity felt like the only option left.

> >   < <

Our family doc and I thought that moving her to a hospice with 24/7 care would allow her to pass in peace. She could finally get the pain medication she needed, as she no longer required all her mental functioning to handle her underfunded staff and ensure they didn't harm her. However, as it turns out, it's not always so easy to die. It's a sacred and special process, and both your mind and body must be totally on board, otherwise, you're stayin' put. The mindbody is for real! Hospitals terrified my mom and for good reason, given her prior experiences of being mistreated by doctors from the age of eight when she was involuntarily used as an experimental birth control subject by Americans in Jamaica. This justified fear is shared by many other Black women+ who, for example, have a maternal death rate twelve times that of white women in New York City hospitals.[16]

My mom was moved to a hospice named after a white saint (cuz aren't they all), and from there I did everything in my power to help her find relief. To help her die. Assisted suicide wasn't yet legal, so we were on our own. Left to whispers behind shut doors and rampaging her drug cabinet for a "killer cocktail."

Being the badass bitch that my mom was, I thought she could just make up her mind and that would be that. Ya know, the old "wish yourself to death" trick. But no such luck. Day in and day out, over the course of three months, I stayed by her bedside. I fought with the doctors about my mom's care, sleeping on the pullout to help her feel secure for the first week. As the only Black folx in the whole hospice, it was immediately apparent to me that we were treated differently. My mom was out of her comfort zone, and the medical staff didn't help her feel safe. After merely a week into Mom's stay the white head nurse suggested that it was perhaps the wrong place for "someone like my mom." The fuck you just say?! To tell a sick, disabled Black person in unspeakable pain that she didn't belong in the only place she had left in the world was appalling. My mom's home was now gone. Her possessions given away. That hospice, that room, it was all she had left, and goddamn it, she was going to die in it.

I took on the role of researcher, trying to find some way I could confidently end my mother's pain. End her life. Including searches like "how to kill your mom" (which I do *not* suggest). In the depths of despair, I considered it all. Considerations that took time and energy I could have otherwise spent at my mother's bedside, supporting her through her pain in her most dire time of need. Had we been treated with adequate care and concern, I could have. In the chasm that is her absence, that's perhaps what angers me most. Finally, the head of palliative care, one of the many all-white doctors, sat me down to mansplain that they couldn't simply drug my mom into oblivion. It wasn't allowed and, even if it was, he wouldn't do it.

"Your mom's not dying," he said. "She could live another ten years. Most of her organs are healthy. Strong even. She's just in constant pain."

"Yah," I responded, "and that's *not* living."

The hospice wanted nothing to do with me, my mom, or our sitchu, and I had some compassion for that. Some. But white supremacy, ableism, and misogynoir, they can all get in the way of supporting a patient, her family, and helping them do what's right and best *for them*. Especially when the patient is a Black disabled woman subject to medical racism and an onslaught of dangerous stereotypes about her mental capacity and tolerance for pain.

THE RACIAL EMPATHY GAP

Numerous studies have shown that there is a pervasive racial empathy gap throughout the medical system, where Black folx are perceived as experiencing less pain than white folx. Some studies have found that the same doctor will prescribe less pain medication to a Black patient versus a white patient exhibiting identical symptoms. White folx from the age of seven years old have been found to exhibit a strong and reliable racial bias concluding that Black people feel less pain.[17] Which leads to us receiving less compassion and inadequate medical care.

It took decades to confirm my mother had MS, her white doctors routinely disregarding her symptoms and ignoring her welfare. And then they misdiagnosed her. At thirteen years old, I was told my mom had Lou Gehrig's disease, a fast-onset degenerative disease, and only had a few years to live. Had she been properly cared for, her MS would not have gotten to the point it did, and now that we were out of options and simply seeking support to help my mom die with dignity, we were once again being brushed aside.

A few mornings after the head nurse had more or less told us to leave the hospice, my mom told me about a white night nurse who yelled at her and refused to change her diaper, once again leaving her utterly helpless and forced to sleep in her own shit. Black folx seek out medical attention to support us in healing from physical and emotional traumas, as anyone would, only we frequently face more harm and oppression under that same system's "care." At my godfather's funeral (which I attended the morning after my mother died), I met a head nurse from another hospice. She had heard what my mom and I endured and expressed that it never should have happened—we shouldn't have had to fight to be treated with basic decency. But we did.

> > < <

"It's not physical pain your mom is experiencing. It's emotional pain," I was told by the hospice counselor as another justification for refusing to increase Mom's pain meds, "it's trauma."

"Yah, cool, I *know*. It's manifesting as physical pain, so what's the damn difference?!"

I was told repeatedly by the nurses, doctors, and counselor there was nothing that could be done. No way to help my mother hasten death or alleviate her suffering, and any thoughts I had to that end were sadly mistaken. Except that wasn't fucking true. My mom's family doctor, a South Asian woman and fucking legend, raised the option of voluntary cessation of eating and drinking, which is fancy terminology for starving and dehydrating yourself to death. Assisted suicide may have been illegal, but straight up suicide was not. The trick, though, was to get the racist jerks at the hospice to move past their oppressive perspectives and help keep mama bear as pain-free as possible during the process. But, because they were racist jerks, they wouldn't make that promise.

So, we called in a medical ethicist, someone specialized in helping solve medical ethics dilemmas—and, folx, we sure as fuck had a dilemma on our hands! In the most important and profound use of my legal training to date, I convinced the ethicist that my mom was absolutely entitled to terminal sedation (in regular speak: to be kept sedated on pain meds until she died). As I walked out, I felt triumphant. Kiss my sweet Black ass! If the medical establishment had just done its job and shown some fucking compassion, it could have saved us from this whole fucking fight. Medical racism struck again. But we. Showed. Them. Or so I thought. I passed by the room next to Mom's and saw that the patient who'd been there since we first arrived months before was gone. There were no feet poking out, no sheets or blankets on the bed. There was just *nothing*. And then it hit me. I had spent so much time and energy fighting, I had barely stopped to settle into what it was I was fighting *for*. My mom would soon be dead. Gone. And I would be alone.

> > < <

Over the next twelve days, I watched and guarded as my mom slowly slipped from this world into the next. It was painful, harrowing, and heartbreaking and simultaneously magical, beautiful, and transcendent. I sat by her bedside in total silence and basked in the glow of a soul that was half in this world and half in the next. I could sense something far, far greater than myself, and over those weeks any doubts I may have had about "the other side" were vanquished. Sometimes Mom was lucid, and she sounded strong and entirely in her body. On one such occasion she asked for her hand mirror, and I held it up so she could see her face. She moved her cheeks around, furrowed her brow, then exclaimed, "Shit. I may be dying but I still look pretty damn good!"

The next day she was unable to speak despite her best efforts.

Those were heartbreaking days. All she could utter were unintelligible sounds. I did my best to fulfill my duty as a guardian and gatekeeper to her transition. I played Deepak Chopra recordings and her favorite songs . . . all Celine! I burned incense (wasn't allowed, but fuck all y'all) and brushed her hair. I did anything and everything that I hope a loved one will do for me when my time comes.

Between her now zombielike state and the burnout from all the running around and managing and guarding and witnessing and fighting—I was at my wit's end. If I'd been exhibiting trauma symptoms before this whole hospice ordeal, you best believe I was in the thick of it now. For twelve weeks I had been living as though every moment could be my mom's last, and for two decades I spent every moment worried about her welfare. I went home that night and debated whether to go back. I had always been the hyper-responsible, dutiful daughter and most of my life I lived under the acute fear that my mom would die well before either of us was ready. I made the hard decision not to go. I was near the brink of something bad, and who knew how much longer this all would last. I went to bed and awoke at two a.m. I felt something odd and contemplated calling the hospice but decided not to. I put my head down to go back to sleep, and eleven minutes later, they rang: "Rachel, your mom has died. We're so sorry."

OPPRESSION KILLS

In the weeks and months that followed, I endured grief unparalleled. It felt like the weight of a lifetime of pain fell down on me all at once. Like a ton of bricks. Not only from physically losing my mom, but from all the losses, oppression, and pain both I and we had endured along the way. I relived the many lifeline alerts

I had received in the middle of the night to rush to her aid and how I lived across the street from her social housing unit in order to do so. I remembered all the times we barely had enough to eat. I could hear the scream she made before I found her lying on our living room floor, the white carpet stained with the blood spilling from her head wound—just days before my first-year law exams. I recalled the way our justified anger was routinely used against us. I reflected on the time I was nearly kicked out of university after my mom drained my student loans to pay rent because she didn't qualify for disability payments and was scared to be subjected to the "Black welfare mom" stereotype. The times I had to call the paramedics when she stopped breathing at four a.m. and then work eighteen-hour days on million-dollar deals to make rich white men richer. I was left to endure the cavernous ache of her absence but also the fact that had white supremacy not forced so much trauma upon her, had she been diagnosed earlier and/or treated with equitable health care, she never would have had to end her life at all. And I wouldn't have had to help kill my own mother. I was mired in pain that comes from combating a racist, misogynist, ableist system that made her dis-ease, her death, and my grief all the worse. With no one to constantly care for anymore, the thick haze of my own trauma, the burden of carrying a lifetime of white supremacist harms, descended upon me. Within three months I had suicidal ideations. Had it not been for my connection to Spirit, the support of a few close friends and my (now) husband, and a stint on antidepressants, I'm not sure I'd still be here. The compounding isolation of my loss and having my experiences constantly invalidated by misogynoir made me want to end my own life.

In the end, I was empowered to get a hold on my situational depression before it caused me or others grave harm, but I wonder how many other Black women+ have died and continue to die as a result of the tremendous trauma systems of oppression inflict on us and our families. Women+ like Erica Garner, who died of a heart attack at twenty-seven after her father, Eric Garner, was murdered on video by NYPD officers who never faced indictment.

As a queer Black woman living in a white supremacist world, the traumas I endure and the impacts on my health are never-ending. The consequence of inherited traumas like PTSS and the daily, lived traumas from enduring misogynoir have had atrocious consequences on both my family's health as well as my own. I suffer from anxiety and adrenal burnout from being forced to live in a near constant state of hypervigilance. My immune system is compromised. My stress hormones have been shot to hell, and it's hard to rest or digest because my body has been in fight or flight for decades if not a lifetime. Black and Indigenous communities around the world are diseased and dying from the impacts of white supremacy. For example:

> Black American women are 7.5 years biologically "older" than white women because our telomeres (ends of chromosomes controlling aging and key biological functions) are shrinking as a result of excessive chronic stress factors, including racism, classism, and sexism.[18]
> In Canada, Black folx have a 60 percent increased risk of psychosis compared with non-Black folx and are most likely to face racism from the medical establishment, increasing their risk of self-harm.[19]
> In South and Central America, Indigenous people endure the highest rates of morbidity and mortality, with the least access to health services compared with the non-Indigenous population.[20]
> In the UK, Black women are the most likely to suffer

from psychological distress, depression, and anxiety, while Black men are ten times more likely to suffer from mental health issues than white men.[21]

All the foregoing health issues are exacerbated in times of global pandemic, like COVID-19, as Black folx who, due to white supremacy, have higher rates of underlying health conditions and are more likely to die when hospitalized. It's no surprise (or mistake) that we're dying at disproportionate rates.[22] Indigenous folx are all too often disregarded by white medical "professionals" and left for dead, much like Joyce Echaquan who was murdered in a Quebec hospital when medical staff administered the wrong drugs then called her dumb and "only good for sex" as she wailed for help.

This is just a glimpse into the health consequences of systemic oppression on Black and Indigenous folx, and we haven't even covered the deaths caused by police brutality, the criminal justice system, or other state-sanctioned murders. Every day, in every way, white supremacy kills. In the midst of the COVID-19 and Black genocide pandemics, government agencies around the world declared what Black folx have known for centuries: anti-Blackness is a public health crisis. I know firsthand how the stress from oppression can kill, and yet I can never fully divest my nervous system from the same systemic web of lived and inherited stressors. I cannot help but wonder: *Am I destined to suffer the same fate?*

TOWARD HEALING

White supremacy creates trauma and causes havoc on the health of humxnity as a whole: BI&PoC as well as white people, LGBTTQIA+ as well as straight folx, both trans and cis beings.

No one is impacted more than the most marginalized, who are traumatized by oppression then further oppressed because of those traumas. Still, we all have harms in need of addressing. When we are not undertaking our inner work, these harms go unacknowledged, unaddressed, and ultimately unhealed. If we repress our emotions, especially our rage, they may very well manifest as dis-ease if not death. Especially for Black and Indigenous women+ who also face systemic oppression, including medical racism and misogyny. For white and other dominant groups, the inability to honor and tend to your inherited and social traumas is not only of great risk to your own health but to the health of Black and Indigenous women+ and other oppressed groups who suffer at the hands of your unhealed wounds. Trauma is not only an experience; it is a structure of oppression.

Right now, we have the privilege and opportunity to help heal ourselves from the inside out, across time and space, for ourselves, our ancestors, and future ancestors. Healing is possible but it requires a deep examination within. As you move through this work, and through the world, pay close attention to the ways your body is talking to you. And your body, if not your ancestors, will tell you when you are in stress—through sensations such as headaches, fatigue, indigestion, insomnia, and more. Do your best to notice when you are disconnecting from yourself and why. Pay attention to the triggering pieces and show yourself care so the emotions they evoke don't lodge within your physical self. Racial justice requires massive upheaval of the mind, body, and Spirit. It demands illumination of not only our own pain, but the pain that has passed down our families for generations and perhaps lifetimes.

We must acknowledge our ancestral history—whatever that may be. However hard that may be. Address the harms your ancestors endured or inflicted, or both. Examine what wounds you have learned, absorbed, or perpetuated. And begin to identify their stories and your feelings. Stop repressing and start expressing. Your life, my life, all of our lives, depend on it. Because white supremacy is killing us all, both internally and externally, Black and Indigenous women+ in particular. And because no one else should be forced to die like my mom did, and no child should be forced to bear witness. Until we do the inner work to address our personal and collective traumas and eradicate white supremacy, more Black and Indigenous children most certainly will.

Spiritual Soulcare Offering/Call to Action

REFLECT AND JOURNAL ON THE FOLLOWING:

> Do you have enslaved ancestors or ancestors who enslaved others in your bloodline? If so, have you acknowledged it? Is it acknowledged in your family? How or how not? How does it make you feel? How can you acknowledge it now? (Note: If you don't know your ancestry, you can research, or tune in and ask them.)

> Is there a history of known trauma in your ancestral line? If so, what? How has it shown up in your family line? Has it ever been addressed?

> How has your race, gender identity, and/or sexual orientation impacted your health (negatively or positively)?

When you've finished, find a quiet space where you can be in solitude for at least ten minutes for the following meditation.

Ancestral Meditation

As this is our first meditation together, let's take a moment to note that we will be partaking in these practices in a culturally informed way. This begins by acknowledging and honoring the ancient peoples of present-day India, my ancestors, who cultivated and shared the potent practice of meditation with the world so we can partake in it today. If it is available to you, extend gratitude to the Indian community for the gift of this practice by supporting them in some way (financially, energetically, or otherwise).

Now let's begin. Find a position that feels most comfortable for you in your body right now. It can be sitting upright with your feet on the earth, lying down, or otherwise. If it feels sufficiently safe, close your eyes. Or lower your gaze. Take a long, slow inhale through your nose, filling your belly and back body with air. Then take a long, slower exhale out through your mouth, emptying the belly completely. Take two more breaths in this manner. Begin to notice where you may be holding on to tension, perhaps in the shoulders, jaw, or brow. Breathe into those spaces.

When you are ready, bring your ancestors into your mind's eye. Ask them to come forth and present themselves to you. You may perceive them through sight, sound, or sensation. Just notice. Ask your ancestors what they most wish for you to know. Perhaps they want acknowledgment of the pain they endured at the hands of oppression. Perhaps they wish to express their apologies for the oppression and harm they inflicted on others. Perhaps both. Tune in, observe, and surrender. If it feels aligned, ask them to help release you from whatever ancestral patterns or stories no longer serve—whether you are aware of them or not. Feel free to share whatever you wish with them as well—affirmation, forgiveness, simply bearing witness. Ask them for support as you move through this work, which offers healing for them as well as you. Then call on all the ancestors of the land you live on, which may include the original Indigenous stewards of the land and/or Black folx kidnapped, enslaved, and brought to your region. Listen to what they have to say.

Finally, thank all the ancestors for communing with you and slowly open your eyes. Know that you can call on your ancestors for protection and guidance whenever possible. And I suggest you do so as we move through this work together. You may also wish to leave your ancestors an offering to show them gratitude—whatever feels best and right for you, be it a glass of water or wine or a hot meal. They are with you always and all ways. You are never alone—in this work or in the world.

≫ ≫   ≪ ≪

For more meditations to support you on your racial justice journey, head to www.rachelricketts.com/meditations.

SIX

> > > > > >

Getting Spiritually Activated

> Every [humxn] must decide whether [they]
> will walk in the light of creative altruism or
> the darkness of destructive selfishness. . . .
> Life's most persistent and urgent question
> is, "What are you doing for others?"
>
> **—MARTIN LUTHER KING JR.,** *STRENGTH TO LOVE*

To approach racial justice in a heart-centered and embodied way is no easy feat. It takes courage and constant compassion, which is supported through our soulcare. We all have a shadow side, but white supremacy intentionally encourages us to deny our challenging emotions and ignore discomfort—ours and others' alike. Consequently, many of us are unable to navigate the most complex, confusing, and critical systems on the planet—ourselves. Luckily, I've created five precursors for getting spiritually activated, as I like to call it, in order to engage in authentic, rather than performative, racial justice

These prompts will help you begin the work of caring for your soul by first illuminating what's there. They have been carefully cultivated based on my work helping thousands of individuals and global companies commit to racial justice, and if you're ready to dive deep and do the work, then they can help you too. There are reflection questions for each of the prompts, and I suggest setting aside some quiet time to be with yourself, journal, and reflect on your answers—all in one go or over a few days. As I've shared, writing using your nondominant hand helps you get into your heart and out of your head, so as always, if it's available to you, I encourage giving it a try for some or all the prompts.

Remember, this work is trying and often triggering, so take good care before you begin. Light a candle, play some music, burn some incense, or have a hot cup of tea on hand to help support you as you move through. There are soulcare offerings throughout this chapter to help you ground and address whatever may arise from going within.

Please know that if you need to take some time to get through these questions, that is okay. Take care of you, but do get through. These tools are an opportunity for you to get raw and real with yo'self. To crack your chest open and witness all that is there, the good, the bad, and the ugly, so you can start the necessary work of standing in your truth, owning your shit, and healing your heart. Then, and only then, can you authentically commit to the work of racial justice. And make no mistake, this work is urgent. It is necessary. And we need *you*. You ready?

#1—Embrace Vulnerability

Before we can commit to authentic anti-racism, we need to be willing to embrace ourselves, our transgressions, our experience, our grief, guilt, shame—and all of this requires us to become vulnerable. Vulnerability is the quality or state of being susceptible to physical, mental, or emotional harm, degradation, or destruction. As author Brené Brown shares, it is uncertainty, risk, and emotional exposure.[1] Vulnerability is a precursor to empathy and essentially every tool required to dismantle white supremacy, such as compassion, ingenuity, and resilience. Embracing vulnerability means trying with the knowing that you may get it wrong. It means dropping your defenses and accepting things as they truly are. It means leaning into your discomfort so you can learn why it's there and using that information to create deep and meaningful change. Racial justice requires courage, and to get there we first need to tap into the parts of ourselves we most often seek to hide.

Journal prompts:

> How have I witnessed vulnerability in myself or others? Do any images, sounds, or sensations come to mind?

> What did I learn about vulnerability growing up? Who, if anyone, modeled vulnerability for me?

> What prevents me from getting vulnerable? What do I find scary or hard about being vulnerable?

> Are there any real threats to my being vulnerable?

> How might vulnerability support me in connecting with others and advancing racial justice?

Connecting with our vulnerability is a major challenge in a world that constantly tells us to be anything but. If you can, finding time to practice the art of surrender can help. Find a quiet space alone, take three long breaths, inhaling and exhaling slowly, then repeat this affirmation:

I am ready, able, and willing to get more comfortable with my discomfort. I surrender, I surrender, I surrender.

Feel free to repeat this as needed however and whenever feels good (during breakfast, at the gym, during a meeting, whenever!).

#2—Get Honest

It is impossible to bring about social change if we're not being true—to ourselves, each other, and the cause. We all comprise light *and* dark, and both play a vital role. Our shadow side is part of who we are and how we experience the world. It is there to help teach us. For my fellow BI&PoC, let's get honest about the harms we've caused ourselves or other BI&PoC, particularly queer and trans Black and Indigenous women+, by internalizing white supremacy. For white folx, getting honest means owning whatever harms you've undoubtedly caused against BI&PoC. All too often white folx exclaim "I didn't know!" about the realities of racism, anti-Blackness, or anti-Indigeneity, and to that I say *bull. Shit.* Y'all knew. Consciously or unconsciously, y'all knew, but you need to face yourselves in order to admit it. What's needed is a serious reality check about our fears, motivations, and actions and how they've impacted ourselves and others, most poignantly the most marginalized.

Journal prompts:

> When was the last time I was truly honest about something hard? How did that feel?
> If I am new to racial justice and anti-oppression work (last few years or less), what took me so long? Why?
> If I had to switch places with a (or another) queer or trans Black or Indigenous woman+, would I? Why or why not? What, if any, privileges do I possess that they don't?
> How have I harmed myself and/or others because of white supremacy? How does it make me feel to recognize this truth?

#3—Acknowledge Your Anger

Anger is a strong feeling of displeasure, annoyance, or hostility, often resulting from some way we feel we've been treated unkindly or unfairly. This emotion has really gotten a bad rap, but *why*? All emotions are useful, informative, and show up for a reason. Anger arrives to inform us that something is wrong, something needs to change, or some boundary needs exerting, and that is some seriously important info for us and those around us to have. It is what some choose to *do* with their anger that has everyone's undies in a twist.

Make no mistake, Martin Luther King Jr. was angry. And he channeled that anger into a movement. Just because you feel anger does not mean you gotta run around calling everyone an asshole. Anger has and continues to be at the forefront of many leading social justice revolutions, so we need to switch up our perspective on and relationship with this particular feeling. Most of us socialized as women were taught that rage is wrong. We were made to feel ashamed or guilty for expressing ourselves in this way, especially Black women and femmes. This is even more true in the spiritual sense, as many "gurus" teach that you can't be both spiritual and angry. Well, I say FUCK. THAT. If you aren't outraged at the injustices in the world then you either don't care or aren't paying attention. So, let's reacquaint ourselves with our good friend anger so we can learn ways to fuel it into positive, progressive change. We'll dive into this further in Chapter 9, but for now, let's start getting familiar.

Journal prompts:

> Do I feel comfortable expressing my anger? Why or why not?
> How have people in my life responded to my anger? How did that make me feel?
> How does it make me feel when others express their anger? Especially Black women+?
> When have I witnessed anger expressed in a way that helped fuel collective change? How can I do the same?

Talking about, let alone diving into, our anger can bring up all kinds of ish. We can feel disconnected from our bodies trying to access an emotion many of us have repressed for decades, if not our entire lives. Many of us will find the ego fights us hard on this one, and anxiety can enter the scene at a fierce and rapid pace to distract us from actually accessing our anger. If you feel like things are getting anxious, swirly, or simply too much, inhale through your nose for four long counts, hold your breath for six counts, then slowly exhale out of your mouth for seven counts. Repeat two or more times until you feel grounded.

#4—Have Integrity

Integrity is the personal choice to hold one's self to consistent standards. There are a lot of performative allies and activists out there, and spiritual bypassing is at an all-time high (we'll get into all-a-dat in Chapter 8). If you think "love and light supremacy" is going to solve the dis-ease that is racism, you aren't really doing the work. And if you believe that your "good intentions" make you incapable of causing harm, guess again, friend. I am *not* (and will never be) down for that shit.

It can be easy to appear to act in allyship, but are your actions aligning with your appearances? Are your teachers' and mentors'? Are you following, supporting, uplifting, checking in on, learning from/about, paying, and centering Black and Indigenous women+? If not, there's a disconnect, my sweets. Irrespective of intentions, what we do and say is what has all the value. Impact over intention all the way. As such, we need to focus on our sincerity to this deep and meaningful work by unearthing the heart of the matter, getting intentional with our word and sticking to it.

Journal prompts:

> Do my actions align with my intention to fight racial injustice? Do my words?
> Do I use spirituality* as a means to defend, deny, or ignore my shadow side and the way it can cause harm in my racial justice efforts?

> Why am I addressing my racism or internalized oppression now? If I'm new to this work (i.e., last few years or less), what took me so long?
> What am I willing to lose in the name of racial justice? What am I willing to gain?

#5—Acceptance and Action

Authentic anti-racism requires us to *act* to bring about change whenever and wherever possible. There is much about ourselves, our community, and the world that can change and needs changing. Still, equally important is finding a level of acceptance for all that has and continues to transpire. The actions we did not take. The injustices we have already suffered. Those who have harmed us and the harm we have caused. Acceptance isn't agreeing with or condoning what has happened. Nor does it mean allowing further transgressions. It means we do our best not to succumb solely to suffering or getting entirely overwhelmed by the thick web of white supremacy. We practice loving kindness toward ourselves for what we did not know or were willfully refusing to acknowledge *and* we do better. We accept that we cannot fix every single issue in the world *and* we devote ourselves to doing the best that we can with the most pressing issues.

Folx get tripped up in the "coulda, shoulda, woulda," and here's the thing: If you're practicing authentic anti-racism, you're going to grow and evolve *every* day. You're going to reflect back in a week and think, *Dang, I needed to wake up!* Feeling guilt, grief, or shame can be part of the process of uncovering your truth and the truth. But if we get stuck there, we won't keep growing and flowing and engaging in this fight. Accept what needs accepting, and then get the fuck to work.

Journal prompts:

> > What do I need to accept about myself or my actions?
> > How can I use my mistakes to create meaningful change?
> > What can I do to support myself when I feel overwhelmed by all the oppression in my life and/or in the world?
> > How can I practice more compassion toward myself and others (especially queer and trans Black and Indigenous women+)?

Okay, that was a real reflective task! How did that feel? You've come a long way. Exploring inward, unearthing your ish, and beginning to address all that's there is hard—and it is necessary. Now let's continue the important work of tending to our hearts.

Energy Cleanse

You've been diving deep, and chances are you're feeling the impact not only emotionally and spiritually but mentally and physically. If/when you can, honor yourself with a long shower as a means to help you cleanse and purify your energetic field. The more we lean into our innate state of BEing, the more we can withstand our discomfort and commit to much-needed personal and collective change. This practice can help!

When you've finished the prompts above, take a shower and/or imagine the water washing away all that no longer serves you. Perhaps it's a now outdated identity, harmful situations you've experienced or harms you've caused others, or fear of embracing your anger. Recall the fear or frustration you named in Chapter 2's exercise. Call on your ancestors to support you in releasing whatever needs accepting and letting go. Imagine it flowing down the drain. Ask the water to help purify you as you do. If emotions arise, let them surface, release, and be cleansed by the water. Scream if you need. Cry if it feels cathartic.

When you feel complete, let the water pour over the top of your head or your heart space. Imagine the water as healing energy nourishing you with all that you need to embrace your hard truths, acknowledge the pain you've caused yourself and others, and commit to helping heal the collective. Repeat whenever you need help letting go.

> > > > > >

SEVEN

Unearthing Our Internalized Oppression

> The spirit of my ancestors did not
> manifest themselves in my soulbones
> to watch me become a convenient
> place for someone else's feet.
>
> —NIKITA GILL

I grew up in a city with a beautiful shoreline. There's a long seawall that wraps its way around the central core, connecting neighborhoods and hosting outdoor activities like running, rowing, and cycling. I don't run often—though this story makes it sound like I do, which I ain't mad at—but I did jog said seawall from time to time. Fighting global systems of white supremacy tends to cause me some stress (like, a lot), and one particular morning I arose and decided that getting my run on was that day's cure. As I laced up my sneakers, I was deliberating over where I wanted to run. Should I head to the seawall like I usually do or switch it up? I decided to spice up my life and run around the neighborhood I lived in at the time. I jogged down my street, turned left, and ran up the next. As I did, I noticed the predominantly white folx passing me by as they made their way to work. As I had the majority of my life, I lived in a predominantly white neighborhood. A nice one, full of heritage homes and green space. Seeing nothing but white faces pass me by was a real regular occurrence. But on this morning, I noticed something else. Something awful. I realized that as I ran I was doing so in a way to appease white comfort. Though I wanted to roam freely up and down the same streets to peep the beautiful homes and gardens in my hood, I wouldn't dare. I knew all too well that the white folx in my surroundings would be alarmed by a Black woman running aimlessly on their block. I could see it on the white and other non-Black faces of those who passed me by, and I could envision the folx in their cushy homes getting concerned. Instead of running where and how I wished, I ensured I appeared as though I was running "with purpose" to some final destination. I ran each street paying careful mind not to seem as though I was lost, directionless, or scoping the scene to steal. I was out on a run to relieve my stress and support my physical and emotional well-being, yet I was being assaulted by the woes of white supremacy telling me I was suspect and didn't belong in my own backyard.

As my own behaviors came to light, I felt disgust. I stopped my run and reflected on the truth: that I had been doing this my entire life—over thirty years at that point. I began to wonder how many other ways white supremacy had reared its ugly head inside of mine. How often had I moved through the world in a way that prioritized white folx and the comfort of whiteness to the detriment of my own? Probably a lot. This is how internalized race-based oppression works—causing myself and other folx of color to internalize negative ideologies about ourselves and other BI&PoC (especially Black and Indigenous women+) and prioritize the comfort and well-being of whiteness. But make no mistake, we don't make this shit up. Internalized oppression is rooted in very real lived and felt experiences. A few weeks prior to my jogging awakening, I had been on a run on the seawall (told you it sounds like I run a lot!). Like I said, I lived in a super white community, so being near Black people was always a cause for celebration. On this run I ran by my Nigerian friend Udokam, as well as a tall Black man a few blocks later. I made a post about it when I got home, because never in my Vancouver life had I seen two other Black people running when I was. It was a good day. After I posted, Udokam informed me that the Black man I saw was a friend of hers, and shortly after I passed him he was stopped by a white person "concerned" that he was lost. The racist assumption is, of course, that a Black person couldn't possibly live in a nice neighborhood or go for a fucking run like the thousands of other non-Black folx in the area. The result is a constant conditioning in Black folx to internalize that oppression within and among ourselves. This story has taken on a whole new meaning in light of the murder of Ahmaud Arbery, who was shot by white men for doing precisely as I, Udokam, and her friend had done—running while Black.

As described by the University of Kansas's Community Tool Box, internalized oppression is when people are targeted, discriminated against, or oppressed over a period of time such that they often internalize—meaning believe and make part of their self-image and internal view of themselves—the myths and misinformation that society communicates to them about their group.[1] This is not to be confused with internalized racism, as only white folx can partake in, let alone internalize, the global system of race-based dominance, and internalized racism is just racism. Periodt! BI&PoC internalize white supremacy, Black folx internalize anti-Blackness, women+ internalize patriarchy,

LGBTTQIA+ internalize homophobia and transphobia, and those living at the intersections of oppression internalize them all. Anyone belonging to a marginalized group or groups is prone to internalize the oppression taught and consumed by the dominant culture. As South African anti-apartheid activist Steve Biko once said, "The most potent weapon in the hands of the oppressor is the mind of the oppressed."[2]

MANIFESTATIONS OF INTERNALIZED OPPRESSION

Internalized oppression, also known as self-oppression or internalized inferiority, manifests in two primary ways through either the individual or group membership. With respect to race or ethnicity, on an individual level we oppress ourselves by internalizing the myths and misinformation spread by white supremacy about our race, gender identity, sexual preference, or ethnicity. This results in hiding our truth, withholding our authentic, fulsome identities, and/or playing into stereotypes leading to self-fulfilling prophecies. For example, when I was twelve years old I had a crush on the class cutie. Paul was blond and blue-eyed with Australian ancestry. One day I saw a photo of Paul and me that a friend had taken, and I quickly concluded our fate: we could never be together. He was the epitome of white male ideals—why would he ever like a "Black girl" like me? And that was that. I put a lid on liking Paul or any of the other guys in my predominantly white class and deemed my Blackness decidedly undesirable. Paul wound up marrying a South Asian woman—whom I adore—and my inner child was nearly moved to tears.

Race- or ethnic-based internalized oppression shows up through group membership when BI&PoC buy into white supremacist myths and misinformation about other members of our own racial or ethnic group and oppress or discriminate against one another instead of fighting those in power (white folx). This results in fighting, isolation, discrimination, criticism, etc. within ethnicities and communities of color. Anti-Blackness within the Black community is an example of internalized oppression on the group level. This plays out when, for example, Black men+ refuse to date Black women+, or Black folx advocate for people in power who actively discriminate and oppress Black people (hello, Kanye!).

Internalized oppression in the individual and group membership contexts leads to the furtherance of white supremacy amidst and between BI&PoC and shows up in all sorts of ways, such as:

> A Nigerian woman+ bleaching her skin to be lighter (i.e., whiter).
> A Mexican child refusing to speak Spanish in public to assimilate with the dominant white language (i.e., English).
> White-passing BI&PoC denying their non-white ancestry to reap the benefits of whiteness.
> An Indigenous person with straight A's only applying to community college because they don't believe they're smart enough to succeed elsewhere.
> The Rwandan genocide (murdering each other based on groupings created by and for the benefit of white colonialists).

I often find it's internalized oppression that fucks me up the most. It has me out in these streets stifling my own damn self and pits other Black folx against me (and me against them). White supremacy has done a damn good job of ensuring we hate ourselves and each other arguably more than white supremacy itself. You'd be hard-pressed to find a BI&PoC who's escaped this vice—not even our greatest heroines.

My mother once told me about the time she had the honor of designing the stage for Maya Angelou at a speaking event. When she went back to the dressing room that she'd designed to meet Ms. Angelou, whom I adore, our poetic prophet was having none of it.

"She can't come in," Ms. Angelou said, pointing to my white-passing mom (after finishing all the hard alcohol my mom had been required to leave in the room). "She's *milk*!"

My fellow Black folx will know that Ms. Angelou was referring to the fact that Black folx come in all shades, from milk white to blue black. My mother was a light-skinned, multiracial Black woman, and Ms. Angelou, of much darker complexion, actively discriminated against her because of it, leaving my mom utterly crushed.

I don't share this to shit on anybody—both my mom and Maya are legends gone too soon in my eyes, and if you've read *I Know Why the Caged Bird Sings*, you know Maya endured some seriously painful stuff. My point is that internalized oppression can get the best of *all* of us. And it's a damn shame.

IMPACTS OF INTERNALIZED OPPRESSION

Irrespective of how it manifests or disseminates, race- or ethnicity-based internalized oppression has serious adverse impacts on the oppressed. These include:

> feeling inherently less worthy, good, capable, deserving, beautiful, accepted, etc. because of your race or ethnicity

- believing there is something wrong with being a BI&PoC
- believing you are not BI&PoC, or less of a BI&PoC, because you are white-passing
- having lowered expectations and limiting your self-potential
- experiencing limited choices to either act in alignment with white supremacy or disrupt the status quo and the internal conflict that creates
- feeling hopeless or overwhelmed by the lack of available possibilities[3]

As Dr. Tarakali shares, it also frequently leads to survival strategies that may include:

- appeasing and caretaking of the oppressor
- staying silent or attempting invisibility
- withdrawing from and avoidance of the oppressor
- isolation
- dissociating and numbing
- hypervigilant scanning and interpreting everything in the social environment as a threat[4]

These impacts are real, lasting, and take a toll on the well-being of the oppressed. As a queer Black woman I have been dealing with adrenal burnout caused by caretaking, hypervigilant scanning, and people pleasing for close to a decade. The consequences are more multifaceted and magnified for those at additional intersections of oppression. A queer, trans, dark-skinned, disabled, fat Indigenous woman will have to unpack further layers of interconnected internalized oppressions, for example.

For multiracial folx with white origins and/or white-passing BI&PoC, the mindfuck continues, as you are likely to both benefit from white privilege (in some form) while also battling internalized oppression caused by white supremacy. For this reason, many white-passing BI&PoC are forced to work double duty to address their shadow side, which often entails the oppression of others while also being oppressed because of race or color.

HOW DO WE HEAL?

White supremacy starts within, and for the oppressed, it festers there, creating a potent cocktail of self-hate and in-group conflict. How do we overcome it? First and foremost, by dismantling white supremacy. It is impossible for BI&PoC to eradicate our internalized oppression so long as its cause, white supremacy, exists. Though it is on white folx to dismantle the oppression they created, we all must fight for racial justice out in the world and make room for BI&PoC, especially queer and trans Black and Indigenous women+, to prioritize our own comfort above that of white supremacy in our hearts and homes. Facing our shadows, showering ourselves with compassion, and supporting ourselves with soulcare are all vital to the resistance, as is coming together in sufficiently safe spaces free from the white gaze to commune over our shared struggles. Acknowledging the ways in which we cause harm to ourselves and others serves to loosen the shackles of oppression. As Audre Lorde once said, "What are the tyrannies you swallow day by day and attempt to make your own, until you will sicken and die of them, still in silence?"[5] Naming internalized oppression when you notice it at play in yourself and others can help to minimize its power. Get clear about your intention to address and overcome your internalized systems of dominance. This intention can reduce your time spent *in tension*. And BI&PoC deserve all the freedom we can get.

REFLECT AND JOURNAL ON THE FOLLOWING:

> How has internalized oppression shown up in my daily life (re: race, ethnicity, gender identity, sexual orientation, etc.)?
> How have I contributed to internalized oppression in others (particularly queer and trans Black and Indigenous women+)?

This can unearth a lot of conflicting feelings, so you may wish to ground yourself before and/or after. If it is available to you, head outside and put your bare feet, hands, or back on the earth (grass, soil, or sand). Getting into nature and connecting to the earth's electrical energy, known as earthing, can alleviate stress and promote well-being. Hence the term "getting grounded"! If nature is inaccessible, all good: if possible, lie on the floor at home and envision roots extending from your spine into the earth below.

Call to Action

IN MOMENTS WHEN YOU FEEL INTERNALIZED OPPRESSION MAY BE AT PLAY, ASK YOURSELF:

> Whose comfort am I prioritizing right now?
> Why?
> What is it costing me and/or others (especially queer and trans Black and Indigenous women+)?

Commit to calling it out in yourself and/or others whenever it is sufficiently safe to do so.

> > > > > >

EIGHT

Spiritual Bypassing & Emotional Violence

> The courage to be authentic is spiritual.
> Unauthorized positivity in order to be
> liked [or] approved of is not.
>
> —UNKNOWN

My father has spent the better part of his life seeking spiritual affirmation. He has changed his name to abide by numerological guidelines, fasted to better commune with his physical vessel, and spent what I'm guessing cost tens of thousands of dollars on (blood) crystals to energetically uplift his environment. When I was eight, he built a meditation hut in his backyard. When I was ten, right after my half sister was born, he spent a month of solitude camping in the jungle in Kauai, searching for Spirit or salvation or whatever the fuck you find living solo in a jungle. When I turned twenty-eight, he moved to Malaysia to live near his guru of the moment. I don't know many people who have spent as much time and energy on their spiritual fitness as my father. And yet, I have not experienced the fruits of all that money and supposed labor. For all of his efforts to connect with his highest self, my father remains entirely, and often incredulously, ill-equipped to face his shadow self or take any responsibility for his actions. Despite practicing yoga and meditation long before it became cool, he remains unable or unwilling to own up to his shit and truly heal his heart. Instead, he uses his spirituality as a cloak to not only disguise his personal imperfections and emotional underdevelopment, but justify them. Actions such as telling my twelve-year-old self I would never amount to anything. Or criticizing me for being unable to "release the past" when I hold him to account for his emotionally, verbally, and physically abusive ways. I've spent much of my life enraged by and resentful of this fact. Now, I mostly feel sad. I have come to realize that my father is partaking in a well-oiled machine of denial, bypassing, and emotional violence. One created and powered by a white supremacist source of spirituality.

Spiritual bypassing is the "tendency to use spiritual ideas and practices to sidestep or avoid facing unresolved emotional issues, psychological wounds, and unfinished developmental tasks . . . to disparage or dismiss relative hum[x]n needs."[1] It is rampant not only in spiritual and wellness circles but in the daily discussions I have with liberal white women+ (especially cis women), who use it to primarily end any discussion about race that makes them uncomfortable. Being pretty much *any* discussion they have with me about race! It's the notion that spirituality means things are always light and positive. It means they bypass addressing or talking about the hard stuff. And that is not spirituality. That is the opposite of spiritual. That's using spiritual tools or offerings as a means to bypass the reality of people's lived experience, to bypass humxn emotions and discomfort. In terms of racism, spiritual bypassing manifests as:

> Constantly seeking "positive vibes only." This is "love and light supremacy," where spirituality is used to avoid an embracing of our shadow selves, conflict, anger, or challenging emotions of any kind.

> Claiming we are all "one race," which denies the very real and divergent lived experiences of BI&PoC.

> Perpetuating the "law of attraction" or "you create your own reality" style of thinking, which denies systemic barriers for BI&PoC and privileges granted to white/white-passing folx, also while blaming BI&PoC for our inability to overcome institutionalized oppression. As tarot reader Corinna Rosella said, "Maybe you manifested it. Maybe it's white privilege."[2]

> Anger-phobia and overemphasis on forgiveness, which denies the full spectrum of humxn emotions, demonizes anger or sadness, and requires BI&PoC to withstand violence while undertaking deeply challenging emotional, mental, and spiritual labor, causing us harm and upholding white supremacy.

> "Stop being divisive," which again denies the lived experiences of BI&PoC and upholds the egregiously divisive status quo that is white supremacy.

The person partaking in spiritual bypassing is keeping *their* comfort prioritized. It's about them, their inability to face their shadow or tolerate their entire emotional spectrum, let alone the spectrum of others, and that's it. There's nothing spiritual about it. It is also often accompanied by a serious level of judgment of others and anything "low vibe," delusional thoughts of being somehow spiritually enlightened, repression of emotions, or a tendency toward mindless compassion. Now, here's the tricky part.

Because nothing is fully black or white (pun intended). There are nuances to all of these things. For example, I very much believe that we are all one. I believe we are interconnected beings. But in order to appreciate and lean into our connection, we must honor the vastly different experiences each of us is having and the ways in which I have been harmed, and have harmed others, at the hands of white supremacy. It's a thin and often shadowy line. But fear not. I got suggestions to help you with this delicate dance.

BOLSTERING AGAINST SPIRITUAL BYPASSING

One of my primary suggestions for recognizing if you are engaging in spiritual bypassing as it relates to racial justice and anti-oppression is to check in with your honest intention *and* its actual impact. Are you trying to make things easier and more comfortable? If so, for whom? If it is for white people or the oppressor in question, chances are something problematic is at play. Spiritual tools and practices are about unity and oneness, but that unity is only authentic if it is bringing folx from all walks of life together to be affirmed and supported equitably for who they truly are and for the breadth of their full lived realities. In order to create real union we need to honor and acknowledge the oppression faced by BI&PoC due to white supremacy; women+ due to patriarchy; trans and queer folx due to transphobia and homophobia; and queer and trans BI&WoC due to all of the above.

Spirituality is a means for us to learn how to withstand our discomfort and unpack and address its origins; it is not intended as a mechanism for constantly feeling lighter or better, for working around or away from challenging emotions. If you are engaging in avoiding discomfort through a spiritual-based excuse, you are spiritual bypassing. That is entirely different from invoking Spirit to help you move through challenging emotions or as a means to help you dive deeper into yourself and the ways in which you can honor and accept wrongdoings, repair harm caused, and expand into a higher, more aligned version of yourself. *That* is the path to Spiritual Activism.

EXPOUNDING EMOTIONAL VIOLENCE

In addition to spiritual bypassing, there are a host of other harmful actions and behaviors that are often present amidst those both inside and outside of spiritual or wellness communities, all of which are forms of emotional violence. Emotional violence can be described as a range of psychological-based behaviors inflicted, intentionally or unintentionally, to manipulate, silence, hurt, coerce, control, belittle, isolate, intimidate, or otherwise psychologically, verbally, emotionally, or spiritually harm another. I include spiritual bypassing as a form of emotional violence because it results in psychological, spiritual, and emotional harm. For example, if I inform a white yoga teacher that I found their class harmful because they did not use inclusive language and the teacher responds by saying I am being divisive or that they "don't see color," the teacher is using spirituality to avoid the issues being raised and derail the conversation at hand. This causes me emotional harm because I have expended time, energy, and labor to raise these concerns, and the result is being met by defensive responses that deny my lived experience and reject my request for connection. Our deepest need as humxns is belonging, so feeling constantly othered, ostracized, and unwanted, especially as a result of speaking truth to your own oppression, is incredibly painful. It causes real and tangible harm. Other forms of racialized emotional violence include:

> **Gaslighting**—This is a covert form of manipulative abuse, again intentional or unintentional, whereby BI&PoC are made to believe that we are not experiencing the racial harm we are experiencing, causing us to doubt our reality. For example, if I tell a white friend they said something racist and that friend responds by saying, "You're just being sensitive," or "That's not what I meant."

> **White wildness**—This is the fragile and ferocious defensive response white folx commonly have in regard to race or racism. For example, when white people get upset when race is mentioned or at the sheer thought that I could know anything about them or their behavior solely because they are white. A white woman named this "white fragility,"* being the "state in which even a minimum amount of racial stress becomes intolerable, triggering a range of defensive moves . . . such as anger, fear, and guilt, and behaviors such as argumentation, silence, and leaving the stress-inducing situation."[3] I've renamed this concept to emphasize the harm it inflicts.

> **White entitlement***—The belief that it is a BI&PoC's duty to educate white folx about race, speak to white folx kindly and calmly about race, and otherwise behave in a way that allows white people to remain coddled and comfortable about their power and privilege—which I won't be doing, so get yourself all the way prepared!

> **Weaponized kindness***—Coined by antibias educator Leesa Renee Hall, this is "using the quality of being friendly, gentle, tender or considerate as a tool to

guilt someone into abandoning their [justified] anger, [loving] boundaries, or much needed self-care."[4]

> **White innocence**—The idea or belief held by a white person that they are a "good" white person somehow excluded from benefiting from and perpetuating systems of white supremacy and causing BI&PoC harm. This ironically causes BI&PoC harm, because when the white person does inflict pain on BI&PoC, the white person refuses to acknowledge or address it.

> **White silence**—When a white person is aware that an act of racism is taking or has taken place but refrains from saying or doing anything about it.

No matter the form of oppression in question, emotional violence is rampant. Especially amidst women and femmes, because emotional violence is the only acceptable form of anger release or expression for women and femmes to exhibit in a heteropatriarchal society. And emotional violence is covert AF! Still, as a result of white supremacy, BI&WoC are subjected to ongoing emotional violence at a greater rate than other women and femmes. And of course, queer, trans, poor, disabled, etc. BI&WoC even more so. As author Soraya Chemaly states, "Middle-class white girls appear to be the most likely to suppress negative feelings and the least likely to be openly angry,"[5] because heteropatriarchal ideals of femininity require a disconnection from one's emotions in order to meet the fucked-up standards of the status quo (think passive, helpless, small, etc.). It makes sense then that cis white women are also some of the most emotionally violent. All of that pent-up anger is just stored up waiting for the minds, bodies, and souls of the niche population that cis white women feel sufficiently safe enough to unleash their scorn on—being BI&WoC

(*especially* Black women, femmes, and femme-presenting folx). Journalist Liz Plank wrote about the impact of patriarchy on cis men, and she concluded that in a heteropatriarchy, for men, "showing violence becomes more acceptable than showing feelings,"[6] and I believe the same to be true for women and femmes, especially cis white women, but the violence is emotional as opposed to physical. Because women and femmes are not generally allowed to express our anger, we instead commit calculated, often untraceable acts of mental and emotional warfare against one another. When I learned what gaslighting was my mind was blown. My (white) best friend at the time had treated me that way our entire relationship, and I had thought I was losing it, which is one of the telltale signs you're being gaslit by the way! Heteropatriarchy would have us believing that women and femmes are not violent, but I beg to disagree. And cis white women, the pinnacle of idealized femininity, take the cake.

So! Let us move forward armed with this awareness. As trauma therapist Meenadchi shares, violent communication arises when we are disconnected from our hearts and bodies and unable to acknowledge or express our needs.[7] Nonviolent communication requires us to deepen our connection to ourselves as well as others and to work toward holding more capacity to meet others in their needs while honoring our own. Let us pledge to put down our weapons of mental and emotional warfare, and for fuck's sake let's express our righteous rage so we can channel it toward collective change rather than perpetuating white supremacist aims (especially you cis white women!).

Skip the Spiritual Bypassing

Below are some helpful questions to ask yourself to help prevent spiritual bypassing and investigate whether spiritual bypassing may be at play:

1) Am I using spirituality as a means to lean into or away from my or another's discomfort?

2) Is my heart or my ego running the show right now?

3) What is my tolerance for challenging emotions or discussions?

4) How am I using spirituality to embrace both light *and* dark?

Instead of bypassing, try the following:

1) Check if your need to be good and right is overriding your commitment to racial justice.

2) Shut up and listen.

3) Believe BI&WoC. If we think it is about race, gender identity, or both, chances are high that it is, and even in the rare instance that it truly is not, do your best to appreciate the toll of constant, daily emotional violence and aggressions. Same for other oppressed identities.

4) Get more comfortable with your discomfort.

5) Name it. Call people out when you feel bypassing may be at play (yourself included).

As always, there is no telltale sign, you will have to explore and practice and investigate on your own in each and every situation. Luckily, you're a smart and fully capable humxn who is absolutely able to do better as and where required (finger snap, neck roll). You got this! That is, so long as you're really willing.

NINE

Spirituality, Anger & Activism

> Those who want an antiracist society
> must understand that terrain extends
> beyond institutions. The battle is—
> at least partly—spiritual.
>
> **—ANDRE HENRY**

SPIRITUAL ACTIVISM & SOULFUL SOCIAL JUSTICE

Spirituality is an ethereal concept with many understandings. In direct opposition to the analytical, tangible, facts-based knowledge adored by white supremacy, spirituality is inherently elusive. It is not visible nor can it be measured. It is a mystical entity. It requires faith. Though spirituality is somewhat unexplainable, I agree with Brené Brown's description:

> *Spirituality is recognizing and celebrating that we are all inextricably connected to each other by a power greater than all of us, and that our connection to that power and to one*

another is grounded in love and compassion. Practicing spir-
ituality brings a sense of perspective, meaning, and purpose
to our lives.[1]

Spirituality is deeply personal and entirely interrelated. It is both a faith and a practice, and it commands an ongoing and honest commitment. Sometimes it is associated with a particular set of beliefs and guidelines, as in organized religions, and sometimes it's not. My spirituality is secular, meaning it is not tied to an organized faith; but that doesn't make it any less potent. Because spirituality and the concept of Spirit (or Higher Power or whatever you wish to call it) is so intangible, it is highly misunderstood and appropriated. To me, spirituality is not about following specific rules or praying to a certain God over another. I'm not knocking those things, but they are not what constitute or create connection among us. To the contrary, they are very often used as a means to divide us. In contrast, my understanding of spirituality is about connecting with ourselves, one another, and the planet. It appreciates the interconnectedness between all living beings, be it on this plane or beyond, and the sacred, infinite, and unwavering energy that binds us all. This spirituality acknowledges that we are all born perfectly imperfect. That we all have purpose and part of that purpose is to call ourselves into our highest version of being, which manifests differently for different folx. It also understands that we have all the tools we need. Everything we need to awaken our fullest potential and self-actualize, in this life or any other, exists within our own hearts. Not a guru or a god. After all, as interconnected beings, I *am* God. As are you. We are one, though our lived experiences greatly differ. I believe we are born knowing this truth, and it is the journey of our lifetime to learn, unlearn, and relearn so we can remember who we really are. The practice of spirituality then becomes the practice of learning how to tap into our interconnectedness, face our inner shadows, and transform our pain into personal and collective change. I won't say my version of spirituality is "right," because that line of reasoning simply perpetuates white supremacy and I ain't here for that shit. But I firmly believe this understanding creates more connection, more belonging, and ultimately more peace. Alternatively, as we'll discuss, there have been far too many instances of folx who have used their version of "spirituality" as a tool for oppression.

Like spirituality, activism can also be a profoundly personal but fundamentally collective practice based in faith and hope while demanding an ongoing commitment. That is, when it's done authentically. Sadly, performative activism is rampant out in these streets. The commodification of "diversity and inclusion" by white supremacist capitalist heteropatriarchy is serving us more of the same, but with a few more Black faces in the marketing materials. Folx are finally understanding that they cannot continue to operate as usual, because the usual is racist, sexist, homophobic, ableist, transphobic, and oppressive in pretty much all ways. But many people are caught up in seeking to be perceived as "woke" without doing the work required to get them there. Performative activism manifests as dropping social justice buzzwords without knowing their history or meaning, calling on others to address their oppression without actively and continuously addressing your own, and seeking cookies (i.e., praise) for sharing a post on socials or otherwise doing the bare minimum. In the wake of George Floyd's murder, it looked like millions of white people demanding education from Black educators only to ignore Black lives and liberation a mere three months later. It is superficial, careless, and the antithesis to spiritual practice. Along with Chris Brown and white boys rocking puka shells—performative activism needs to become a thing of the past. Conversely, authentic activism is a deeply spiritual enterprise. It demands our presence. It requires us to get right with ourselves before ever attempting to call in* others, and it includes a constant assessment and reassessment of ourselves, our values, and when and how we are out of alignment. It is a practice of soul-filled social justice.

> > < <

I rejected the term "activist" for a long time. It didn't feel right to employ a word used to name my ancestors who fought day in and day out on the front lines. Who risked their livelihoods, lives, and families' lives in the name of collective justice. But I came to realize that as a Black woman, sharing my truth is absolutely a revolutionary act and one that attracts a lot of violence. In a divinely feminine understanding, baring yourself in such a vulnerable way and being met by ongoing emotional and spiritual assault and/or abandonment is undoubtedly an act of activism. Activism isn't, nor need it be, solely relegated to subjecting yourself to physical harm. I have lost countless friends and community. I have declined many well-paying opportunities because capitalism always perpetuates white supremacy even when it has a Black face on it. I am routinely exposed to threats to my life, health, and well-being. I am an activist, and my activism is a spiritual practice.

I believe spirituality is a necessary element of activism and activism is a vital element of spirituality. Spirituality is an active, not passive, undertaking. It requires not only conviction but effort. It seeks to both practice and create connection between humxns and Spirit, to dismantle that which prevents us from aligning with each other, our greatest good, and the Most High.

Spiritual Activism, then, is my take on how we call folx of all races into the work of activating their hearts as well as taking active measures necessary for racial justice. Spiritual Activism is racial justice and anti-oppression work entrenched in connection, soul, Spirit, and collective consciousness. It is an embodied approach to activism and the element of racial justice most often missing. But it is an essential part of the puzzle. Soulful social justice is anti-oppression work that begins with *us*. It is centered around the inner work we must first undertake in order to contribute to collective healing and dismantling all forms of oppression.

Spiritual Activism is about the activism work that I, as a queer Black woman, was called to do. And who is considered an activist should be very carefully considered. If you do not face the same odds as the oppressed identities in question, you do not have the same consequences. You can act in allyship, but you are not an activist simply because you are spiritual and/or seek to end oppression. Seeking to end oppression doesn't make you special or extraordinary, nor should you seek to end oppression in order to *be* special or extraordinary. Committing to racial justice makes you a humxn connected to the collective. And our unified healing. MLK Jr., Harriet Tubman, and Malcolm X practiced forms of Spiritual Activism in different ways, and what we need now is a culmination of the practices they commenced with divinely feminine intervention.

Spiritual Activism, comprising an embodied, heart-centered approach to racial justice, is the path toward our collective salvation. It's about outward action but also doing the inner emotional work required to overthrow systems of oppression. And it requires we acknowledge the violence that those claiming to be spiritual have and continue to inflict, particularly on communities of color.

SPIRITUAL SINS

It is impossible to talk about white supremacy without discussing the role of religion. Organized religion is often a masterful mind-control tactic used by whiteness to control Black, Indigenous, and other populations. Myself included.

When I was nine years old my mom and I visited my aunt in North Carolina. In true southern form, my aunt is a devout born-again Christian, so when Sunday morning rolled around my mother and I put on a good face and joined her and my cousins at their predominantly white church. To this day, I can recall the grandeur of the chapel, the size of the ministry, *and* the terrifying sermon by the priest. As he was preaching, he proclaimed that it was the duty of all those in the pews to recruit all non-Christians to the faith otherwise we too would burn in hell. At my impressionable age this deliverance rocked me to my core. I exited the church in tears, my mother taking me away to assuage my fears and ensure me that hell was not a place I would be going simply because I did not do as a white man on a pulpit commanded.

I am a secular spiritualist but am all for those who subscribe to a specific faith. The problem I have—the serious and pervasive problem that needs to be addressed—is the ways in which organized religion, guised as spirituality, has been and continues to be utilized as a tool to dominate, exploit, and oppress BI&PoC, women+, LGBTTQIA+, and all those who do not adherently abide by whatever particular scripture they happen to spew. For example:

> The Spaniards used Catholicism to dominate much of the Philippines.

> Israel continues to use violent force against Palestinians in the name of Jewish occupation.

> Canadian and American settlers used Christianity to strip Indigenous peoples of their culture and spiritual beliefs.

> The Arabs who enslaved Africans for hundreds of years did so under Islam.

Religion also supported the creation of modern-day racism, with Christianity playing a major part in advancing the hierarchal concept of race way back when. Colonialism was motivated not only by gold and glory, but God. Missionaries and colonizers alike felt it was their Christian duty to spread religion and convert non-white "savages" to the faith.[2] As Showing Up for Racial Justice says, "Christian church[es] have played central roles in reproducing the idea of white supremacy (i.e. that white is 'normal,' 'better,' 'smarter,' 'holy')."[3] Not to mention the ongoing and intimate connection between Christianity and the most violent white supremacist organization the world over, the Ku Klux Klan. Many organized faiths are also homophobic and transphobic, particularly Fundamentalist Christian sects that promote an egregious act of terrorism against LGBTTQIA+ folx they coin "conversion therapy."[4]

A lot of fucked-up, oppressive shit has been done in the name of religion and spirituality. But I'm not coming for religion as a whole. As I said, I support those who subscribe to organized faith insofar as that faith is not based in the subjugation of others for any reason. What is entirely unacceptable is when religion, or any form of spirituality, disguises a quest for power and control under the cloak of spiritual freedom. Spiritual freedom has nothing to do with either. Whether it's in the name of Osho or

Jesus Christ, I don't care. What I do care about is how your faith is (or is not) used to cultivate connection and not only acknowledge but address oppression, both personally and collectively. Embracing spirituality and practicing Spiritual Activism mean acknowledging the harms that certain sects of spirituality have inflicted against BI&PoC, especially queer and trans Black and Indigenous women+, and following marginalized communities' lead as a means to right the wrongs already inflicted as well as prevent future harms. Spiritual Activism also requires us to embrace the fullness of our emotional experience—including, if not especially, our anger.

THE ROLE OF RIGHTEOUS RAGE

"Rage" is not a word most of us are comfortable with, especially not in spiritual circles. We usually connote anger and all related emotions as deviant and destructive, but our anger is a vital part of our emotional well-being. Anger tells us when a boundary's been crossed or an injustice suffered. And rage, an intensified form of anger, does precisely the same. Though rage is often perceived as inherently uncontrollable and violent, that understanding is yet another tool of white supremacy. And with good reason! The rage we witness under white supremacy most often *is* violent and uncontrolled—and manipulative. Most of us have succumbed to an unchecked form of rage at some point or another—I most certainly have and it ain't pretty. I have wielded my rage abusively through shaming, condescension, and coercion. It's not a rage I'm proud of nor promote, and certainly not the rage I'm proposing (obviously). I'm talking about a rage that includes love and compassion. For ourselves and others. Righteous rage is motivated by, and results in, deeper connection as opposed to desire for domination. It demands discernment. It is forceful anger that is asserted when a grave harm has transpired and it commands accountability. Accountability seeks to remedy harm, restore trust, and reestablish severed bonds. Righteous rage is infused by and with Spirit. This kind of rage is a reflection of our mental, emotional, and spiritual vitality.

Feeling intensified anger can actually be a sign of your health. For example, if you feel rage in response to being abused, your rage is an indication that you care about yourself and your well-being; it is calling you into action to ensure you are not subject to such maltreatment in the future. Rage, like anger, can be channeled and transmuted for good. It is at the core of many of the most notorious social movements of our time. Righteous rage can, and very often has, changed the world for the better. Marsha P. Johnson channeled her rage into coordinating the Stonewall uprising to uphold gay rights. Martin Luther King Jr., fueled by his anger at the poverty and plight of Black Americans, mobilized millions into creating more equity for all. Angela Davis's outrage at the social and political inequalities of women helped solidify the feminist movement. Indeed, without anger we may never have had the likes of the LGBTTQIA+, civil rights, or women's movements. It is important to note how the rage of the oppressed is particularly demonized and policed by white supremacy. For example, Black rage channeled in support of Black liberation very often requires civil disobedience as a means to combat the overwhelmingly oppressive systems of state-sanctioned brutality (like Minneapolis and Portland being set ablaze after George Floyd's murder). Black folx who took to the streets during this civil uprising were named thugs and terrorists, with many non-Black folx calling for strictly "peaceful protest." But, as anti-oppression educator

McKensie Mack says, "That rage is not about control and dominance, that rage is about fatigue. That rage is rooted in being on the receiving end of global white supremacist murder and abuse for centuries."[5] This too is righteous. And revolutionary.

Righteous rage is a powerful vehicle to propel personal and collective change because it inherently contains additional inertia. The potency of our rage is exactly what is required to help propel us to take on the challenging inner and outer work required to commit to racial justice. To accept and incite the changes needed to keep promises to ourselves as well as to others, and to call on ourselves and others to dismantle the oppressive status quo systems as they currently exist. The changes required to bring about racial justice are not meager. They are lofty, robust, and all-encompassing. Rage is one of the most powerful tools to get us there but only when channeled effectively. It requires unlearning the powerful ways of white supremacy we have all consumed and, instead, finding the capacity and tolerance to hold compassion alongside our rage. No. Easy. Ask.

At first, tapping into your rage may seem an insurmountable task. After all, you've likely been conditioned to avoid anger and rage for the majority of your life (I was!). This is especially true for those socialized as women and femmes. And doubly so if you are a Black woman+ living under the constant threat of being labeled angry simply for breathing. Still, what is undoubtedly more of a challenge is learning how to hold your rage *and* compassion in the same breath. Righteous rage beckons both. It holds space for the harms that have been trespassed on you and/or the most marginalized and motivates you to hold those causing such harm to account, *and* it asks you to hold space for the perfectly imperfect humxnity in others, including yourself. Not because you need to skip into some superhumxn state of forgiveness toward those who have been oppressive (or anybody!), but because activating your righteous rage is ultimately about healing, and healing requires our full and complete selves. This is where your spiritual self gets kicked into high gear!

Oftentimes our rage is very much connected to or spawned from love. If you do not have love for a person, situation, or system, then it is unlikely you will feel the intensified anger that is rage when that person, situation, or system—be it a friend, foe, or the collective—does you (or is done) dirty. In the words of homegirl Solange, "You got the right to be mad."[6] When you can tap into your rage while also maintaining compassion for yourself and others, it helps you better tolerate, and therefore utilize, the intensity of emotions you are feeling. Especially when those emotions are mixed. For example, if a white friend says something racist, I will likely feel rage but I'm also still likely to feel affection, because, after all, that person is my friend. If I want to be best equipped to employ my righteous rage, then it is helpful for me to accept that I can possess both rage and compassion in the same instance. If I have feelings of rage because of my friend's actions but I also feel compassion for them and I don't know how to tolerate both, I am more likely to self-censor my rage and instead attack or shame myself for *feeling* rage, because that is easier on my nervous system than tolerating my mixed emotions. The end result is: (a) disconnection from my friend because I'm not empowered to employ my righteous rage and hold them to account, (b) my friend's harmful actions going unaddressed, and (c) mental duress caused by self-criticism, shame, and other painful forms of self-attack deriving from an inability to hold both my rage and compassion at once. Not a cute look.

I can have compassion for you *and* rage against you or your actions. Our compassion does not negate our rage and our rage need not negate our compassion. It's not easy to tolerate both emotions at once, but expanding our capacity to tolerate our discomfort is part of our commitment to Spiritual Activism. I can want nothing to do with you and wish you well. Or forgive you and still tell you to fuck off (energetically or otherwise). I can express the harms you've inflicted and the anger I feel as a result while still honoring your full self and acknowledging your pain, sadness, and remorse. When we fail to hold space for the full spectrum of our mixed and multifaceted emotions, we rob ourselves of the full expression of our humxnity, as well as the humxnity of others, and we may cause ourselves harm by turning our rage inward rather than transmuting it into much-needed change. A fail on all accounts.

So lean into that righteous rage and compassionate anger. Spiritual Activism is a loving and challenging call to embrace our righteous rage, to know when that rage is righteous rather than violent, and to move in and from heart-centered action. It is a call to align with Spirit in order to do the deep inner work that precipitates any external or collective shift. And to motivate ourselves into being the change we wish to become. Spiritual Activism is an active opportunity to observe and accept yourself and your role in perpetuating white supremacy for what it is, so you can get to work on making the change necessary to stop causing harm and start helping the revolution.

Connecting with Our Righteous Rage

Find a quiet space, take a deep breath, and ask yourself the following:

> Where does rage live in my body?

> What does my rage want to do (or what *has* my rage wanted to do)?

> If my rage could talk, what would it say?

Journal, draw, voice note, or otherwise record your answers however feels best.

THERE IS NO "RIGHT" WAY TO EXPRESS OUR RAGE, ESPECIALLY FOR THOSE SUBJECTED TO CENTURIES OF MURDER AND ENSLAVEMENT. WHEN YOU FIND YOURSELF FEELING RAGE, TRY EXPLORING THE FOLLOWING:

1) Acknowledge your rage and surrender to its existence.

2) Get curious about any other emotion that may live beneath or beside the rage (for example, sadness or grief).

3) Practice tending to your rage. For example:

> Journal answers to the above and burn them (safely please!).

> Punch into a pillow—and keep punching until you feel your rage has done what it needs to do.

> Take a time-out to reflect or take three deep breaths.

> Scream at the top of your lungs in your shower, car, or room with music on blast (my personal fave).

4) Connect with your ancestors. Sometimes our rage is compounded by the rage our ancestors felt or the feelings we hold because of what they did or endured (especially for Black and Indigenous folx). Honor that, and them.

5) If it feels available to you (and it may not), sense if you also feel love, compassion, or other conflicting feelings for the person or situation. If so, let yourself hold space for both (it's a mindfuck, so just try it out).

6) Focus on connection rather than domination.

7) Tap into your inner child to explore what boundary has been crossed, injustice inflicted, or need requires attention. Observe what your rage *and* loving compassion (for yourself and others and particularly the most marginalized) want to do about it and act from *that* place.

TEN

> > > > > >

Intersectional Spirituality

> Never learn your ancestral ways
> from those that benefit from your
> ancestor's pain.
>
> —GLORIA LUCAS, NALGONA POSITIVITY PRIDE

Spiritual Activism offers insight and wisdom about ourselves and others while arming us with an embodied presence to confront our racial shadows and better withstand our discomfort—all of which are critical in order to achieve racial justice. Still, simply being spiritual or partaking in spiritual practices is not enough. *How* we tap into Spirit—whom we invite into our shared spiritual spaces and for whose benefit—is all part of the racial justice effort. Many spiritual wellness offerings that were primarily created by and for communities of color have been co-opted by whiteness. Many BI&PoC and other oppressed folx have been excluded from supposedly spiritual spaces using practices created by *our* ancestors. There is an epidemic of wellness platforms and influencers inflicting harm on BI&PoC and other marginalized folx and refusing to foster respectful relationships with people and offerings from cultures that are not their own. Spirituality and wellness are more mainstream than ever before, but they have also become bigger sources of segregation and suffering rather than communion and healing. What we need is an intersectional form of spirituality.

Intersectional spirituality* is a means to aid us in invoking a multifaceted approach to wellness that promotes culturally informed, racially sensitive, and non-appropriative spiritual teachings and practices as the path forward for healing the collective divide. It provides a framework for embracing spiritual and wellness practices as a way to unpack our privileges, help heal our hearts, and dismantle white supremacy while also acknowledging the ways some of those practices have been and continue to be used to do the exact opposite. To engage in intersectional spirituality is to practice spiritual wellness in a way that honors the impact of those practices not only on our own lives but on the lives of others, particularly the communities from which the practices and offerings originated—including the ways in which spirituality and wellness have resulted in their oppression. Specifically for white people whose ancestors have a long history of violence against the communities who created today's most popular wellness practices. Intersectional spirituality helps us to examine how harm arises and the complex nuances inherent in partaking in practices that can both build up and break down the oppressive systems we seek to stop. Together we'll explore how the wellness industry and its spiritual foundations have bolstered white supremacy and how we can better utilize spiritual wellness as a means to eradicate, rather than enforce, global systems of oppression.

WHY "WEALTH & HELLNESS"?

The first time I heard the phrase "wealth and hellness," it was a slip of someone's tongue. The host of a feminist gathering accidentally swapped the "h" and the "w" when referring to the health and wellness industry and the room filled with resonant laughter. Though many of us turn to health, wellness, and spirituality as a means to improve our well-being and connect with the collective, there is much about these industries causing harm and degrading the very things we seek. They lead to a culture of "hellness," especially for the oppressed folx they exclude, while creating great wealth for all those who cultivate them, often cis, white, non-disabled, and otherwise privileged folx. The global wellness market is valued at over $4 trillion[1] and has become entirely subsumed with colonialist and capitalist forces. Consequently, it is no surprise that the majority of the industry is inaccessible and harmful to communities of color.

To me wellness means peace, vitality, and safety in an emotional, spiritual, psychological, mental, and physical way. Wellness is a full-body, comprehensive, 360-degree state of being in alignment with your highest and best self. It is an inherently spiritual act. But wellness isn't possible for the majority of us when much of the modern-day wellness industry is created by and for rich, young, white, hetero, thin, cis, non-disabled women, to the exclusion and harm of everyone else. There are systemic barriers to wellness for most people on the planet due to oppression rooted in race, gender identity, sexual orientation, ethnicity, ability, and more. Barriers that have been strategically set in place both intentionally and otherwise. But impact trumps intention. Take, for example, in 2019, when *Yoga Journal* invited Nicole Cardoza, a Black woman, to be featured on its cover—an invitation only a few other Black women had received since the magazine's inception in 1975—then rescinded that invite. Instead, the editors asked their online community to vote between Nicole's cover and a cover with a white woman. As Nicole shares, "They were worried that my image wouldn't sell, and they wanted the data to prove it."[2] Earlier that year yoga culture advocate Susanna Barkataki publicly shared how *Yoga Journal* had an opportunity to showcase herself and four other Desi women on its June cover—you know, women whose ancestors actually *created* yoga.[3] Instead the editors chose a white woman holding mala beads. For a cover that actually refers to articles by Susanna and others on "honoring the roots of yoga." Fucking appalling. Sort of like when Lululemon, the most problematic yoga company on the planet, hosted a "Worth 100" panel for International Women's Day with predominantly white, non-disabled, thin, young, upper-middle-class women. I guess they're the only ones Lululemon deems worth a damn. In my personal experience, the company has made that clear many times over.

In addition to being racist, anti-Black, ableist, and fatphobic, wellness is also mired in heteropatriarchy. Spiritual subservience and manipulation, key elements of toxic masculinity, promote the notion that we are not our own healers. But we are. You are your own guru. Nobody knows you, your mind, or your body better than you. The purpose of spirituality is to teach you how to access your own innate healing power, not rely on powers outside of you for constant support.

On the whole, wellness today is classist, racist, ableist, homophobic, fatphobic, transphobic, ageist, and otherwise overwhelmingly oppressive. It is an agent of injustice. But true wellness should not be for a select few. It is our birthright. Each and every one of us. The current culture of wealth and hellness contradicts everything wellness is truly about it. It is a hierarchy enforcing insidious beliefs about who has the right to wellness and, more important, who does not. It's entirely unsurprising then that so many BI&WoC and other marginalized folx are unwelcome in the modern-day wealth and hellness industry, be it personally or professionally.

WELLNESS SO WHITE

I have always felt like an outsider in the wealth and hellness industry because it neither speaks to nor includes me. Until two hot minutes ago, Black women+ have rarely been represented in spiritual or wellness images, marketing efforts, or leadership, and any act of noninclusion is in and of itself an action. A telling one. One of the biggest ways wellness excludes all BI&WoC is by failing to create inclusive, equitable, and sufficiently safe spaces. Despite my intimate involvement in wellness, there are very few wellness spaces I feel sufficiently safe to enter as a Black woman. Most people aren't doing their racial justice work, so they are ill-equipped to create authentic healing spaces. Most of my spiritual wellness occurs at home or in spaces solely for BI&PoC, which are very rare spaces to find. I do this because I've had so many violent experiences in wellness spaces with white women. It doesn't matter that I was introduced to yoga and meditation when I was eight or started frequenting a naturopath at eleven; the white-washed world of wellness treats me as an outsider. I am perceived as less knowledgeable, less abundant, and less worthy of care. From spiritual mediums who criticized my suicidal ideations as "unspiritual" to spiritual development courses demanding I call and apologize to my abusers, I have faced harm in a wide range of wellness spaces. And it's not just me. Many of my clients are white women in wellness, and the stories they share about the racist actions of their white staff or colleagues are distressing. Stories of front desk staff asking Black women walking in if they were trying to find the women's shelter downstairs (i.e., you don't belong here) or of white yoga teachers refusing to meet the gaze of the sole Indigenous woman in class. In my experience, there is no wellness practice that has treated BI&WoC with more disdain or discrimination than yoga. Cis white women teaching yoga to be precise.

> >   < <

Where I come from yoga is its own religion. Lululemon, the world's largest yoga apparel company, started there, and a large proportion of Vancouverites, the majority of whom are white and wealthy, regularly partake in the world of yoga. For a long time I avoided the whole scene, as I was disturbed at the way in which this sacred spiritual practice, created by ancient Indian communities, was becoming a cash cow for the white, rich, and powerful. I was finally reacquainted when a good friend started teaching and let me guest her classes for free (cuz shit was expensive!). I was reminded of the origins of the practice, its great power to aid us in overcoming adversities, and the ways it can serve as a vehicle for much-needed change. Years later, I signed up for yoga teacher training as a means to bring this potent practice to Black women+ and other marginalized communities. At the time my only option was to take this training from a white woman. It certainly wasn't my first choice, but she was the longtime partner of someone I knew, so I chose to give it a go. Big. Mistake.

It began with an energetic inkling, as these things usually do. Though the teacher and I had some rapport, something still felt off. As the only Black person in the class, I thought it was just in my head (as internalized oppression had taught me to do), but then the aggressions began. When I asked questions during lessons on the origins of yoga, the teacher promptly shut me down. There was no sense of being a lifelong learner of the practice or culture herself, instead I was not to challenge her know-how in any way. Then she told me that my energy was overbearing. That I needed to be wary of intimidating my future students. I was regularly criticized for the way I held and took up space, so much so that I began to question myself and whether I was actually aware of my environment and impact on others, both on and off the mat. I had some strong feelings about the way I was being treated, but those feelings weren't "spiritual," so I spiraled into self-doubt, which then turned into self-attack. *Maybe this isn't what I think it is? Maybe she just doesn't like me? Am I a bad person for thinking this is fucked up?* During the last few days of training, all the students led one another through sequences. The teacher carefully curated groups of twos and threes, and on every occasion I was matched with the loudest and most space-consuming cis white man in our class.

Is this because I can handle his shit? Or is this because she's telling me we're aligned energetically? I could barely focus, not only because he was constantly in my fucking face, but because the overall message I was being sent throughout the training was that I was too much. That I wasn't cut out to teach and my way of being would cause my students harm. I was ostracized for being who I am. My Black, bubbly, and boisterous self wasn't the right fit for yoga. At least not according to the white woman who was teaching me about it. The training left me so dubious and depleted I barely had any desire to teach yoga asanas at all. I still don't.

I wish my story was unique, but it's not. The white-washing of wellness has resulted in white supremacist standards as the norm, and it is causing BI&WoC, LGBTTQIA+ folx, and others mad harm. Below are some of the specific ways the spiritual and wellness industry both exclude and cause harm to BI&WoC (as well as many other marginalized folx).

#1—Profit over People

Many wealth and hellness offerings are made by and for the white and wealthy, so they ain't cheap. There are an array of wellness spaces charging upward of $30 per class! I will never say that BI&WoC can't or don't have money, because of course we can and we do, but there are systemic and institutional obstacles in place that result in many BI&WoC earning far less than men+ and white women+ for the same work, especially Black and Indigenous women+. As well as Latinx women+. Charging major chunks of change means we are being excluded from the opportunity to participate or are forced to sacrifice more in order to do so. It also means that if and when we do partake, we are likely to be only one of a few BI&WoC in the space. When I was a spin instructor (a few lives ago), our classes were pricey and I was left teaching rooms full of white folx, so even as an instructor I was the outsider. It was isolating—not to mention exhausting. I mean, you try teaching an all-white class how to ride on beat in unison. Way above my pay grade!

BI&WoC are also frequently priced out of things like retreats, courses, and nutritional wellness. Buying organic or going vegan is great in theory, but it is not a practical or financial reality for many who are otherwise oppressed and then shamed for their inability to afford the lifestyle choices proclaimed "healthy" by whiteness. Most wellness spaces are also entirely inaccessible to disabled folx, be it physically or otherwise. Minor changes could foster massive inclusion, but these spaces remain inept and exclusive. When wellness is devised within the racist, ableist, capitalist, heteropatriarchal status quo, it prioritizes profits over people and denigrates the sacred practices created to bring unity, not division.

#2—Cultural Appropriation*

Many things we place under the "wellness" umbrella today are practices and offerings created by and for communities of color that have been co-opted and appropriated by whiteness. Cultural appropriation refers to a particular power dynamic in which members of a dominant culture steal intellectual, spiritual, cultural, and/or informational wealth from a culture of people who have been systematically oppressed by that dominant group. With respect to race relations, this means white folx who steal cultural elements from any BI&PoC community are appropriating, and because of universal oppression against Black and Indigenous folx, any person who steals from Black or Indigenous communities is appropriating. As with any form of theft, it is inherently harmful. I'm not saying white folx can't practice offerings from BI&PoC cultures (or non-Black folx from Black culture), but very often when they do it lacks any connection with the community of color that created it and is thus appropriative. In some cases, it even goes so far as being an assault on what the original practice actually is, the origins of that practice, and the community that created it. For example, a roomful of white women+ practicing "hip-hop yoga" is offensive in all kinds of ways. First, it's not yoga. It's movement that has benefits, but it is not linked to the tradition of yoga. Call it something else. To honor the roots of yoga is to honor the eight limbs of yoga (seven of which are non-physical). It also requires honoring the ancient Indians who created the practice Westerners are most familiar with today, *and* the ancient Egyptians (i.e—Africans) whose Kemetic yoga practice is said to predate yoga from ancient India.[4] Second, hip-hop is a specific art form created by Black Americans as a means to navigate the pain of anti-Blackness most predominantly caused by, guess who? White folx! To appropriate a sacred Indian and African spiritual practice while listening to Black American music created for Black folx' survival is a hell no. Listening to our music requires first listening to and addressing the ways you oppress us. Most white folx who partake in those kinds of classes do so without any understanding of the roots of yoga or of Black music and are doing diddly-squat to support, uplift, or give back to Indian, African, or Black American communities or combat the oppression we regularly face as a result of the white supremacy these same white folx are perpetuating. Given that white supremacy is the status quo, it is safe to say that most white yoga instructors are appropriating, causing harm, and should likely stop. ASAP. The same holds true for engaging with other spiritual practices, cultural and spiritual relics used on altars or otherwise, clothing, food, music, art, plant medicine, etc. originating from communities of color.

Cultural appreciation*, which involves a respect for the roots of the practice or item while acknowledging, honoring, uplifting, and giving back to (financially or otherwise) the communities from which it originates is all good.[5] Still, as professor and author Brittney Cooper asserts, "White people don't share. They take over."[6] Things like yoga, meditation, and breathwork became acceptable only when white people started doing them, and then white people became the leaders in the space even though the practices derived from communities of color. White people extract, use, and abuse. As a result, BI&PoC aren't leading the charge for those practices, nor is there an honoring of what the roots of those sacred practices are. Many of the things white people practice as "wellness" now were specifically prohibited by white people in the past. It was one of the white colonizers' many weapons of cultural destruction. Yoga being banned by Brits when they invaded India is one example.[7] Colonizers restricting the burning of sage by Indigenous tribes in North America is another.[8] As a Black woman, appropriation causes me harm because it is yet another form of colonialism. Of whiteness stealing from communities of color for its own spiritual, emotional, physical, and financial gain. It means BI&WoC are not welcomed in wellness spaces, and it creates cultures where BI&WoC are socialized to believe we don't have the right to pursue wellness. We ask ourselves, "Who am I to heal and be free?" when the world tells us we are not allowed. On the contrary, we have every right to our own awakening. BI&WoC's healing, especially that of queer and trans Black and Indigenous women+, has and will lead the racial justice revolution.

#3—Exploiting Communities of Color

Wellness, like any other industry, prioritizes the comfort, well-being, and bottom line of white folx first, and this often results in the outright exploitation of communities of color. For example, crystals have become a hot commodity. I *love* me some crystals and have had a collection since I was a girl, but I've come to learn that most of these beautiful, healing gems are frequently mined in a manner that oppresses the African, Asian, Indigenous, and other communities of color they come from.[9] The person who is extracting that crystal might be enslaved or an indentured laborer earning pennies per hour. Having the energetic benefits of the crystal is not a comprehensive element of wellness if the person who extracted that crystal for you is being oppressed, because their oppression is linked to your oppression. Same goes for sacred plants like white sage and palo santo, which have been cultivated and used by Indigenous North and South American communities for centuries and now face extinction, a huge threat to the spiritual practices of these communities, due to white demand.[10] We also need to be more cognizant of how we treat the limited resources from the earth and the ways in which our degradation of the environment, even in the name of "wellness," disproportionately impacts Black and Indigenous people. All of this leads to a hierarchy of wellness, with white folx, their wellness and well-being, reigning supreme.

This is also true in terms of global access to wellness and cultural offerings. Pre-COVID-19, the wellness tourism was valued at nearly $650 billion and increasing at double the rate of regular tourism. The largest growing wellness destination is Asia, in countries comprising communities of color like India and Indonesia, where predominantly white wellness tourists go to extract sacred healing for pennies on the dollar.[11] I was recently in Bali and had an intensely disturbing experience. I saw the ways in which it was being pillaged by whiteness. The resources are being extracted and the land is being overdeveloped for predominantly white foreigners, who extract the elements of Balinese culture, healing, and land that work for them so they can rejuvenate, get rich, or both. At the expense of the Balinese. Talking to the locals, who are often at the behest of white tourists and bosses, it was clear that this system was serving white interests first.

All of this leads to a hierarchy of healing happening in our local communities, cities, nations, and across the globe. I don't believe it's my right to oppress other communities for my own healing, nor should it be necessary. We need to be more integral; we need to follow the traces of these things that we call wellness down to their source and figure out whose wellness they're for, whom they oppress, and how we can promote global wellness from the beginning of the extraction of whatever the offering or item is, up until our use of it. If we find that those offerings aren't actually promoting global wellness for *everyone*, then they shouldn't be considered tools of wellness at all.

#4—Stealing BI&PoC's Language

Words matter. Language is a critical part of racial justice and we have a responsibility to be discerning in the words we use because words cause harm. It has become a trend for white-owned wellness businesses to steal, and thus appropriate, words from communities of color. For example, "tribe" is a common description for our close peoples—"your vibe attracts your tribe" and all that. But Indigenous (including Indigenous African) folx all over the world have been oppressed for centuries, and continue to be, as a result of belonging to a tribe, so this is not a simple word that should be used to describe some people who want to support one another while they become "spiritually awakened." As Chris Lowe writes in his article "The Trouble with Tribe," "tribe" was a concept used by European colonizers to subjugate Africans, and "for the most part ['tribe'] does not convey truths but myths, stereotypes and prejudices."[12] There are better words to use that do not cause harm, so use them!

Similarly, spirit animals* are constantly appropriated out of their Indigenous context. Only specific Indigenous nations have something akin to a spirit animal, and for those that do, it serves a sacred function. To call your pet or favorite sweater your spirit animal is an assault to those tribes and their beliefs.

In this same vein, all non-Black folx need to stop using African American Vernacular English (AAVE). Immediately! It was created by Black Americans, predominantly from the queer and trans community, as a means to navigate and survive anti-Blackness and white supremacy. The use of "woke," "slay," "preach," "yaaas," "honey," "dope," "queen," "sis," etc. are not up for grabs (pretty much every other word from *Queer Eye* star JVN's mouth . . . love them, but hard NO). Stop using it to sell your classes and products. It ain't for you, and your use of it is appropriative and violent. So long as Black communities the world over are oppressed by the anti-Black systems *you* benefit from (especially for using the exact same terms)—keep our language outta your mouth. You are *not* a "spiritual gangster," you cannot "namaslay," and if you're using "woke" you're anything but. Similarly, using Sanskrit words like "namaste" without an understanding of their meaning and cultural history, as well as the ways whiteness sought to stamp them out, is a no from me.

You're not entitled to use whatever words you want to however you wish. White supremacy has afforded white and white-passing folx the privilege of believing they can and should use whatever language they choose, but co-opting words from the marginalized is oppressive. When I witness wellness spaces appropriating language from communities of color it tells me they are not doing their work. They do not understand the ongoing harm this causes and how it enforces their power and privilege at my and other BI&PoC's expense. There are so many other ways to express your point, and if you know or even suspect the words you use have the potential to cause the most oppressed harm and you refuse to change them, you are prioritizing your comfort and that of the oppressor.

#5—Colonial Offerings

Many modern-day spiritual teachings are rooted in white supremacy and are thus inherently oppressive. Teachings like the law of attraction and books like *The Secret* or *A Return to Love* claim you can improve your health, wealth, and personal relationships solely through the power of love or positive thought, but they fail to take into account the very real systemic obstacles BI&PoC face as a result of white supremacy. Being in spaces that blame me for supposed weaknesses that are actually attributable to racism, sexism, patriarchy, capitalism, and other globally oppressive forces is to subject myself to violence. This is made all the worse when the space I entered was intended to be one of reprieve for my healing.

➤ ➤   ◂ ◂

Everything. Is. Political. The personal and the spiritual, meaning wellness is no exception. If you consider yourself to be in wellness, especially if you are leading these spaces or practices, then it's imperative you do your racial justice work and create offerings that are inclusive, accessible, and welcoming. To all. Not just a select few. So long as we equate wellness with whiteness, BI&PoC will always lose. It is vital to practice an intersectional form of spirituality, otherwise your practice *is* causing harm.

Intersectional spirituality creates conscientious wellness. It means no longer having a hierarchy of healing. Wellness won't be created by and for a mere few to the detriment and exclusion of all who are already marginalized. I want to observe connected thought and intention around what wellness is and whose wellness we're prioritizing. I want wellness to understand that centering Black women and femmes healing is a form of collective care. And I want more of us to tap into our own ancestral healing wisdom. We *all* have ancestral practices and know-how from our own races, ethnicities, and cultures. What would it mean for white folx to tap into their own lineage and healing first, as opposed to exploiting healing practices and modalities that don't belong to them and have been actively oppressed by their ancestors? I want wellness to prioritize the needs, comfort, and well-being of the most marginalized communities because to date wellness has done the opposite.

A huge part of this practice is learning to appreciate rather than appropriate. Good thing I have some tangible ways to better welcome BI&PoC and other oppressed folx and commit to intersectional spirituality. Your calls to action are below!

Observation Exercise

REFLECT ON THE FOLLOWING:

> Who are the biggest names in health and wellness right now? Why? What race/ethnicity/gender identity/sexual orientation/ability are they? What are the cultural roots of the practices they are sharing? Do they acknowledge those roots?

> Pop over to the Instagram or web page of your favorite wellness brands and leaders. What are they doing to promote racial justice and anti-oppression? Did they make any commitments to address anti-Blackness following the Black liberation uprisings in 2020 or otherwise? If so, have those come to fruition in a transparent way? How can you hold them accountable?

> What race/ethnicity/gender identity/sexual orientation/ability are your spiritual, health, and/or wellness teachers? Do you learn from teachers, gurus, or mentors from marginalized races or other identities? Why or why not? Do any of your teachers originate from the cultures your practice is from? If so, how? If not, why?

> What are three ways you can tap into and learn about your own ancestral spiritual wisdom?

Canceling Cultural Appropriation

We touched on the harm caused by cultural appropriation in the spiritual wellness context, though it's important to note that appropriation occurs in all kinds of ways, so it is vital to face your shadows, examine your behaviors, and challenge yourself so you can best discern if and when you are being appropriative. Below are some considerations to help you determine if, when, and how you are appropriating:

> Am I a member of a dominant group that does and/or has oppressed the community from which the practice, offering, clothing, food, music, etc. (the "Action") originates?

> What is the history of my race/ethnicity with the community that the Action originates from? Was harm inflicted? If so, how?

> Am I acknowledging and crediting the community that the Action originates from? If so, how? If not, why? And how will I change that?

> Am I honoring the origin of the Action? If so, how? If not, why? And how will I ensure to do so?

> Is the Action in alignment with the roots and history of the Action? If so, how? If not, why? And how can I do so?

> Am I giving back to the communities of the culture from which the Action originated (financially and otherwise)? If so, how? If not, why? And how will I change that?

> Are Black and Indigenous folx being involved and centered? Are the communities from which the Action originated leading the Action? If so, how? If not, why? And how can that be rectified?

> Who is making money off the Action (if anyone)? Are those earning the most from the Action also from the Action's origin community? If so, how? If not, why? And how can that be rectified?

PART TWO

RING THE ALARM

Nothing will work unless you do.

—MAYA ANGELOU

> > > > > >

ELEVEN

Impact over Intention

> My experiences, my hum[x]nity and my
> life will never be negotiated on the altar
> of evil cloaked as inane intellectualism.
>
> **—ENWONGO C. CLEOPAS**

It was a gray October day just a few weeks after I had left my life and livelihood as a corporate attorney behind. It wasn't raining, but the air was moist, as it often is given Vancouver's lengthy coastal shore. I was rushing. Off to some meeting or other in a hurried state, and I opted to take a car share in one of those cute and compact Smart cars. I held the membership card to the vehicle dash, waited for the car doors to unlock, and away I went.

Less than ten minutes into my drive I found myself at a red light on Main Street. I looked into my rearview mirror and I saw an SUV barreling down the road directly behind me. I could tell it was going fast. Too fast. It wasn't going to stop before it reached me. With only seconds to spare I thought about swerving my little hunk of metal into the lane on my left to avoid a collision, but there wasn't time. I sat still, powerless, and braced for impact. There was a single moment of silence before my world turned into a two-car orchestra of metal on metal and the sound of my own screams. When the screeching finally ceased, I looked over to the sidewalk and saw people stopped and staring. A man had come out of his shop to locate the source of all the noise. It was, at least in part, me.

I moved the compact car to the side of the road as the man who had hit me did the same. Then, I sat in shock. What just happened? Why did it happen? Did I do something wrong?

One of the women on the sidewalk came to my car door. She asked if I was okay and, as I was apt to do, I responded "yes" before checking in with the truth of my reply. She gave me her information to use as a witness statement before she went on her way to resume her run. The driver of the other vehicle, a middle-aged white man whom I'll call Sir Speedy, came out of his car and immediately apologized.

"I'm so sorry! Are you okay?" he said. He could tell that I was not.

Sir Speedy saw my tears as I emerged from the driver's seat and gave me a hug, which I found oddly comforting given he was a random white man who'd just caused me bodily harm. He said he had been reaching for something in his glove compartment and wasn't paying attention. *No shit,* I thought. I leaned back, still in shock. We exchanged information, as you do in these kinds of situations, and Sir Speedy went on his way.

Though I was grateful to have walked away from an accident that could have been much worse, I was scared and shaken up. My mind immediately ran into overdrive, as it so often does.

Let's not make a mountain out of a mole hill, Rachel—my inner critic, always quick to take up the chance for ridicule.

I was free from scratches and bruises. There was no blood or bones evidently out of place. Still, inside I was anything but okay. I had just absorbed the inertia of nearly nine thousand combined pounds of moving metal colliding. I was on the side of the road. Alone. And all I could do was cry. I called my now-husband, Tyler, to tell him what happened. As he insisted on leaving work to pick me up and take me to the hospital, I couldn't help but feel silly. As if this whole thing were being blown out of proportion.

"It's not a big deal!" I said. "I'm fine." I had lied to myself so many times by then I was beginning to believe it myself.

"I'm on my way," he exclaimed as he hung up the phone to rush to my aid.

Within half an hour I was at emergency. The doctor was polite while informing me that I had sustained whiplash to my neck and shoulders, but you could tell he didn't have much time for minor injuries (plus, I'm Black, so my pain doesn't matter). Once again, I felt foolish. Why was I wasting this medical professional's time to confirm what I already knew? I was FINE. At least on the outside.

As the months and years went on, my injuries turned into chronic pain, which took a serious toll on my mental, emotional, spiritual, and physical well-being. This car accident had, and continues to have, major ramifications for my life and livelihood. Still, I was and remain grateful because the man who drove into me immediately owned his mistake. Sir Speedy could have come out of his car with an array of accusations:

"What the hell were you doing?"

"Why didn't you get out of the way?!"

"This wasn't my fault!"

It all happened so fast that had he blamed me in some way, I would have likely felt I had indeed done something wrong. But I hadn't.

Do I believe Sir Speedy intended to run into me with his car? Absolutely not. But it doesn't matter. Because he did, and I was harmed as a result. Instead of proclaiming that he hadn't meant to hit me and driving away, he stopped on the side of the road and dealt with the consequence of his actions. Hell, I even got a hug. Does he deserve a medal for owning up to his harms and being a half-decent humxn? Surely not. I doubt any of us would intentionally run into another person (though we've witnessed several white men at Black Lives Matter rallies do just that). But if and when we do, we own our actions and seek to remedy whatever harm we've caused. Right?

Well, when it comes to racial justice, we need to behave precisely this same way. We need to own our IMPACT over our INTENTION. Yet, this is very rarely the response received when an oppressed being graciously explains that harm has been committed against them. Rarely are we met with hugs, acknowledgments, and apologies when asking others for accountability, but rather entitlement, defensiveness, and violence.

F.Y.I. (FUCK YOUR INTENTIONS)*

Let's get something all the way clear, right away. When it comes to racial justice, your intentions are more or less irrelevant. Whether you did or did not mean to exclude a disabled person, create an unsafe space for Black women+, or make a transphobic joke doesn't matter a whole hell of a lot. What matters most is the impact that action has on the marginalized person(s) in question. I have personally and professionally endured one too many a white woman+ who dug their heels all the way into the idea that the harm they caused was unintentional. What they're really saying is "I care more about how I am perceived and feeling as though I am a good person than I do about the actual harm I've caused another, particularly someone with less power and privilege than I have, or how or why I've caused that harm." The accusation of causing harm is treated as worse than the actual harm that was inflicted, and that is entirely unacceptable. You may not intend to cause harm. In fact, you may authentically intend to *avoid* harm, but in the end your intention doesn't really mean shit. Whether you intended to cause harm or not is truly not the point. The point is that you did. Periodt.

Am I saying that having good intentions executed poorly is the same as the folx who have a true intention of causing harm to oppressed folx? Of course not. What I *am* saying is that we shouldn't be so damn focused on intention either way. It is possible for well-intentioned folx to cause the same, if not more, harm than those with ill intent. The majority of harms inflicted against me in my life have been from those in my innermost circle. Our priority should always rest with those who are enduring the harms, the specifics of the harms in question, and how those harms can be rectified, as opposed to the inner mental workings of the perpetrator, which does nothing for the person who has been harmed whilst invalidating their experience and negating a remedy. This line of reasoning, or lack thereof, perpetuates the white supremacist status quo by focusing on the perpetrator, emphasizing ingrained entitlement, and further oppressing the person who was harmed by silencing, rejecting, and/or ignoring. Prioritizing intention over impact is a tricky and deviant little mindfuck that allows oppressors to avoid taking ownership and essentially shuts down an opportunity for accountability, growth, and connection, all of which are precipitated by an ability to better tolerate your discomfort and own your shit.

This is also why "not knowing" about white supremacy or

how to engage with it is not an excuse. The extent to which you are able to operate in your day-to-day without any clue of the atrocities inflicted upon the oppressed is the extent to which your privilege is preventing you from observing the realities of the world. Black and Indigenous women+ are forced to swim through swamps of murky aggressions, never mind blatant white supremacist violence, all day every day. Does it matter that the vast majority of folx who perpetuate white supremacy do not intend to cause myself and others harm? Not much. Am I still forced to spend an exorbitant amount of time, money, emotional labor, and energy healing my heart from all the pain incessantly inflicted upon me by "well-intentioned white folx"? I sure as heck do. And it's all the worse for Black trans women.

Black folx have been yelling from the rooftops about racial justice century after century, and still here we are, hundreds of years later, and so many of y'all still don't get it. Whatever the intentions of your words, actions, inactions, thoughts, behaviors, perspectives, opinions, all are secondary to the actual IMPACT they have on Black bodies, Black joy, Black lives, and Black liberation.

Irrespective of whether your objective is to perpetuate white supremacy, anti-Blackness, or anti-Indigeneity, in the absence of proactive, daily work to combat your racism, prejudice, or internalized oppression, you are. This is precisely why doing your deep inner work is necessary and urgent.

In the face of causing harm I say F.Y.I., dear ones. *Fuck. Your. Intentions.* And, as a member of my online community once astutely added: Feel. Your. Impact. The next time you're called out or in, take a breath. Listen to what's being said. Believe them. Challenge your shadow's tempting whispers to defend, deny, and object. Apologize. Take ownership and examine why you did what you did or said what you did (or why you failed to). And understand that your intention is irrelevant. Actions matter.

MONITORING IMPACT OVER INTENTION

Prioritizing impact over intention and feeling your impact are key. The next time someone holds you accountable, try practicing the following to help you through:

1) Take a breath—Our breath activates our parasympathetic nervous system, which helps to calm the body down, and long, deep breaths have proven particularly helpful in quelling anxiety, fear, and other emotions that arise when we're feeling targeted.

2) Receive—Attend to what is being said. You may not need to respond for a while, so actively receive what's being shared. Ask thoughtful, respectful questions only if you need more clarity, but do not feel entitled to answers. Google is also your friend if you have access.

3) Believe—Have generous assumptions of what is being shared with you and the person sharing it. Lean into the totality of your wrongdoing, not because it proves you're a bad person (it doesn't), but because it is an opportunity to learn, grow, and ultimately do better.

4) Apologize—Verbally and through changed behavior (more on this in the next chapter).

5) Reflect—Use this as an opportunity to learn, grow, and minimize harm moving forward. Yes, you will still cause harm. Keep going and growing.

If you are committed to ending oppression in all forms, you will fuck up. You will cause harm. You will have a negative impact despite intentions to the contrary and you will have to atone for that. This is not an *if*; it is a *when* and a *how*. The goal here is not, nor should it ever be, perfection, which is a concept created by and for perpetuating white supremacy. Prioritizing impact creates a heart-centered gauge for the work you are seeking to do in the world and if, when, and how it is actually dismantling oppression. It is an opportunity to check in with yourself and others, especially those most oppressed and/or impacted by your actions, acknowledge how and where you can improve your efforts and lean into your spiritually aligned tools for doing better.

Owning My Impact

Using the table provided, write out three actions or inactions you have taken that caused a (or another) queer and trans Black or Indigenous woman+ harm. For example, an action may be expecting us to undertake some form of work for you without remuneration (emotional or otherwise), or an inaction may be staying silent instead of speaking up when racist remarks were made against us in your presence. These can be regarding a person you know personally, professionally, or otherwise. For example, it may be a total stranger, like a store manager, or someone you know of but have never met, like Janet Mock. As always, you can focus this exercise on another BI&PoC or other marginalized folx as well or in lieu of queer and trans Black or Indigenous women+ if necessary.

Action or Inaction against a Black or Indigenous woman+.	What was my intention for that action or inaction?	What do I believe or know to be the actual impact of that action or inaction on the Black or Indigenous woman+ in question?	What, if anything, needs to be done to remedy my harm?	What have I learned?
1.	1.	1.	1.	1.
2.	2.	2.	2.	2.
3.	3.	3.	3.	3.

Do your best to recall the intention you had at the time (or still possess), and then critically reflect on your actual impact, which may have become clear to you at the time and/or may be something you have a better understanding of now in hindsight. Do your best to recall instances where your intentions and your impact did not align—noting where they did can be helpful, but the purpose here is to note where they did *not* and reflect on how to do better moving forward.

Forgiveness Reflection

When you finish, take a moment to digest the harm you've experienced and/or caused, own your impact, and acknowledge what you've learned. Then, if it feels aligned, connect to your heart space and practice the following forgiveness mantra, as adapted from the meditation teacher and community organizer La Sarmiento:

> *I create space for myself to be imperfect.*
> *I create space for myself to make mistakes.*
> *I create space for myself to be a learner, still learning life's lessons.*
> *I forgive myself.*
> *And if I cannot forgive myself now, may I forgive myself sometime in the future.*[13]

Please Note: This exercise is likely to bring up some strong discomfort, do your best to simply be with what arises and do NOT rush out to contact those whom you have harmed. You still have more work to do, my love, keep reading and if, at the end of the book, you think reaching out prioritizes healing for the person you harmed, proceed to do so.

> > > > > >

TWELVE

Magnifying "Microaggressions"

I understood "microaggressions" to
mean "little bullshit acts of racism."

—GABBY RIVERA

It is impossible to talk about impact and intention without a discussion about "microaggressions"*, the common culprit most notably responsible for unintentional harms. A "microaggression" can be defined as "the everyday verbal, nonverbal, and environmental slights, snubs, or insults, whether intentional or unintentional, which communicate hostile, derogatory, or negative messages to target persons based solely upon their marginalized group membership."[1] As Columbia University psychology professor Dr. Derald Wing Sue states, "In many cases, these hidden messages may invalidate the group identity or experiential reality of target persons, demean them on a personal or group level, communicate they are lesser hum[x]n beings, suggest they do not belong with the majority group, threaten and intimidate, or relegate them to inferior status and treatment."[2] These behaviors can be inflicted upon a person or group marginalized for any reason and come in a wide range of shapes and sizes, a plethora of which I have experienced, from homophobia to misogynoir.

I can recount only a few instances of being called a "nigger" to my face. The first was when I was just thirteen, walking down a busy shopping street alongside my white friends, when a white man experiencing houselessness looked at me and yelled, "You nigger!" in my direction. I was shocked but did what I had always been socialized to do: I prioritized the comfort of my white friends, who were visibly embarrassed, and laughed the whole thing off. As a Black woman, I'm considered lucky to have only a few such run-ins, and though I may have been spared from other overt assaults, I have been treated as a nigger through looks, actions, and misdeeds more times that I can count. I am constantly subjected to daily racist "microaggressions," many of which are entirely unintentional.

I grew up surrounded by well-intentioned white women who made statements like "I never thought of you as Black," insinuating that my intelligence, speech, demeanor, etc. were outside of the monolithic "ghetto" personification they affiliated with Blackness and therefore I didn't belong to my own community. Several friends I had known for many decades invalidated my experience of racial oppression with claims that I must be mistaken. From bedrooms to boardrooms and beyond, every facet of my daily life is policed by white supremacy through the arsenal of inconspicuous but aggressive acts. Some other examples include:

> Constantly being labeled angry for the slightest inflection in speech, and I am assumed to be hotheaded or harder to deal with and thus given less leeway in negotiating conflict.

> I am frequently flagged for secondary screening or pulled out of line at the airport to have my luggage checked when the white or non-Black folx around me are not.
> Being followed around in stores by people of all races, because the presumption is that I'm poor and criminal.
> The process of publishing this very book has been rife with non-Black folx' tone-policing my narrative or arguing with my experience and expertise.

Non-race-based harms include acts like misgendering* someone, commenting on someone's health based solely on their weight, or when a man+ talks over a woman+.

"Microaggressions" are in fact anything *but* micro. I place the term in quotes because it's a bunch of bullshit. It is yet another tool to minimize the harms against the marginalized and perpetuate white supremacy. For that reason, "microaggressions" should really just be labeled what they are—aggressions. Another form of violence, but white supremacy covers these acts of harm in the guise of "micro" and thus insignificant. Or, as I like to call them, Heartbreaking Acts of Racism (or other oppressive bullshit) formerly known as "microaggressions" (H.A.R.M.)*. Intentional or not, physical or otherwise, H.A.R.M. cause meaningful and lasting damage with severe and deleterious impacts. Every time I leave my front door, I put on an artillery mask so I can handle the ceaseless plague of white supremacist violence that undoubtedly comes streaming my way. All of this on top of dealing with the everyday ups and downs of life. It is a nonstop, never-ending state of WTF?!, and it's worn myself and so many other Black and Indigenous women+ down.

Let's head back to my car accident for a hot minute. Sir Speedy did not intend to ram into me with his vehicle, but he did. And the impact was major. It wasn't visible, to him or to me at first. The totality of my harm manifested after Sir Speedy was long gone. What I endured during that accident is akin to what I endure every time I am slighted by a racist, homophobic, or sexist aggression—doubt and disbelief. I immediately wondered what I, the person who was in the car completely stopped at a light, had done wrong. I internalized my own oppression and perpetuated white supremacy by devaluing my nonvisible harms and repressing my anger at having been slammed into. To drive this analogy home (pun intended), my gratitude for Sir Speedy's accountability was also based in my conditioning to H.A.R.M. Had he not taken ownership for the accident, the likelihood that he, a middle-aged white man, would be believed by the police or insurer over me, a young Black woman, would have been (and remains) incredibly high, with serious adverse consequences.

As Dr. Roberto Montenegro, a chief fellow in child and adolescent psychiatry at Seattle Children's Hospital who studies the biological effects of discrimination, states, "['Microaggressions' aren't] about having your feelings hurt. It's about how being repeatedly dismissed and alienated and insulted and invalidated reinforces the differences in power and privilege, and how this perpetuates racism and discrimination."[3] As we've discussed, this has deleterious impacts on the physical and mental health of BI&PoC, particularly Black women+.

AGGRESSIONS & OUR ANGER

H.A.R.M. are also known as death by a thousand paper cuts. They are akin to walking down a busy street with your hands by your sides, while everyone else walking past you has their arms outstretched making windmill-like motions constantly and punching you as you pass. At a certain point, you're going to get fed the heck up with the incessant blows to your body and you're likely to lose your shit on whomever hit you last. And that last aggravator will almost certainly experience the wrath of every blow that impacted you prior to theirs. The cumulative trauma of enduring never-ending injury from a system created by folx who do not acknowledge, let alone remedy, the harms they've inflicted results in those hits becoming indistinguishable. Who is more to blame—the first person who hit you or the last? The entire system works together as a whole, both intentionally and otherwise, to ensure the oppressed remain ostracized and othered.

Oppressed folx have every right to be angry about these ongoing assaults. But, as Brittney Cooper explains, "If you are Black and hope to live to adulthood, micromanaging your feelings is necessary for survival."[4] We have learned to let these aggressions slide, to play them down, to stay hidden and silent lest we disrupt the powerful and privileged, but this undertaking only leads to more anger. And resentment. Whether we're conscious of it or not.

Embracing our own anger allows us to embrace the anger in others. I've experienced many H.A.R.M., but I am also no saint. I have clutched my purse walking by a Black man with a hood at night. I have used the wrong pronouns*, and I have made fatphobic statements. I've also worked hard to do better. And when I am held accountable for causing such harms, the last thing I could ever imagine doing is telling the person who was gracious enough to expend the time, energy, and emotional labor educating me on my mistake that they have no clue what they're talking about or the right to explain their own lived experience.

CALLING OUT VERSUS CALLING IN

There is an ongoing debate regarding call-out versus call-in culture and the ways in which the oppressed are "allowed" to express themselves when naming harms caused or asking for accountability. This debate is entirely rooted in the discomfort we have with anger, ours and others—particularly the anger expressed by Black women and femmes who are constantly vilified as angry. One of the most problematic occasions upon which white women+'s anger is unleashed is when they are named racist by a Black person. White entitlement leads white women+ to believe that, as a Black woman, I am obligated to speak to them with a smile and ensure their comfort above all else, even when I am explaining the harm they've inflicted against me. You know who else had that expectation? Enslavers and colonizers (I hope you're picturing my side-eye). As racial and gender justice disruptor Ericka Hart says, "Call outs are love. Call outs are necessary . . . Call outs are survivor-centered."[5]

When I name the impact your action had on me, I am calling on you to be accountable for the harm you've caused. No matter my tone. If you are more concerned with *how* I express what I have to say than *what* I am saying, you are further contributing to my oppression. As I've made very clear by now, Black women+ have damn good reason to be angry. Our lives and livelihoods are constantly threatened, cast aside, and terminated as a collective result of these ongoing assaults to our dignity. Does this mean I have license to perpetuate physical or emotional violence against others? Absolutely not. Does my expression of anger often get *perceived* as violence solely as a result of white supremacist stereotypes to the benefit of all white (and non-Black) people? Every damn day. Even former First Lady Michelle Obama faces this challenge, most notably when the media demonized her during the 2008 presidential race. As she says, "For a minute there, I was [labeled] an angry [B]lack woman who was emasculating her husband."[6] All of that's about white supremacist norms, not Michelle's or my actual behavior. Because of white supremacy, non-Black folx are often intimidated by us, but that does not mean we *are* intimidating. When Black women+ are forced to mask our true emotions in order to prioritize the oppressor's comfort, especially when attempting to address *our* oppression, the battle is already lost. Calling out is a form of accountability required for healing and justice.

Call out or call in, call it what you want, just don't call the cops. Learn how to embrace anger—especially from those who have been labeled angry as a weaponized means to silence, ignore, and dehumxnize. Practice having compassion for the anger that understandably occurs when someone faces perpetual assaults toward everything from their hair to their heels, and drop the expectation for the oppressed to kindly unpack why and how to treat them with decency. As cultural critic Sydette Harry tweeted, "Why do I have to watch my language for fear of alienating allies, when they can watch us die without fear of anything?"[7]

THE ART OF APOLOGIZING

When we cause harm, we need to take intentional actions to address the consequences. The best form of apology is changed behavior. Still, a verbal apology prior to the changed behavior, when authentic and sincere, can have a meaningful impact toward restoring trust. More times than I can count I've received half-hearted or downright fake-ass apologies from men+ and white women+. They sound like "I'm sorry you're hurt" or "I apologize, but . . . ," or my all-time favorite, "I'm sorry you took it that way." None of these own the harm caused or acknowledge the impact. They aren't actual apologies. So then, what's the best way to apologize for oppressive harms? Well, it's impossible to move through all possible scenarios, and it will always depend on the specific person involved and the harm that was caused, but I certainly have some guidelines that can be of help when discerning if, when, and how to broach an apology for a racist (or other oppressive) action.

Before extending an apology to the person in question, I strongly suggest doing deep inner work to first address your racism, internalized oppression, anti-Blackness, or whatever oppression is in question. Attempting an apology without addressing your own role in perpetuating white supremacy can only get you so far, and the chances of inflicting more harm are incredibly high. For example, it may require more time, energy, and emotional labor from the person you seek to apologize to or cause them to reexperience the harms inflicted. So, do your work first and do it for a while (not just a workshop or a week). Ask yourself the tough questions. Get more comfortable with your discomfort and unpack why it is you caused the person harm to begin with.

Then get clear on *why* you want to apologize and *whom* the apology is for. Is it for the person you've harmed, or is it really for you? Are you seeking to acknowledge the harm you have caused for the other person's benefit, or are you really seeking to absolve yourself of guilt, grief, shame, whatever? If the apology is about you, don't do it (that's not an authentic apology). If the apology is so you can explain yourself, so you can feel better about yourself (which may be a by-product but should not be the primary purpose), or for your own knowledge or understanding, please stop. Your apology will likely cause more damage. Also, if you feel the need to get into your intentions, just don't. They don't matter (remember, F.Y.I.!). If, however, the apology centers and is for the other person so that they can know that you know you were wrong, are taking accountability for your behavior, and are taking action to try to rectify the harm you have caused them (and do better moving forward), then you have the groundwork for an authentic apology. But there's more.

You can declare whatever you want (and I've heard it all), but without an active change, it's bullshit. In the words of #MeToo founder Tarana J. Burke, "Apologies are not work. They precede work."[8] An apology without change is manipulation. Periodt! So, your apology should be specific in addressing the harm you caused, taking responsibility, and naming it for what it was (i.e., racist or otherwise oppressive). And it should include a clear statement about what you're doing to address that behavior. Inquire and respect the other person's desire or willingness for an apology. If the apology is truly for the other person (and not for you), then you first need to check in with the person as to whether they want to talk to you or discuss the issue at all. I have personally been subjected to a myriad of "apologies" from white folx for their racist behavior, and not one has ever checked in with me first or taken a moment to think about whether their reaching out or engaging in such a discussion would be painful or harmful for *me*. They just launch into whatever it is they need to say because they need to "get it off their chest," which is all about *them*. It's white centering*. Don't treat people as your emotional trash can please and thanks.

Lastly, money is not an apology. Yes, remuneration and reparations are a part of contributing to racial justice, but they do not *replace* changed behavior. Using money to avoid doing the deep inner work required to sustainably act in solidarity and overturn the systems that allowed you to have the wealth privilege you possess in the first place is an act of oppression. Growing up in a white and wealthy community means I've had endless encounters with white and wealth privilege being used as a means to remedy harm rather than the harder but more important act of addressing wrongs and changing behavior. As Leesa Renee Hall aptly states, "To someone who has wealth privilege (notice I didn't say class privilege—understand the difference), it is not expensive to them to throw money to make mistakes go away. They can go through life not being held accountable for the harm they cause because all they need to do is fix it with money."[9] This is particularly true for white folx, who have the most wealth privilege as a result of the economic exploitation of BI&PoC worldwide, particularly Black and Indigenous folx. For centuries. Leesa also cites her brother-in-law, who said, "Money is the cheapest investment."[10] I could not agree more. Okay, let's break this all down.

Some Questions to Consider to Make an Authentic Apology

1) Have I done my inner work to dive into my racism, internalized oppression, or other oppressive harm? If so, for how long? What have I learned?

2) Why do I want to apologize? Why now?

3) Who is the apology primarily for—me, or the person I've harmed?

4) Am I clear on the harm I caused and ready to name it for what it was (i.e., white supremacy)? Can I speak to the specific actions I have taken and will continue to take to change and cause less harm moving forward?

5) Have I checked in with the person in question and asked them if they are willing to engage with me so that I can apologize? Have I respected their decision?

6) Am I attempting to weaponize my wealth or other privilege as a means to remedy my harm rather than actually changing my behaviors?

7) Am I ready to ask for an apology without *any* expectations of the person I'm apologizing to (not forgiveness, not a certain response, NOTHING)? Only apologize if/when you can do so with zero strings attached.

Here's an example apology to address harms inflicted by perpetuating white supremacy . . .

1) Check in:

I have been doing some deep inner work around white supremacy, and I have come to realize that I caused you harm. I would like to apologize for my behavior and the harm I caused you if you would be willing to receive my apology. I will respect your decision either way.

2) Apologize:

Thank you for giving me the opportunity to apologize to you. I am doing my best to account for the way(s) I caused you harm. I am still learning and I may fuck this up. If I say anything here that causes you more harm and you feel sufficiently safe/have the emotional energy to let me know, please do. If you want to stop communicating with me at any point, please let me know. No explanation required.

I apologize for [name your specific act of violence]. I realize that it was [racist OR a result of my internalized oppression] because [explain why] and it caused you harm. I take full accountability for my actions and I am committed to [insert the actions you have/will continue to take] to reduce harm moving forward. I understand that if my actions or inactions do not change, this apology is insincere. I appreciate you and I am sorry. If there is anything you would like to share or let me know about my actions, apology, or anything else—it would be a privilege to receive what you have to share. I appreciate that would necessitate your time, energy, and emotional labor and may require reexperiencing the harm I have caused; I also understand the impact my actions have had and may continue to have on you. Should you wish to engage with me further, I will do my best to minimize further additional labor on your end. In deep gratitude.

It's time we all caused less H.A.R.M. Sadly, many of us (and certainly all BI&PoC) will experience H.A.R.M. all too often. Below is an offering to support you in protecting your energy before, after, or even during such acts of violence.

Spiritual Soulcare Offering

Aura-Shielding Meditation for Energetic Sovereignty

If you find yourself facing H.A.R.M. or other violence, this is a simple meditation that can assist you in getting back into your body and reclaiming your power. Our aura (the energy field surrounding the body) may expand to help defend us when we are subject to harm, which can then create more holes or tears in our auric field, leading to emotional, mental, or physical unrest. This exercise promotes energetic sovereignty by calling your power back and releasing unwanted and/or harmful energies that may have attached to you.

Find a quiet space and close or lower your eyes if it feels safe to do so. You can lie down or find any position that feels comfortable for you and your body right now.

Connect with your breath and begin to envision and tap into your auric field, which extends six feet out in all directions around you. Take a moment to notice what your aura feels like. Are there any areas calling for your attention? No need to overthink, just send your energy where it feels needed. Imagine a healing white light pouring over you and cleansing your entire auric field, filling in any holes or tears. Call your power and energy back across all space and time, and release any and all unwanted lingering, corded, or otherwise connected energies. When you feel your aura is restored and repaired, envision guards protecting you and your aura. These may be in the form of shielding light in a color of your choice, trees, or animals. I like to envision a ring of my matriarchal ancestors surrounding me and sending me healing, loving light, with another ring of ancestral warriors guarding me with huge shields.

When you're done, rub your hands together in front of your heart center if that's available to you. Then place your hands over your heart and feel the loving energy you can create for and give to yourself. Take a deep exhale, releasing anything that needs releasing. As always, give thanks to the ancient Indian elders who cultivated this potent practice so that you can partake in it today. Open your eyes and journal, sing, dance, rest, cry, scream, set your boundaries, and/or share your truth as feels best for you (in a manner that prioritizes the well-being of the most marginalized). If you are able, please pay homage to the Indian communities that cultivated this practice for you to enjoy—energetically, financially, or otherwise.

> > > > > >

THIRTEEN

Why White Women+
Need to Get Out the Way

We can't become what we need to be
by remaining what we are.

—OPRAH WINFREY

In all my workshops, white women+ show up with heavy hearts. Often overwhelmed at how and where to start the work of addressing their own racism but mistakenly believing they can and should lead the way toward ending white supremacy. There is an epidemic of white women+, especially cis women, partaking in performative activism and attempting to distance themselves from white supremacy by spearheading anti-racist education. When it comes to racial justice, white women+ must learn how and when to follow—not lead. White women+ need to do their part to uplift, learn from, follow, and support Black and Indigenous women+ in dismantling white supremacy. White women+ have a huge and necessary role in racial justice, but they need to actively address their white supremacy and minimize harm, give up their privileges wherever possible, and call in all of their fellow white people to do the same (with tangible consequences for failing to do so). But actively engaging in racial justice does *not* mean presenting yourself as an educator or making money off anti-racism in any way. Still, y'all keep doing it. As I write this, a white woman's book about "white fragility" is the highest-selling anti-racism book worldwide (and she reportedly commands $20,000 for a workshop!).[11] In the wake of the Black Lives Matter uprising amidst the COVID-19 pandemic, more white women swooped in like moths to a flame to cash in on anti-racism (especially in the "wealth and hellness" biz). They are earning a living from the exact systems of oppression they're claiming to fight. Meanwhile, Black and Indigenous racial justice activists and educators who've been preaching similar shit for decades still can't pay their rent. This is white supremacy at its finest. And it's *unacceptable*.

There are many common pitfalls that white women+ seeking to engage in anti-racism frequently succumb to and that BI&WoC, steeped in our internalized oppression, are quick to enable. That ends here. And now. Let's uncover these mistakes so we can all do better at advancing racial justice and preventing harm toward the most marginalized. Our work is urgent.

> > < <

White women+, as a whole, need to get out the dang way—metaphorically as well as physically. A common experience I and many other Black women+ discuss in our work is how white women+ literally refuse to move out of the way for us in physical spaces. Walking down the street. In the grocery aisle. At the airport. White women+ are conditioned to expect, often unconsciously, that Black women+ will move out of their way and defer to their physical superiority. White women+ are not the only ones, by any means, but they are often the most egregious. Especially cis white women. This aggression plays out day after day, and most white women+ have no conscious clue they're doing it. Since I am no longer prioritizing white comfort, I now make a point to stay in place when this arises, which often results in white women+ body-checking me. Then one of two things happens: either the woman+ continues on as though they didn't just slam themselves into my being, or they say something like "Sorry, I didn't see you."

When it comes to racial justice, this phenomenon is a telling one. Because white women+ so rarely acknowledge Black women+ or other WoC*, and even when they do, they do not acknowledge the harms they cause, let alone care to remedy those harms. It shows how far white women+ need to go in order to engage in authentic anti-racism and why they are absolutely not the ones to lead the way.

SHOCK & AWE

The majority of white women+ couldn't survive a solitary day dealing with what Black women+ and other WoC must go through. The experiences we endure. The looks—the way we're stared at and entirely ignored in the same moment—the tones, the silencing, the constant policing of our thoughts, emotions, bodies, words, and faces. White women+ have been socialized to be crappy at coping. With anything. Especially their own violence. One of the reasons white women+ cannot lead anti-racism is because they remain in a state of disbelief and disillusionment around racial realities. For example, there's been a shit ton of white women+ in shock the last few years, be it from the 2016 U.S. presidential election, the Brexit referendum, systemic anti-Blackness amplified during the COVID-19 pandemic, and the like. Though these outcomes have been alarming for sure, the "shock" that I have witnessed and continue to witness from white women+ is not only played out. It's triggering. The political appointment of racist, xenophobic misogynists should come as *no* surprise. Nor should state-sanctioned killings of Black lives. Not. At. All. The system is set up by white supremacy for white supremacy to prevail. White women+'s dismay is simply a consequence of their white privilege. When it comes to the electoral system, what is happening amidst all the "heartbreak" and "hopelessness" is an expectation. An earnest belief that if they just roll up their sleeves to canvas for a cause, have a few hard conversations, and work solely within a white supremacist system, then shit *will* change. And that expectation is white supremacy at play. Because Black and Indigenous women+ have been rallying, kicking, and screaming *for centuries*, and our truths have been actively suppressed by whiteness—including white women+. This is why I have always wholeheartedly believed Trump would win another term, and that the same if not more white women would vote for him! As a queer Black woman, I have no faith in a system that allowed him to become President, or remain in office, in the first place. White supremacy thrives through the systems it created. Still, when Trump wins, white women will once again express their shock and awe. I hope I'm proven wrong (and by the time you're reading this, we'll know) but I'm not holding my breath! I personally believe it is my duty to vote because the consequences of not casting my ballot can lead to more harm. But I also know voting is just one small (and not particularly effective) way to fight injustice and Black people should in no way be expected to participate in a structure built to eradicate us. The system as a whole is a racist, homophobic, transphobic, classist, ableist, ageist, and misogynist mess. It is not enough to throw all your weight and hopes for change behind an oppressive electoral process then do fuck all the rest of your days—but too many white women+ do just that, then sink into despair when shit doesn't go their way (smh).

White women+ need to collect their wigs and their people. But collecting their people does not and cannot mean *leading* anti-racist education or efforts, because—newsflash—they don't sufficiently know or understand racism! I would never take up space as a leader in fighting ableism, because as a non-disabled person, I cannot comprehend the depth of the experience of those with disabilities and could never speak to what is best to end a form of oppression I participate in. It is not my place. And believing that it is only further harms folx with disabilities who are forced to fight to have their stories shared instead of non-disabled assholes like me. Same goes for gender identity, sexual orientation, and all oppressions, including race. White folx, and all oppressors, need to know their limit and play within it.

White women+ benefit from white supremacy and are thus unable to lead the way toward dismantling it. As my friend and activist ShiShi Rose shares, "White women specifically choose not to fight racism even when they are being oppressed because they would rather remain as close to power as they can even if that means feeding the beast that harms them too."[12] A-fucking-woman.

There are also some who argue that white women+ need to call in other white folx who won't receive information shared by BI&WoC, but white folx who refuse to acknowledge what I, as a Black woman, have to say about racial justice are also refusing to acknowledge my humxnity. And if you aren't willing to acknowledge my humxnity, how the hell are you going to undertake the immense inner and outer work required to fight for my liberation? You're not. Next!

GLEANINGS FROM GLENNON

A prime example of why white women+ should not lead anti-racist efforts comes from one of America's most beloved white women: Glennon Doyle. As she wrote about in her book *Untamed*, in the fall of 2018 Glennon made a post on Instagram about a webinar for white women to discuss race that she and another white woman were leading.[13] This, my loves, is a stunning example of white women getting way the hell out their lane. Why? Say it with me! Because white people have no place leading anti-racism education. There are lots of important and informative tidbits that came out of Glennongate, so let's unpack and learn, shall we? We shall!

Let me make it clear that I'm not here to rip Glennon a new one. She made an effort and she fucked it up. That's just part of doing the work, and for better or worse, she is in no way exceptional. Let's start there—reiterating that she, like every other white woman, celebrity or otherwise, is not exceptional. White women+ are all included in the hot mess that is whiteness. Together. Let me remind y'all that all white women+ benefit from white supremacy, they all belong to it, and nearly all perpetuate it (even if they're trans, gender non-conforming*, LGBTTQIA+, poor, immigrant, disabled, or the like). But white women+ keep feeling like they've transcended to some exceptional place after one hot minute's worth of anti-racism, granting them the right and ability to educate other white women+ on race. It's white exceptionalism at its finest, and in this instance many agreed. Hundreds, if not thousands, of BI&WoC, along with white women+ authentically engaged in racial justice, pointed out how problematic Glennon's webinar was. First, white women+ do not need a "safe space," as was promoted, to discuss race. This infers that spaces with BI&PoC are somehow unsafe, and that's a racist proposition; and BI&WoC sure AF don't get "safe spaces" away from white supremacy.

More concerning was the notion that Glennon or the cohost, a white woman who came from a highly criticized all-white "racial justice group" (mayjah eyeroll from me), was qualified to lead a conversation on race. That an anti-racism discussion among white women+, led by white women, was a helpful event. Wrong again! Let me repeat: white people, aka those who intentionally and unintentionally oppress BI&PoC to maintain power and privilege to the exclusion of all others, cannot *lead* the revolution against the very thing they most benefit from. Any anti-racist dialogue led by white folx occurs through the lens of white supremacy and is thus inherently flawed and harmful.

Lastly, there's the fact that this educational webinar was offered for free or by donation, which undermines and depreciates the tireless work of Black racial justice educators like myself—which was the point I raised with Glennon. Now, when and how white folx *should* take independent action is in fact an ongoing debate within the racial justice realm, and Glennon was encouraged to host that webinar by a council of BI&WoC who believe white people need to lead in this way (smh); but I was also informed by a Black activist who spoke with Glennon that the council advising her was comprised of very few Black or Indigenous women+, let alone queer and trans Black and Indigenous women+ racial justice educators (aka the folx we all *ought* to be learning from and listening to). Fail!

When I say follow Black and Indigenous women+, I don't mean that one colleague you had way back when. I mean those of us trained, educated, and continuously and actively engaged in racial justice and intersectional anti-oppression, full stop. I mean prioritizing queer and trans Black and Indigenous women+ activists who have and continue to pave the way for our collective liberation. The great majority of queer and trans Black and Indigenous racial justice activists agree that white people have *no* business leading racial justice, and when they do, they co-opt the movement, white-wash the discourse, and cause BI&PoC harm.

All in all, the white woman webinar was a fail. What happened next was arguably worse. Glennon ultimately decided to call off the webinar—no applause there, as it never should have existed. She also tagged me and two other Black anti-racism educators in the post (since removed) sharing what she had learned from the perspectives we had offered in our responses on her post announcing the webinar. Then, like clockwork, came the violent comments from white women attacking Black women and displaying white women+'s omnipresent allegiance to white supremacy. These comments went unaddressed and uncensored on Glennon's page *for days*. In the meantime, myself and other Black women were subjected to ongoing harm, with some white women harassing us in our own DMs. This is yet another reason white women+ cannot lead conversations about race—they can't or won't rein in their own people. Allowing white women+ to attack Black women+ in any space is straight-up racist. White silence is indeed violent, and anyone who would allow that to take place is not doing enough of their own work, let alone able to lead others through theirs. Was Glennon's attempt at allyship a full-out fuckup? No. She sent me a small sum of money to remunerate my energy and education. I received a flock of new followers who were seemingly ready to do better. And it was a prime and public example of what *not* to do, which many white women+ learned from. Another example of what *not* to do is Glennon's chapter about this incident in her book, which fails to name or credit a single BI&WoC for the themes and ideas she presents or the education she received in becoming "racially sober," as she calls it. As Glennon herself said, "I will keep getting it wrong, which is the closest I can come to getting it right."[14] Glennon, like all white women+, can, and really should, do better. Few things are entirely wrong or bad, and dismantling oppression is far more complex than a binary perspective can withstand. Still, there are better ways to try than others, and white women+ need to stop, think, and follow rather than rush, perform, and lead.

In this same vein, I disagree with the Chelsea Handlers of the world who create works about white privilege that they can lead and profit from *because of their white privilege*! Her 2019 Netflix special on this topic was sixty-four minutes of white centering in action. Hard pass. Had Chelsea produced a documentary that was coproduced, directed, and hosted by Black and Indigenous women+ (who were paid well!) and/or directed all profits to an organization supporting us, then I could get behind it. But she didn't.

> > < <

All of this goes to show why simply educating white people, or other dominant groups, is insufficient to create critical change. Many BI&WoC are critical of efforts to educate white people. ShiShi Rose argues that white people have the information to dismantle racism but are choosing not to, because they know it requires them to give up power.[15] And yes, white women+ HAVE power. Some even suggest white folx tend to believe or portray that they are less capable or knowledgeable than they really are when it comes to racism. I don't disagree. There are a host of social justice issues white people take on and have no problem researching, finding solutions, and acting on (e.g., climate change, animal cruelty, etc.), but when it comes to racism, white people become incapable. "When you know better you do better" doesn't necessarily apply here, as knowledge about white supremacy alone does not equate to action, and action is what's required.

SO, WHAT IS WHITE WOMEN+'S ROLE?

As I said, white women+ are absolutely needed in the fight for racial justice and they need to play a way bigger role than they have to date. Voting and talking among themselves is not enough, so how *should* white women+ help dismantle white supremacy? And how can BI&WoC support that? Great question! I've shared a few of my hot tips below.

#1—Understanding White Folx Ain't the Ones

First off, we all need to understand that white folx, who have never experienced systemic or institutionalized oppression as a result of race, should not and cannot adequately educate on that topic in any formal way. White folx' work is to follow, center, support, uplift, learn from, and pay queer and trans Black and Indigenous women+ activists and educators, who are the most versed on dismantling white supremacy. Then absorb that knowledge into your daily life to spend your power and privilege however and wherever necessary. To collect other white women+ is to (1) point them in the direction of the melanated women+ rightfully leading this work, (2) explain to other white women+ what they've personally learned from those educators and why they personally find anti-racism important for *everyone*, and (3) get them on board with also spending *their* power and privilege.

White-passing BI&WoC can do the same: collect your white-passing people and preach as to the need for *all* to be unpacking the ways they perpetuate white supremacy and cause non-white-passing BI&WoC harm. No matter your race or ethnicity, let us stop applauding white women+ for doing the bare minimum and discontinue our support of white women+ who are attempting to lead the charge in a way that does not follow, credit, and remunerate the centuries of racial justice guidance and gospel from Black and Indigenous women+, unless it's leading the charge against white folx doing just that. And any white woman+ making a penny of profit off racial justice doesn't understand what the fuck racial justice is.

Many BI&WoC have allowed white women+ to get away with this shit because they'll offer us a seat at a table of power and privilege we hadn't had access to before. But the price of admission is greater than any nourishment we believe we'll receive. We too need to address the ways internalized oppression causes ourselves and each other harm; to prioritize our experiences, work, and wisdom; and to hold white folx to account when they try to co-opt the movement. Anything otherwise causes harm.

#2—Hold Other White Folx Accountable

There's a difference between white women+ trying to be educators, which is a no-no, and holding other white folx accountable, which needs to be done *immediately*! When white women+ witness their people acting out of turn—friends, family, coworkers, strangers, elected officials, whomever—they should be calling those folx out. Racist, sexist, anti-Black, transphobic, or homophobic comments, oppressive actions, etc. need to be condemned and tangible consequences need to be established. Like losing a job, family member, or customer. White women+ need to make it clear that white supremacy will not be tolerated and take action to hold folx accountable when it does. And here's the kicker: if you are doing your own internal work to face white supremacy, it makes speaking up against injustice easier, because there's no other option. That *is* the work. You simply will not allow it any longer. It becomes unacceptable for you, and your integrity mandates you align your actions with your values and your impact over your intention and the intentions of others. A clear indicator that you are committed to racial justice is an inner circle free from all who are not. Read that again and take action as necessary.

Guide any and all white folx to the Black and Indigenous educators they can learn from, and share what it is you personally learned from those educators and why you find racial justice imperative. Make it clear to all those in your midst what your values are, including those specific to racial justice, and engage in dialogue with those who need help understanding. I've shared guidance as to how to best do that in Chapter 14. Credit the Black and Indigenous women+ who've taught you, call in your people to do the work alongside you, and encourage other white folx to follow, support, nurture, learn from, and pay the Black and Indigenous women+ leading the way. Remember, your work is not to be a voice for those whose voices have been oppressed. Your work is to spend your privilege.

#3—Spend Your Privilege

One of the best ways white women+ can dismantle white supremacy is through leading by example. That starts by calling in your people to do their own work as per the above, but go further by giving up your power and getting out the way. Step down from roles to create space for Black and Indigenous women+. Mandate anti-racist hiring policies. Offer your gifts, talents, and services to BI&PoC, particularly queer and trans Black and

Indigenous women and femmes, and other oppressed folx for free. Make introductions to support our access to power. Pay micro-reparations regularly. Continuously ask what you can give up, then make it happen. White folx will never be able to repay the debts owed to Black and Indigenous folx, but it is imperative that they try. Lead the way in not only acknowledging your privilege but actively giving it up.

#4—Critically Examine White-Only Initiatives and Spaces

I get a lot of questions from white women+ confused about when they need to act alone and when they need to call on BI&WoC for help. I appreciate this concern, because despite the fact that Black and Indigenous women+ can and must spearhead racial justice, *we cannot be expected to bear the brunt of the labor.* Black and Indigenous women+ will lead the way, but white women+ ought to do the majority of the work. Think of it like a choreographer and their dancers—queer and trans Black and Indigenous women+ are the masterminds, expending our high-level gifts and guidance to create the way forward and support the dancers (white folx!) in executing the precise routine of the master vision: equity for all.

Generally, if all participants in an all-white initiative have engaged and are continuing to actively engage in racial justice work led by Black and Indigenous women+ and the intention of the gathering is to act primarily as support for one another in their unlearning, with a goal of always centering and prioritizing the well-being of BI&WoC, then, and only then, can it be acceptable to gather. If the intention is for the white-only group to act as a source of racial justice education, then it is a no. Unpacking and supporting one another through this work is education in and of itself, but not of the same type that ought to be left to Black and Indigenous racial justice educators.

Even in the best of circumstances, it must be acknowledged that any all-white initiative addressing race is inherently problematic, as all issues and discussions will take place through the lens of white supremacy. There is no work-around for this fact. However, one way to help counter it is to bring in (and pay) a Black or Indigenous anti-racist educator to help check and moderate your white initiative and assist with your ongoing education. It is also imperative that any participant in such a group has taken not just one kind of education from one educator, but many. It is unacceptable to take one webinar or work through one workbook, then rush to an all-white space or start an all-white initiative. Many, if not all, of your queries can be addressed by simply doing more of your own work as led by and through Black and Indigenous women+.

Lastly, it is always critical to ask: Why do I feel I need a white-only space or initiative? Get real and get honest. With yourself and others. As a queer Black woman, there is no space on Earth that is truly safe for me, so your ability to gather in such a way to work through and process your racism—the thing that has resulted in both my ancestors and present-day community being starved, raped, lynched, enslaved, and murdered—is a product of your white privilege. If you truly feel it is necessary, do it authentically, do it rarely, and know that a group of white folx gathering to discuss racism is rarely in and of itself anti-racist; rather it is supplemental support to one's anti-racist efforts.

If you are seeking to be in a white-only space solely in order to process your feelings about your racial justice work, then go for it. Because the BI&PoC in your life are not compost bins for white feelings. We're exhausted from simply trying to survive.

To recap on some of the dos and don'ts for white folx taking independent initiative to fight racial injustice . . .

Some Dos for White Folx

> Take any and all initiatives to give up your power and privilege whenever and however possible and organize other white folx to do the same.

> Take it upon yourself to conceive solutions and take action that is: (a) rooted in the inner work you've learned from Black women+, and (b) centers queer and trans Black and Indigenous women+.

> Actively create ongoing and equitable opportunities for queer and trans Black and Indigenous women+ and call in your people to do the same (for example, hire us, share the mic, mandate equitable practices in your personal and professional life, etc.).

> Engage your fellow white folx in the work of learning from, financially investing in, and following queer and trans Black and Indigenous women+ educators.

> Hold white people accountable for their harmful actions or inactions and create consequences for those who refuse.

> Remain accountable to and led by queer and trans Black and Indigenous women+ educators/activists.

> Actively and continuously educate yourself by reading books, listening to podcasts, taking racial justice courses, etc. led by queer and trans Black and Indigenous women+ racial justice educators and activists.

> Center the well-being of queer and trans Black and

Indigenous women+ in ALL of your efforts and constantly ask yourself and your accountability partners if and how you are doing so.

> Amplify the work of those Black and Indigenous women+ you are learning from, always giving us credit for our work and specifically sharing what you've learned.

> Hold space to help fellow white folx move through the grief and other conflicting emotions that arise from undertaking racial justice.

> Stay in your lane and follow, follow, follow the lead of Black and Indigenous women+.

Some Don'ts for White Folx

> Fancy yourself an anti-racism educator or leader in any way, shape, or form (and for the love of Blackness, *stop* writing anti-racism books and facilitating workshops).

> Profit from racial justice or anti-racism work in any way (and if by chance you do, redirect those funds immediately).

> Assume your one Black friend (or anyone other than a qualified Black or Indigenous racial justice educator/ activist) to be an expert on race from whom you can learn about anti-racism.

> Hold space for white people to have pity parties or prioritize their own discomfort over the discomfort of (or straight up violence committed against) BI&WoC.

> Start an organization or nonprofit to help BI&WoC. (Instead, research BI&WoC-owned and -operated

organizations already doing the work and fund/support *them*. You can even get a group of white folx together to raise funds.)
> Center white people's education or well-being over the liberation and well-being of BI&WoC.
> Do not attempt to lead, do not attempt to lead, do not attempt to lead.

> > < <

Authentic anti-racism is about prioritizing Black and Indigenous women+ and finding ways for all BI&PoC to access and maintain the power and privilege that we have been traditionally excluded from. It necessitates all of us, myself included, following and learning from the most marginalized—the old, poor, fat, non-English-speaking, disabled, immigrant, dark-skinned, queer and trans Black and Indigenous women+. It requires critically identifying and engaging with the Black and Indigenous educators and activists truly committed to ending all forms of oppression, while being conscientious not to solely follow and support the cis, straight, light-skinned, pretty, or polite educators who keep you in your comfort zone.

Racial justice has been and will continue to be led by women+. What I'm telling you, without a shadow of a doubt, is that those women+ will not be white. I firmly believe change is coming. But it can only come if all women+ work every single day, inside and out, to dismantle white supremacy (not just come election time or when a video of Black murder goes viral); and we all must accept that queer and trans Black and Indigenous women+ educated in racial justice must lead the way.

Setting Your Racial Justice Values

This is an exercise for you to both clarify and commit to personal racial justice values no matter your race or identity. These values will help guide you to discern when and how to take action toward ending white supremacy, day in and day out. To start, head back to the intention you set at the beginning of the book. Review it, meditate on it, and consider how it may have changed since you first began this journey into Spiritual Activism. Think about the values that lie underneath. You may notice underlying values like: connection, equity, love, integrity, authenticity, intersectionality, community, acceptance, etc. Grab a dictionary or thesaurus (or hop online) and find five to ten words that best sum up your values as they relate to combating white supremacy.

When you feel good about the values and descriptions you've landed on, set a timer on your phone or watch for two minutes, then pick your top three to five values, crossing out all others before the timer goes off. (Tip: Start by crossing off your least important value and go from there. Also, you may find some words incorporate more than one value, so go with those.) When you're done, write out your top three to five anti-oppressive values (and their definitions). Write out a short description to explain what each word means to you.

If you need help, head to www.rachelricketts.com/vision-and-values and check out mine. Then put them up somewhere you will acknowledge them every day, like your desk, bathroom mirror, or fridge. Try them on for a week or two and update them as and when needed on an ongoing basis. Use these values to help inform how and when you show up to dismantle oppression. As you dive deeper in this work your values will change, as will you.

Declaring Your Anti-Oppressive Goals

Now that you have your anti-oppressive values, let's put them to werrrrk! Pick three actionable goals to help dismantle white supremacy this month. Write them down. Be specific and set deadlines for each. Then pick three larger, more long-term goals to help dismantle oppression in the next six months. Put them somewhere you can affirm them every day, and hold yourself accountable (call in support to help you)!

FOURTEEN

Acting in Allyship

> The thing with activism is that it doesn't
> build character, it reveals character.
>
> **—JANAYA "FUTURE" KHAN**

The term "ally" has been a hot commodity as of late. Every cis white woman and her dog are jumping on the ally* train. There's a lot of self-appointed aggrandizing going on and none if it is for the actual benefit of those most oppressed. So, what actually is an ally? How can we best act in allyship? And where are we getting allyship all wrong? Lemme tell ya.

WHAT IS AN ALLY?

An ally is a person who uses their privilege to advocate for someone who doesn't hold that same privilege. Some argue being an ally shouldn't be the goal at all but rather an accomplice or co-agitator. Someone who actively disrupts shit in order to create change. For my purposes, I'm going to lump those terms in with "ally," because unless you're doing all of those things, I don't think you're worthy of any damn term whatsoever. Contrary to the widely held (often white) belief, the term "ally" is not a noun. You cannot name yourself an ally. Ever. The term is one that can be granted to you by the specifically oppressed group with which you seek to act as an ally. Especially not when you're doing so solely because you dislike a certain oppression. Disliking or disagreeing does not an ally make. Which is precisely why I argue that you can never actually *be* an ally but you can *act* in allyship. I cannot take off my Blackness. I *am* Black. But acting in allyship, or not, is a choice. One that is required to be made time and time again, day in and day out, for the rest of your days. White people can act in allyship with BI&PoC, men+ can act in allyship with women+, non-disabled folx can act in allyship with disabled folx, cis folx can act in allyship with trans folx, and so on. The moments of acting as an ally are defined by the choices, behaviors, actions, or inactions made. We all have allyship to undertake and we will all, at one point or another, fail to take it. One can never act in allyship 24/7, which is why one cannot *be* an ally. And then there are the ways we oversimplify the intersectionality our allyship demands. For example, maybe you are a hetero and non-disabled South Asian woman who decides to act in allyship with a Black woman but haven't given much thought to the oppression faced by LGBTTQIA+ folx or disabled folx. In which case, you aren't acting in allyship for *all* Black women+. Only those who are straight and non-disabled.

When we acknowledge that allyship is an action, and one that requires commitment and constant tuning and retuning, we can get over this notion of it being a sense of who we are or element of our identity. It's not. Nor does it need to be. As racial and gender justice disruptor Ericka Hart shares, "I think there is a higher drive to call yourself something more than taking actions to end the injustice(s) . . . I just take actions, speak up, disrupt, I don't need a label."[1] Just do the damn work and get over yourself. Aight?

EXAMPLES OF ACTING IN ALLYSHIP

Because acting in allyship is so multifaceted and inherently intersectional, it is impossible to share an exhaustive list of ways we can best act in allyship. Still, there are some clear suggestions and starting places as they specifically pertain to acting in allyship with BI&WoC and, of course, queer and trans Black and Indigenous women+ in particular. As Black Indigenous activist Kénta Xiadani Ch'umil shares, acting in allyship comes in micro forms (like donating or calling out racist behaviors) and macro forms (like withdrawing from a job and mandating your replacement be a Black or Indigenous women+ or using your privilege to help defund the police).[2] Ideally you partake in them all (not necessarily all at once). I always find the best place to start is with real-world examples, so I have shared some of the ways people in my life have shown up and acted in allyship with me as a Black woman. These include:

> A white client checking her racist white colleague when the colleague interrupted our conversation to reject my claim regarding cultural appropriation.
> White friends dropping dinner off for me after multiple violent murders of Black folx.
> My husband gathering his men+ to join me at a march for women's rights.

> My East Asian friend acknowledging the ways in which I face additional oppression due to misogynoir in our discussions about racism.
> A white client in the wellness industry holding a fundraiser to pay for my travel expenses to host a racial justice workshop at SXSW.
> My straight friends acknowledging and affirming my bisexuality when I came out.
> A white friend using her power and privilege at a major national business to get the company to hire my services.
> Folx sending me financial contributions when they have learned something from me IRL or online (without asking or sharing, just doing).

These are only but a few of many ways you can show up for those who hold less power and privilege than you in some or all instances. Below I've shared some additional (but in no way exhaustive) examples of ways to act in allyship. I have separated these into two categories, external and internal acts of allyship, which are by no means black and white, because it is important not only to act in allyship in outward, tangible ways but also inner, abstract ones. Truly acting in allyship requires both. As always, I have highlighted acting in allyship with queer and trans Black and Indigenous women+, but many of these are applicable for BI&PoC generally and/or other or additionally marginalized folx. There's also space at the bottom of each for you to add your own ideas for doing better, because we're here for critical, independent engagement!

Examples of External Acts of Allyship

> Lobby for government reparations from all countries that participated in and benefited from the transatlantic slave trade to all Black folx in such countries.

> In the words of Rihanna, tell your friends to "pull up." Engage them in your racial justice learnings and direct them to your queer and trans Black and Indigenous women+ educators, ensuring never to attempt to *lead* racial justice efforts if you are white.

> Divest your money and support from brands, celebrities, and influencers who do not actively support racial justice and anti-oppression, and support Black and Indigenous folx and brands. Call on your people to do the same.

> Address harm when it arises, whether it originated from you or not. Believe queer and trans Black women+ and understand that, no matter your race, continuing to work with, defend, or befriend people who have been shown to harm queer and trans Black women+ is also an act of violence.

> Set aside a monthly budget for ongoing micro-reparations to queer and trans Black and Indigenous women+.

> Use your light-skinned privilege to amplify darker-skinned folx and dismantle colorism.

> Speak to the organizers of conferences, panels, and events that do not feature and remunerate multiple queer and trans Black and Indigenous women+ (one ain't enough) and boycott if they refuse to do so.

> Support queer and trans Black- and Indigenous-owned and -operated businesses as the standard rather than the

exception (head to www.rachelricketts.com/buy-black
for a list of places to start).

> Advocate to defund the police and abolish the
  prison-industrial complex, including the school-to-
  prison pipeline, while reinvesting funds into Black
  communities.

> Demand and support an entirely new, anti-oppressive
  political system and vote for queer and trans Black and
  Indigenous women+ in the interim.

> Learn the names and history of the Indigenous
  peoples whose stolen land you live, work, and play on.
  Acknowledge them and their land at every opportunity,
  and support them or their descendants energetically,
  financially, and otherwise.

> Withdraw from capitalism, wealth accumulation, and
  all forms of extraction and exploitation in ideology and
  lived reality.

> Amplify queer and trans Black and Indigenous women+
  racial justice educators/activists, and share the specifics
  of what *you* have learned from us.

> Stop appropriating Black American culture (see Chapter
  10). Be considerate of how you consume their music,
  language, style, hair. If you aren't actively supporting
  an end to anti-Blackness personally and collectively,
  you have no right to indulge in Black culture (especially
  when we are oppressed in a way you're not for doing the
  same thing, like rocking cornrows).

> End the white-washing of wellness: Stop using white
  sage, palo santo, and other sacred and endangered
  Indigenous herbal medicines. Stop frequenting

businesses that treat yoga or other BI&PoC practices as a commodity instead of honoring the roots and intentions of the practice. Follow, support, and pay BI&WoC teachers and mentors.

> Defund the gross wealth accumulation of the Christian and Catholic Church (and the oppressive powers that wealth affords them).

> Support Indigenous land and water protectors: write your governments in support of Indigenous rights and use your power to amplify their message.

> Put your body on the line to protect Black and Indigenous people from physical violence or arrest.

> Use inclusive language, including but not limited to asking for and stating your own pronouns—always, not just in the presence of those you believe aren't cisgender. And stop using ableist language (like crazy, dumb, blindspot, etc.).

> Apologize when you cause harm and change your behavior (see Chapter 11).

> _____

> _____

Examples of Internal Acts of Allyship

> Do your personal inner-healing work to better withstand your own discomfort and address the ways

you oppress others. For example, through talk therapy, asking for help, processing and communicating your emotions, connecting with yourself, etc.

> Take full ownership over dismantling oppressive systems you and the dominant group you belong to created and perpetuate.

> Contemplate the ways in which all forms of oppression are connected and how you can best address allyship in the most intersectional way.

> Question whose comfort you're prioritizing. (Is it the person with the most or least power, and why?)

> Unpack and address how colorism shows up for you and causes you and others harm (especially darker-skinned folx).

> Stop lumping all BI&PoC into one group and address our specific harms individually, prioritizing anti-Blackness and anti-Indigeneity.

> Notice and challenge your oppressive thoughts as and when they arise.

> Challenge your inner ableism when you feel pressure to be "productive" rather than simply be.

> Ask yourself: Whom could this action or inaction hurt today and/or in the future? And at the same time ask: Whom could this help?

> Notice the inequity present in the spaces you visit and occupy and how they impact those not represented or welcomed.

> Reflect on the queer and trans Black and Indigenous stories and narratives you experience through music, art, books, film, or otherwise. Ask how they make you feel and process why.

> Practice soulcare and give yourself support to best support others (via community and otherwise).
> Reflect on how much you/this world takes from Black and Indigenous communities (music, food, style, language, resources, land, spiritual practices) and how little you/it gives back.
> Care more about acting in allyship than signaling to others that you are an "ally."
> Constantly check in to ensure your allyship centers queer and trans Black and Indigenous women+.
> _____

  _____

  _____

> _____

  _____

  _____

There is an entirely inexhaustible number of actions you can take (well beyond this list), and the ifs, whens, and hows of acting in allyship will always depend on the specific circumstances you're in. Resist the urge to rush out and check this list off so you can feel better about your privilege—shit doesn't work like that and this isn't about _you_. Whatever actions we seek to take or not take in order to act in allyship, the most helpful guiding question will always be: How does this serve, or not serve, those _most_ oppressed? In the words of Dr. Dori Tunstall, we can ask how our actions or inactions might "assist the most vulnerable in their ability to cope with the conditions that are causing their vulnerability" and, I would add, dismantle the systems creating that vulnerability altogether.[3] In addition, so many folx acting in allyship do so as a result of the work of those most marginalized. And we deserve credit! As Pro-Intersectional Feminism (@iwritefeminism) suggests, "Ask yourself—who taught me this? What have I done for them in return? Am I giving them credit for their labor? To whom do I owe my growth?"[4] Those most oppressed do not owe you thanks for acting in allyship (it's just the right thing to do), but we deserve gratitude for showing you the way. For teaching you, holding space for you, and leading the charge toward our collective liberation. Gratitude means crediting our words and work, remunerating us, and otherwise supporting us physically, mentally, emotionally, and energetically. We don't need you to be a voice for the voiceless, because nobody is without a (metaphorical) voice. We just need you to pass the damn mic.

PERFORMATIVE ACTIVISM

It is important to not only get clear on what acting in allyship is but also what it isn't. Allyship doesn't mean hitting up a protest and posting it all over social media to ensure everyone knows you were there. Nor does it mean wielding your greater economic power (which you likely have as a result of white supremacy) to try to absolve your role as oppressor or rectify harms you've caused. Performative activism or allyship, also known as slacktivism, is a well-intended social justice gesture with no real teeth or substance. It is more about signaling your "goodness" than it is supporting the oppressed. And this shit is flagrant. The rise and increasing power of social media has allowed for more messages and discourse to spread to a wider audience, a great thing for oppressed voices; but when it comes to activism, it has created a community of individuals who fall under the false impression that clicking a "like" button, posting a black square, or otherwise partaking in outward activities for the sake of ensuring everyone all over the internet is aware of how liberal/great/non-oppressive you are makes you an activist. It doesn't. Not even fucking close. Performative allyship is not only offensive, it's dangerous. Take, for example, the safety pin movement where white people in the United States and UK, following Trump's 2016 election and the Brexit vote, took to wearing safety pins to signify solidarity and label themselves "safe" for BI&PoC. Wearing a pin will not address your racism—you can and likely will still cause harm to the BI&PoC you seek to provide safety for. And, more important, violent white supremacist groups quickly saw this as an opportunity to prey on already vulnerable populations, donning safety pins in order to cause harm to any BI&PoC who wished to approach them.[5] If you really want to act in allyship, you need to take action. Both internally and externally. You need to try. And yes, that may mean being called out and doing better the next go-around. Allyship isn't about doing it perfectly (nothing is), it's about growing and apologizing and continuously being and doing better. In the words of my Insta-friend Florence Given, "Real change happens when we give up power, without telling anyone we did it."[6]

HOW TO ENGAGE IN TOUGH CONVOS

One of the major ways we can act in allyship is to call out those who are perpetuating white supremacy, anti-Blackness, and other forms of oppression. Especially with the family, friends, and colleagues closest to us. Below are some suggestions for doing just that.

#1—Set Boundaries

First, set tangible boundaries for yourself—emotionally, mentally, spiritually, verbally, and physically. Get clear on what your deal breakers are and let those closest to you and/or whom you most spend time with know what they are. This helps you know when you need to call yourself into action and how. For example, I have zero tolerance for racist or misogynist jokes or commentary. If they're said in my presence, I will call it out on the spot. If I have the energy and feel sufficiently safe, I'll explain why what was said or done was problematic and why I refuse to be around it. If you're white and/or hold other privileges, this is one of the eight million times per day when you get to choose if you will act in allyship or not. As a queer Black woman I am exhausted at calling out and educating on white supremacy all day every day, and there are tangible consequences for my life and livelihood when I do so. Even more so for my friends living at the intersection of additionally oppressed identities such as trans, poor, fat, immigrant, old, disabled, etc. White and otherwise privileged folx have a lot more work to do, so I really implore y'all to speak up and out, even and especially when it feels uncomfortable. All that said, also remember that you aren't an anti-oppression educator (unless, of course, you are!). Either way, you don't need to head into these situations guns blazing, ready to change the minds of every last oppressor you encounter. If that's your mission, well, you're setting yourself up for failure. Your role is to follow the queer and trans Black and Indigenous racial justice educators leading this work and to call white and other privileged folx on their shit when it arises around you and let them know why it's not okay. State your piece and know you can never convince anyone of anything but rather offer them an invitation to cause less harm.

If you set clear boundaries but Uncle Reg the Racist refuses to rectify the harm he's causing over holiday hors d'oeuvres, then make it clear that your boundaries have been crossed and that you refuse to be in that person's company for the remainder of the event. If the behavior is particularly egregious, you may need to state that one of you has gotta go. Regardless, after the fact ensure everyone who needs to know is aware of the boundaries that were crossed and that you will not be in situations with said person moving forward so long as their oppressive behavior continues, no matter who they are. Sharing a bloodline with someone does not excuse their bullshit behavior. Seem harsh? So are oppressive beliefs and perspectives that uphold a system of white supremacy murdering marginalized folx every day without repercussion. Make no mistake—shit is dire and there is no time to waste. You're either contributing to change, or you're not.

#2—Discuss Values Not Issues

If you're stuck in a disagreement with someone who is genuinely willing to learn about their oppressive ways (and worth your time, energy, and free emotional labor), it can help to approach the conversation from a values perspective rather than homing in on a specific issue. For example, I value social equality* for all, freedom, and fairness, and these values inform why I find racial justice imperative. Sometimes we have similar values as others but seek to have the needs aligned with our values met in different ways, so we're just talking past one another.

Many conservatives value justice and liberty, and though they usually apply those values to their right to bear arms and say whatever the fuck they want (major eye roll), you may be able to appeal to those values with respect to racial justice. This isn't easy, and certainly not always warranted, but if you're in the mood to really try with someone, it's worth a shot (and Goddess-speed!). Do note that sometimes, if not most times, your values simply will not align and that's a good time to call the convo quits. You can't change the minds or hearts of those who are committed to disagreeing with you or your humxnity, and that's why having clear boundaries is the most important piece.

#3—Protect Your Energy

I also suggest mindful tactics to protect your energy before engaging in dicey dialogue, if you know it's coming, such as partaking in a culturally sensitive form of meditation (as we've been doing here), breathwork, and/or visualizing yourself protected by a healing cloak of white light that serves as a buffer between you and unwanted energy. First ask yourself if you have sufficient energy for the conversation. If and when you get into it, in addition to sticking to your values and explaining problematic behavior whenever warranted, do something to release that energy as soon as possible following the discussion. Suggestions include:

> - mindfully washing your hands and forearms while envisioning the talk's and/or other person's energy being rinsed down the sink (extra helpful during global pandemics)
> - a few deep, cleansing exhales
> - making big movements with your body, such as dancing, running on the spot, or safely punching the air to help any trauma from that engagement release

My mayjah takeaway is this: if you are genuinely committed to dismantling white supremacy, then you will call folx out, even your next of kin, however and whenever necessary. This does not mean you lose your shit or cause yourself or others harm, but it does mean that staying quiet or allowing oppressive statements or behaviors to go unaddressed is a choice to prioritize your comfort and/or the comfort of oppressors.

If you're the target of oppression, suss out the sitchu and do you. Lord knows most of us do enough every other day of the year, not to mention that we are subjected to actual, tangible harm if and when we do call it like it is. But if you're feeling sufficiently safe, I encourage you to stay affirmed in who you are and what shit you will and will not allow around you. You deserve to be supported and believed. Always. Especially around those closest to you and with whom you spend the most time.

> >   < <

Get clear on your values and why they're important to you, then engage with others in a mindful manner that prioritizes your values, your well-being, and, most important, the well-being of the most marginalized. Always remember, acting in allyship is not the goal, dismantling all forms of oppression as they currently exist is. Call in support—you can't do this alone. And if your anti-racism is not about centering and supporting queer and trans Black and Indigenous women+, then it's bullshit.

You Betta Act in Allyship List

Review the lists of acts of allyship above, then engage in one to three acts of allyship to support those most oppressed, especially queer and trans Black and Indigenous women+, this week and, at a minimum, every week for the next month. No matter your class, education, ability, or the like, there are options that are accessible and actionable now. Like, this minute. Get to it! Then reflect as follows:

> What were the one to three acts of allyship I did this week, and how did they support the most oppressed?

> What did I notice about myself as I did them? Did I seek cookies or other forms of praise (either internally or externally)? Did I tell myself I was "good" or otherwise separate myself from belonging to a group of oppressors (disavowal!)?

> How did I or can I protect my energy while prioritizing the needs of the most oppressed?

> How can I ensure I continue to act in allyship? (For example, setting up recurring monthly payments, having someone hold me accountable, etc.)

FIFTEEN

Better Befriending Black Women+

> No person is your friend (or kin)
> who demands your silence,
> or denies your right to grow.
>
> **—ALICE WALKER**

Friendships are some of the most enduring and important relationships in our lives. So what are the implications for Black women+ and other WoC who befriend white women+ in a white supremacist society? Fraught AF. I've endured countless experiences of being betrayed by white women+ friends in a variety of ways. When I think back on the relationships that have hurt me most, it's not the (mostly white) men I dated. Not even close. It is a history of violence at the hands of the cis white women closest to me. There was the time my best friend told me I looked like I had been dipped in poo when I was eight. The many friends throughout high school who loved the cool factor of having a Black friend but were entirely disinterested in Black struggles. Or the "liberal feminist" who explicitly refused to hang out with me after reading one of my articles asking white women+ to address their racism. Then there's one of the most egregious offenses, when a close friend removed me as the MC of her wedding after I confronted one of her racist bridesmaids. Needless to say, I never went to that wedding, and we're no longer friends.

These are only a few examples, and they are painful to recall. I am in no way proposing to be a saint (I'm not), and I take responsibility for the ways in which I contributed to these toxic relationships (#internalizedoppression), but the white women on the other side seldom do. In the end, it was clear that the comfort and well-being of whiteness was their ultimate priority.

The community within which I was raised is a battlefield of white supremacy, and I, as the only Black person, let alone Black woman, in the mix at the time did the best I could simply to survive. Though in hindsight I understand the ways in which the white women I once called friends have been beautiful teachers in my life. Folx who have played an integral role in helping me get clear on what I will not endure and fully affirm my power—but that doesn't take away from the fact that I suffered great heartbreak. Much like many other Black women+. Here's a hard hit of realness that white folx have the privilege of ignoring: as a Black woman, the majority of the time being your friend or acquaintance means biting my tongue and hiding the truth of who I am. For your white benefit and comfort, at grave detriment to my own.

> > < <

I've broken up with nearly every best friend I've ever had. Almost all of them have been white. That certainly says something about me, and it undoubtedly says a lot about the women I was befriending. One of my closest friendships was with a white woman I met while working at a restaurant when I was nineteen; we'll call her Andy. I remember the first day Andy and I met. She was impeccably dressed, bubbly, and bright. A woman I could get down with! We became fast friends, and though we stayed in touch as I moved on to law school, our friendship solidified when we both went through big breakups with longtime partners. We lived only a few blocks apart, and I regularly went to her apartment to cook us meals to pair with her homemade kombucha, all of which culminated with watching some trashy show to keep us amused and assuage our post-breakup agony. I taught her how to cook; she introduced me to plant-based meals and got me back into yoga. I joined her family for holiday celebrations; my mother helped her cleanse her ex's presence from her apartment. We spent a Christmas at da club dancing until we were soaked in sweat. We helped each other heal. When I went on a three-month backpacking excursion the summer after I graduated from law school, she was the person I was most excited to return home to (other than moms obvi). I loved her, and I know without question that love was mutual. But in time, I understood that the ways we supported each other as our whole, full selves was not.

Many years later, Andy and I became roommates. I had been concerned about the impact it may have on our friendship. I knew Andy had qualities that rubbed me the wrong way, but I always struggled to name them. At first, it was great. Sharing space on a daily basis only served to strengthen our already formidable bond. But ten months in, everything changed.

I received the call from my mother telling me she no longer wished to live, and I was thrust into a state of action and anguish. I knew supporting my mother as she transitioned was going to take everything I had. So I called in support. I asked Andy and a few other close friends for help, and, as my therapist advised me, I was crystal clear as to the ways they could help. I asked them to show up—both in word and in action. I asked them to check in on me, to be with me as I cried, and to help me with errands. It was the biggest call for help I had ever made, especially for someone who had been caring for others her whole life. Sadly, all of those white folx I called on for support let me down. Especially Andy. When I first told her about my mother, she was entirely present. She even offered to go to the funeral home with me for my mother's cremation when the time came. She said a lot of amazing, caring, and supportive things, but when push came to shove, Andy's talk was cheap. As my mother entered hospice, and the weeks of suffering dragged on into months, Andy became increasingly scarce. She never once came to visit me or my mom in the hospice where I essentially lived for three months. She rarely called or otherwise checked in. And then one day, as I sat alone crying next to my dying mother's bedside, on the same day my beloved godfather passed away, shit all came to a head. I was scrolling on Instagram after having made a post honoring my departed godfather's life and legacy, when I saw that Andy was out of town. She was hosting a healing retreat for other (mostly white) women. I recalled her briefly telling me about it a month or so prior but when you're busy tending to your dying mother you need some support remembering what day it is let alone someone else's schedule. Andy leaving without notice felt like a slap in the face. Not long before her unexpected departure I had called to let her know that my mom had finally been granted proper pain support from the hospice, and we expected she would die within the week. Andy never mentioned that she was leaving town.

Four days later my mother was dead. After staying vigil with my mother's body and preparing her corpse for cremation, I sat and waited for the funeral home to collect her body. I started to make calls. And though I was hurt and angered by Andy's actions, I was also in desperate need of my best friend. I phoned her up at four a.m., an ungodly hour, but your mom only dies once. I hoped she would have kept her phone on awaiting this very moment. She knew the end was near. She knew I was more or less alone. When I got Andy's voice mail I knew that was it. My mom had just died, my favorite person and closest family. And my best friend was nowhere to be found. When Andy finally reached out, she left a message that felt altogether laissez-faire. Like my mother leaving this world wasn't earth-shattering in every way.

The loss of my best friend on top of losing my mother was more than I could take. Then one week later, when I bared my soul to a grief group, the counselor asked me if I was surprised by Andy's actions. If her lack of support at a time I needed her most was misaligned with how she had otherwise shown up in our friendship. And that's when I realized that Andy hadn't been a very supportive friend at all. Not in the ways that mattered. This isn't to say she didn't show me love in many ways, because she absolutely did—through hugs and talks and notes and gifts (cuz, #whitewealth)—but it is to say that when I needed her the most she had a history of leaning away. I recalled all the times she bailed on me last minute. And the ways she would ghost me once a man entered her life. I recounted the ways she talked down to me and made fun of my most sensitive imperfections, both in private and in public. But mostly I remembered the ways in which she would gaslight me when I asked for more care, leaving me feeling needy, troubled, and rejected. What made these actions all the more painful was that Andy is praised in her predominantly white spiritual community for being a champion for women's healing. Just not her (Black) best friend's. Because of her power and privilege as an ambassador for one of the most problematic yoga companies on the planet, I was afraid to say anything about my pain. I knew I would face more gaslighting, as many in my midst wouldn't believe that the person they hailed as their yoga guru could be so violent. Especially since people rarely care about the harm inflicted on Black women+.

I avoided Andy as much as I could, and she didn't make much effort to reach out. Many months after my mom died, I eventually let Andy know how I felt, and though she apologized, once again her actions weren't aligned with her words. I focused on healing my heart from the great grief caused by the loss of my mom, and eventually Andy and I lost touch.

Years later I ran into Andy's mom and learned that her dad had nearly died a few months prior. I texted Andy to send my condolences. Though we hadn't spoken in years, I know better than most how harrowing it is to witness a parent in pain. We wound up meeting for coffee, and Andy shared that she had gone MIA because she was afraid of my pain. Of witnessing the person she had always known to be so strong fall apart. And because I am so strong, she didn't think I needed her. Of all the things she had done and said, this sentiment hurt the most. It was heart-wrenching to know firsthand that the friend you loved most in the world was unable to show up for you when you were most in need, the way you had repeatedly shown up for her, because she couldn't withstand your pain and felt you were "strong enough" to endure it without her (even when you had expressly said otherwise). It was also racist. Black women+ are constantly viewed as strong, independent, capable, and tenacious, and therefore, we're entirely deprived of care. By family, friends, and partners alike. This notion that I, and all Black women+ like me, can and should carry the brunt of life's load on our own is steeped in white supremacy; and as we've already discussed, the emotional, mental, spiritual, and physical strife it creates is very literally killing us. And white women+, especially cis women, are more than comfortable letting us die.

Andy and I never rekindled our friendship. She took me for coffees here and there and hired me for some legal support. She still can't seem to grasp how to fix her fuckup because, like so many white women+ in this world, she's making the situation about *her*. My Black anger, presumed vicious by whiteness, is used as a justifiable excuse not to try. If I had a penny for every white friend who proclaimed, "I don't know what else I can do," when they haven't actually done a damn thing. I'd be rich. In dollars. Still under-resourced in community.

I believe Andy still loves me, and though I am angered and saddened by her actions, in many ways I still love her. When the COVID-19 pandemic erupted in New York City, I again reached out to check in on her, as she's immunocompromised, and, friends or not, I wanted to make sure she was okay (she was, because her privilege allowed her to stay in Canada during the worst of it). Unsurprisingly, when the global health crisis evolved into state-led Black genocide, Andy was silent as a stone.

I still want what's best for her, but I am prioritizing care for myself. Because the only true apology is changed behavior. To not only admit the specific ways she caused harm but to do the inner work to address her white supremacy, where she went wrong, then actively show up and remedy her mistakes. My door remains open to those who put in the work to do better, but I ain't holding my breath.

> > < <

We don't talk about friend breakups or the considerable hurt they cause, especially as women and femmes, and all the more so as BI&WoC. I've never much felt like I fit in anywhere and have spent a lifetime cycling through friends searching for belonging from other women+.

Though I've had many white friends express the extreme

closeness they felt we had, it often left me perplexed. I rarely felt the same, because they didn't really know or care to know me. Doing so would require them to own up to their privilege, unpack their racism and the harm they'd caused me and other Black and Indigenous women+, and these women were not about to do that. If you haven't talked about racism with your BI&PoC friends, decolonization with your Indigenous friends, or anti-Blackness with your Black friends, y'all just ain't that close. Periodt.

I used to internalize my stream of failed friendships and attack myself for them. My first suicidal ideation, at thirteen, arose after being ostracized by two white girlfriends. Then I realized the common theme: almost everyone in question was a wealthy white person who refused to acknowledge or affirm me as a Black woman—meaning they failed to accept ME. I still frequently feel as though I wasn't meant to have good friends. Being a racial justice activist makes meeting new friends all the harder. And the pervasive gaslighting I've endured from white women+ makes it hard to trust myself or others. Sadly, my experiences are not rare. I have heard countless stories from Black women+ about the toxic friendships they experience with white women+, the depression it causes, and how they choose to isolate themselves as a means to prevent further harm. Almost all of which occurs to the willful ignorance of the white women+ in question. This shit has got. To. Stop. Let's explore some other common harms white women+ inflict on Black women+ and other WoC so we can help kick this crap to the curb.

OTHER FRIENDSHIP FAILS

As with any intimate relationship, harm occurs in all close friendships between folx of all races and identities. The potency of the harm that occurs between women or femmes is of particular note, given its insidious nature. We may not punch each other in the face, but we sure as hell know how to take one another out at the knees. Through passive-aggressive remarks, silence, ganging up, criticism, and the like, women and femmes are no strangers to inflicting violence on those closest to us. Naturally, this is magnified in friendships between white women/femmes and Black women/femmes because racial power dynamics create inherently uneven relationships and aggravated forms of assault. For example, when a Black woman and her white friend get into a disagreement, the Black woman knows she will be perceived as "angry" for merely expressing herself. Our white women and femme friends, as a result of their anti-Blackness, are prone to misconstrue our emotional expression, *any* emotional expression, as anger. And when white women and femmes face anger, especially from Black women and femmes, it's considered abuse. Any meaningful dialogue between friends ends, the voices of Black women and femmes silenced and our behaviors policed. Moreover, when cis white women cry, the whole damn world stops. Everyone caters to their tears, and they expect it to be so. Emmett Till, an innocent Black child, was even murdered because of one white woman's tears!

Growing up in an incredibly white space, I accrued a bunch of white women who became my friends on the condition that I didn't challenge them or the system of racist oppression they both perpetuated and benefited from. And for a long time, I didn't—constantly, though unconsciously, ensuring that the white folx surrounding me weren't made to acknowledge racism in any way, because it would almost surely result in violence. White wildness, H.A.R.M., white entitlement, gaslighting, spiritual bypassing, white exceptionalism—you name it, I've endured it a million times over. Black women and femmes rarely trust white women and femmes because of all the violence we've encountered from them. Many of us explicitly refuse to befriend white women or femmes as a result. As Brittney Cooper writes in her book *Eloquent Rage*, "I have always known of white women's great capacity to be treacherous."[1] Below are some additional examples of ways white women and femmes cause their Black women and femme friends harm:

#1—Insensitivity & Selfishness

I once went to visit friends at their apartment, and when I got there, they were both nearly in tears because they were "broke." One of the women exclaimed, "We're living below the poverty line!" and I almost lost my whole shit. I should have. They lived in a two-bedroom apartment on the thirty-second floor of a brand-new development in the heart of one of the most gentrified neighborhoods in North America. One friend drove her dad's BMW, the other a MINI Cooper her parents bought her at sixteen. Meanwhile, my mother was disabled, on welfare, and pleading with the government to give her enough funding to pay for adequate care, and I was busting my ass to pay off student loans and support us both—which my friends were well aware of. Lacking the wherewithal to check your privilege, especially in front of your Black friend, and particularly doing so from your ivory tower surrounded by displaced and disenfranchised Indigenous folx, is all kinds of NO. We're also seeing this collectively with multiple accounts of white women losing their shit when asked to wear a mask to prevent others (mostly Black and Indigenous folx) from contracting COVID-19. Selfish (and violent) as fuck.

#2—Bullying, Solidarity & Silence

It took me thirty-three years to properly understand what bullying from a woman feels like. And when I finally did, I realized I'd been subject to it at the hands of white women+ my whole life. One of the worst instances was at that bachelorette party for a close friend. When I called out a woman for her racist remark, four other women jumped in to "defend" her by outright attacking me in white solidarity. "That's not what she said!" "She didn't mean it that way." "We're just trying to have a good time." As I sat in the center of an almost entirely white circle, I was made out to be the villain. Not one mention was made about the harmful statement the white woman had made. And what was worse than the wealthy, white, and wretched cis women yelling at me was the silence of the other white women present. Those I called friends who knew I was being treated unjustly and did absolutely nothing to stop it. When we returned home from the trip, I spent the next week helping the white bride-to-be navigate *her* feelings about the harm *I* endured at her behest. In a breathtaking act of white solidarity, she then removed me as the MC of her wedding "because of who would be in attendance," though I was still allowed to be a bridesmaid—thanks *so* much! She couldn't even tell me herself—I was informed in an email sent by her fucking fiancé! No words.

Bullying can be big and egregious like the foregoing, but it can also be slight and sneaky, like an ultra passive-aggressive friend who constantly called me and my actions "silly." No matter its form, bullying is brutal. And bullying Black women+, who already endure oppression at every turn, even more so.

#3—Subjugating

Sometimes when I think back on the harms I've experienced in my friendships with white women, it's less the big behaviors and words that hurt my heart and more the daily forms of dismissal. I can still hear the way my high-school bestie would scoff at me and my suggestions. I can picture the eye rolls and looks of disapproval. I am amazed at the ways I was made to constantly cater to, comfort, and center her and her well-being, be it always eating when and where *she* wanted or simply doing what worked best for her. The ways I was made to feel uppity and chronically told to "chill." Forgiving myself for allowing these harms is an ongoing process. Some of the worst violence comes from actions so tenuous they could almost go unnoticed. Almost. It's an often unintentional but entirely ingrained way of subjugating Black women+. As a queer Black woman, my colonial role is to avoid naming or rocking my white friend's boat in any way, or suffer immense emotional, spiritual, mental, and/or physical harm by their hand dare I act out of line.

Another major way I have been subjugated by white women, especially cis white women, is through the use of money. Almost every close white friend I've ever had has used money in an attempt to repair harm, address their guilt, or otherwise make up for their inability to emotionally support me. Whether they knew it—and many of them didn't—their buying me shit or whisking me off to their million-dollar "cabins" created a deeper division within our already off-kilter power dynamic. It made them feel like good friends for doing the bare minimum and left me feeling less able to call them on their bad behavior because "generous" friends must be good friends. Right? Wrong.

#4—White Feminism

Ah, white feminism and all its fuckery. I had a longtime friend who had taken my workshops and one evening, after many a beverage, wanted to talk to me about my racial justice "journey." She shared a desire to support me and my work but was concerned as to her role in it as my white friend. On the surface, and at the time, this seemed like a compassionate sentiment. But what I came to realize is that her concern was actually about her comfort. She was uneasy about what our friendship meant when I would no longer be prioritizing her comfort within it. Just a few weeks later we were out for dinner, and I vulnerably shared the way I am frequently called intimidating because of my Blackness. She immediately belittled me for the mere thought, stating, "That's not because of your race, silly, I get called that all the time. It's because we're loud women!" Ohhhh, is *that* it? Thank you so much for educating me on my own experience. This tendency to center whiteness and dismiss the experiences of Black women+ is classic white feminist bullshit, and I have *no* time for it.

> >   < <

What's most telling is that my relationships with Black women+ are different. They're deeper. And void of the same kinds of violence. The level of intimacy and understanding that comes from navigating the same systems of race- and gender identity–based oppression, and the toll that takes, is immeasurable. Don't get it twisted, all skinfolk ain't kinfolk, but in my experience we usually understand and support one another better.

White and non-Black PoC women and femmes, whether you're friends with Black women+ or otherwise, you gotta do better. Like, *way* better. I've said it many times before and I'll say it again: y'all are causing Black women+, myself included, mad harm. For those thinking, *Not me*—yes, absolutely you. Overtly or otherwise and in many ways unbeknownst to you. I know a lot of it feels unintentional and I know it's 2021—not knowing about racial harm *is* intentional. And entirely unacceptable. Your ignorance is violent. So, what the fuck to do?

HOW TO BETTER SUPPORT BLACK WOMEN+

When it comes to better supporting Black women+ in friendships (and beyond), there's no one size fits all. We have various life experiences, privileges, worldviews, triggers, etc. and our needs and wants for friendship will differ. What I *can* share are five suggestions for how white and other non-Black folx wishing to be *my* friend can begin to authentically engage with and support me personally. I believe many other Black women+ will benefit from the same.

These actions aren't a surefire way to friendship, because nothing is. But given the grave amount of harm I and so many Black women+ have and continue to endure at the hands of non-Black women+, and cis white women in particular, these are my current precursors to rules of engagement with any non-Black woman+ seeking friendship moving forward. I encourage you to check in with the Black women+ in your life to understand if and how this will be of benefit to them, and take similar action to address your relationships with other BI&WoC.

#1—Admit You're Racist and/or Anti-Black

Whether you intend it or not, racism is the status quo of whiteness, and anti-Blackness is inherent in all races. If you are committed to minimizing harm to myself and other Black women+, then you will acknowledge and address your learned white supremacy and its consequences. If you can't recognize that you belong to a race that as a whole has oppressed Black people to build and maintain your privilege and understand the power dynamics at play in our relationship as a result, you're not someone I can feel safe with or trust. This means educating yourself. Reading books is great (thanks for your support!), but passive education is insufficient, especially in the absence of critical analysis from Black and Indigenous women+. I suggest the best way to begin is ongoing active education led by Black and Indigenous racial justice educators. This also means engaging in conversations about racism, white privilege, and anti-Blackness (and not in a manner that requires the unpaid time, energy, and emotional labor of Black women+), learning and using proper terminology, committing to doing better, owning and apologizing when you fuck up and cause harm—because you still will—and continuing to dismantle your white supremacy and/or non-Black privilege for the rest of your days. It is also imperative you own your other privileges, be it from class, gender identity, sexual orientation, ability, age, religion, or otherwise, especially in friendships with Black women+ living at additional intersections of oppression. There's no silver bullet and your work will never be finished, but it's on you to do it every single day for the rest of your life. Or not, but that means you and I can't be homies #sorrynotsorry.

#2—Do Your Inner Work

I can't say it enough times and there aren't enough ways to say it. In addition to admitting your participation in anti-Black systems and all the ways it (and you) have caused Black women+ harm, there's the deep inner work of actively addressing that racism and/

or anti-Blackness and doing your own healing work to address your grief and trauma in order to show up and take action in support of Black liberation. If you haven't addressed your ancestral legacy, inherited trauma, and the areas keeping you stuck, you can't engage in racial justice in a meaningful and sustainable way.

#3—Acknowledge Me

This sounds incredibly simple, doesn't it? Yet I've found it unbelievably challenging for non-Black women and femmes to do. If you want to authentically engage with me, then you need to fully acknowledge me, as in *all* parts of me. Not just the parts you like or want to co-opt. Not just the bits that you understand. Certainly not just the parts that make you comfortable. *ALL* of me. Including my Blackness. I am humxn, just like you. Shit ain't hard (especially if you're addressing your own anti-Blackness). Accept me. Acknowledge me and my experiences. Support me in my anger and do your best to appreciate how and why centuries of misogynoir would leave me so damn pissed off. Believe me. Even and especially when my experiences make you uncomfortable. In the words of Audre Lorde, "The history of white women who are unable to hear Black women's words, or to maintain dialogue with us, is long and discouraging."[2] Same holds true for many other non-Black women+. Acknowledge. Us.

#4—Stop Centering Yourself

Not everything is about *you*. This may come across as facetious, but it's a simple truth pill many white and non-Black women+ have a tough time swallowing. If you expect me to educate you on race (unpaid and outside of my role as an educator), comfort you as you process your anti-Blackness, send you love and light after you've caused me harm, or engage in discussions about *your* hurt feelings re: anti-Blackness (or my resulting boundaries), you're making this entire thing about you. It's not. Countering your misogynoir with the discrimination you face as a woman+ and/or non-Black humxn does nothing but silence Black women+ and perpetuate more oppression. Conduct an honest review of our friendship, of race-based harms you've caused myself and other Black women+, and figure out if you can honestly and earnestly attempt to fix that harm—for *our* benefit. Not just yours. I'm tired and I don't owe whiteness a dang thing, including an explanation.

Ceasing to center yourself also means you understand that you cannot and will never understand my experiences as a Black woman because you have never endured anti-Blackness. White women+ have never endured white supremacy (and if you disagree, then we can call this whole "let's try to be friends" thing quits right now). If there are things I've shared or tried to explain, or behaviors I've exhibited, that you simply don't understand—have some fucking compassion. I am enduring a daily onslaught of hate and discrimination that you could not begin to fathom. If I say it's about anti-Blackness—it almost certainly is. Your attempts to tell me otherwise are usually violent and about your need for comfort over mine. Stop it. Lastly, prioritize and fight for the needs, wants, and comfort of myself and other Black women+, even and especially when you don't feel you directly benefit—not just in the wake of Black death or other times you seek to "feel better."

#5—Support Me

Support means nurturing and uplifting myself and other Black women+ emotionally, mentally, spiritually, and physically. That means checking in on me regularly. Ya know, like a friend. Having to constantly navigate global anti-Blackness is painful and exhausting on a good day, not to mention in the wake of, say, Breonna Taylor's murder or a global pandemic disproportionately claiming Black lives due to four hundred years of anti-Blackness. Support the work to dismantle anti-Blackness and white supremacy by partaking in it yourself and helping spread the word to other white and non-Black folx. Support my humxnity by, as a start, calling out other non-Black folx who partake in anti-Black acts toward myself or others, paying Black women+, using your privilege to address racial justice and anti-Blackness, and ceasing to associate with folx who refuse to do the work. If you believe you're "doing the work" but your BFFs, hubby, clients, and closest circle aren't—you're lying to yourself.

Still with me? Good! I just spilled some mayjah tea, but these are some hard but incredibly important truths you needed to receive. I'm not asking you to become an activist (and when it comes to racial justice I don't believe white people are worthy of the term), but you *do* need a willingness and capacity to face your discomfort and unpack your privilege.

Unplug from the matrix of white supremacy and help us *all*, yourself included, get free.

WHEN WHITE WOMEN+ WAKE UP

Let me change gears for a moment and share some insight as to the wonderful relationships I have with white women+ doing their work. I don't want to leave anyone with the impression that white women+ and BI&WoC (or non-Black WoC and Black women+) cannot be friends. We can. We are. And if we are ever to have a fighting chance at ending oppression, our friendships must continue. Though my relationships with white women+ have caused me a lifetime of serious suffering, those I've been able to forge with white women+ committed to racial justice have been invigorating and inspiring. When white women+ start doing their work, they realize that being a part of the system of white supremacy hasn't just been about causing harm to others—though it has, and they need to reconcile that—but they also learn the ways in which they've caused harm to themselves and had to disconnect from their own heart space in order to buy into this system of dominance. It's similar to how men+ can understand that heteropatriarchy is a system of toxic masculinity that actually also causes them harm—to a lesser degree than women+, of course. These women+ have been cracked open and are now able to cultivate truly integral and intimate relationships, not only with me but with themselves and so many others. They are doing the work of facing their shadow and tolerating their discomfort. And as a result, they are empowered to support themselves and, most important, Black women+, better. For example, one such friend joined me on a retreat I spoke at in Peru that was entirely Black aside from her and an East Asian woman. I invited her myself, an invitation I was happy to extend only because I know her to be doing her racial justice work in authentic and active ways. At the retreat, she led a room otherwise entirely full of Black women+ through a deeply impactful session where she explicitly addressed her privilege and created a space where we could all feel supported and sufficiently safe. I don't think many, if any, of the Black women+ in that room had felt that kind of support from a white woman before—and they all deserve to.

Some of my closest and longest friendships are still with white women+. They understand their role as oppressed oppressors. They are unpacking their need to be good and right, to people please, and to avoid conflict. They work toward causing less harm and dismantling white supremacy every damn day. These women are the exception, but that does not make them exceptional. They are white women+ doing their work, just as all white women+ ought to be. Until we dismantle white supremacy, white women+ will cause Black women+ and all WoC harm any time they engage in any kind of relationship with us. And anti-Blackness from all BI&PoC will also continue to cause Black women+ harm. You must understand that the most unprotected person in this *world* is a Black woman+, and to authentically engage with us means you must acknowledge the harms inflicted by white supremacy, including the personal harms inflicted by *you*. In the words of healer Destiny Turner-Vanlear, "I don't expect anyone to come into my life fully whole and healed because I know I'm still walking the path to remembering myself . . . I just expect you to be eager to heal, and to be willing to do the necessary work."[3] So do more. Do better. And do it now. You're already centuries behind.

Spiritual Soulcare Offering/Call to Action

Below is an opportunity to explore the racial and other power dynamics within your friendships, how and when (not if) race plays a role, and the harms you've caused and/or been subjected to within them.

Friendspection Exercise

REFLECT ON THE FOLLOWING:

> Which friend do you feel most safe with (if anyone)? Why? Are they the same race as you? Why do you think that is?

> Is race acknowledged in any of your friendships, especially with friends of a different race? If so, how? If not, why?

> How many friends from different races do you have? Why or why not? Who holds more privilege in your friendship(s)? Do you acknowledge and address the way differing power and privileges is likely causing harm? If not, why? If so, how?

> Have you ever been oppressive toward or oppressed by a friend because of race? If so, how? Have you ever been oppressive toward or oppressed by a friend based on other identities (ethnicity, shade, sexual orientation, gender identity, class, age, body size, etc.)? If so, how?

> How does white supremacy impact your friendships and the power relations inherent within them?

> For Black women+: Do your friendships with white women+ and non-Black WoC nurture, uplift, affirm, and support you as your whole Black self? Are these friends actively addressing their anti-Blackness? Whose comfort most gets prioritized, and why?

When you finish, examine the why and why nots of your answers and marinate on the implications they have for you, your friendships, and, most important, your most oppressed friends. Journal if you need. After you've taken at least a few days to digest, if you feel you have sufficient tools to do so, ask any friends who may be impacted by your answers if they are able, open, and willing to discuss or review this exercise with you. Ensure any request is first and foremost about the friend with the least power and privilege (whether that's you or them) and that person's well-being. Respect your friend's right to decline, as well as your right to amend (or end) your friendship as and how needed.

> > > > > >

SIXTEEN

What's Love Got to Do with It?

The moment we choose to love
we begin to move against domination,
against oppression. The moment we
choose to love we begin to move towards
freedom, to act in ways that liberate
ourselves and others.

—BELL HOOKS,

"LOVE AS THE PRACTICE OF FREEDOM"

White supremacy not only invades our friendships, it harms all of our loving relationships, especially our most intimate ones. It robs us of vulnerable connections, subjugates the well-being of women+ and demands our unacknowledged emotional labor. This oppressive dynamic has specific consequences for Black women, who, as online user data has proven, are consistently deemed the least romantically desirable (alongside Asian men).[1] It is no surprise that as a Black woman I always felt it was my job to work for love. To prove that I was lovable or risk love evading me altogether. The oppressive harms that played out in my intimate relationships started from a young age. I had no role models of healthy or lasting love to draw upon—both my paternal and maternal ancestry are rife with physical and sexual abuse, infidelity, and other relational traumas. An experience that is rooted in systemic racism and anti-Blackness. My father, born and raised in colonial-ruled Jamaica, was emotionally unavailable on a good day, physically, verbally, and emotionally abusive on a bad one. Having suffered grave violence and trauma himself, violence and trauma his parents had handed down as learned from enslavers and colonial rulers, he continued the cycle of abuse and oppression. When I was just two years old, my mother witnessed my dad strike me across the face and left the next day. Their divorce soon followed. The interactions I had with my dad growing up always left me longing for more—more love, more support, more protection. But he has neither the tools nor willingness to show up for himself, let alone his (many) children.

If there was anything my father failed at more than birth control, it was containing his deep-seated ancestral rage. My earliest childhood memory is of my father trying to attack my cowering mother with a knife while I stood in the middle, wearing nothing but diapers, refusing to let him touch her. My mother, a victim of sexual abuse and a descendant of a slave and her enslaver, could barely defend herself, let alone her baby. I was left with a deep knowing that there was no one who was going to protect *me*. In my two-year-old mind, I internalized this violence, assuming it must be because I wasn't worthy of their care. And if I wasn't worthy of care from my own parents, was I worthy at all? I didn't really think so, and neither did the society surrounding me.

As I grew up, my inner unworthiness increased, as I was inundated with reminders that I wasn't white, thin, blond, blue-eyed, or any of the things deemed desirable by Eurocentric standards. This was made all the harder because most of my Barbie-looking friends were. I was constantly ignored and felt a consistent sense of isolation even in rooms full of others. On the whole, I felt unwelcome, unwanted, and uncared for. This is a common experience for Black women+ whose sense of unworthiness in our intimate relationships are a reflection of the lack of care we are shown in and from the world, especially behind closed doors. Black American women are nearly three times more likely to die as a result of domestic or intimate partner violence than white women+, making domestic and intimate partner violence one of the leading causes of death for Black women between fifteen and thirty-five. We endure intimate partner violence at a rate twenty-two times that of non-Black WoC, and our rates of incest, nonfamilial sexual assault, and domestic violence are also disproportionately high compared with other women.[2] Black men, historically robbed of power by white men, feel compelled to prove their masculinity through control, usually exhibited as violence toward Black women+ and LGBTTQIA+ folx.

Black women+ are uncared for by everyone and become the world's wastebasket for the collective's familial and societal disdain. We are oppressed (and murdered) by men at the hands of heteropatriarchy and discriminated by other women+ because of racism and anti-Blackness. Just ask Megan Thee Stallion! When people take to the streets to fight for Black Lives Matter, it is rarely as a result of a Black woman+'s murder, nor do our murders go avenged. Breonna Taylor was murdered in her own home, in her own bed, and *still* the three white cops who killed her weren't charged. Black women+ continue to die in childbirth at epidemic rates without anyone held to account. Still, Black women+ are expected to, and often do, serve as champions for our Black communities, men+ included, and help educate and lead the way for *all* women+. Like Oluwatoyin Salau, a nineteen-year-old Black Lives Matter activist who was kidnapped, raped, and murdered by a Black man. As Brittney Cooper shares, "This cultural and intimate hatred of Black women is a feminist issue."[3] On the whole, Black women+ are all very much left in a violent epicenter just as I was as a toddler—with men+ on one side and all non-Black women+ on the other—wondering who the fuck is going to care for *us*. The answer we continuously return to is: ourselves.

The world does not love Black women+, but that does not stop us from seeking affection. My wanting to be validated as my whole Black self has played out in all of my relationships, including, and especially, romantic ones. I went into relationships seeking to heal my wounds of rejection and took on the role of serving others because it was the only way I knew to find intimacy. Love was not something I had the privilege of falling into, it was something I had to go out and earn. I searched for worth, validation, and completion in men+, usually white ones, which put me in some seriously scary situations.

LOVE ON THE ROCKS

The first time I met him he asked me what "my mix" was. He was one of those white guys who felt he had a claim on Blackness. Huge. Red. Flag. But I got drunk at da club, as one is prime to do at twenty years old, and awoke one morning to find the man I now call "The Ex" in my bed. Awake. Staring at me. He wanted to know my life story, and I wanted to know how quickly I could get him to leave. I ran into my roomie's room begging to borrow her car and came back jovially to declare I could now drop him off. I wanted nothing to do with this dude, but after weeks of wearing me down to go on a date, I finally relented. I was no match for his charm, and we were inseparable from that day onward. The Ex turned out to be a cocaine and sex addict and the lead character in my most tumultuous relationship to date, and there have been a few! I ignored many warning signs, especially those from my intuition, and what started as a passionate love affair quickly spiraled into dysfunction and despair. There was the time he grabbed my hand and made me repeatedly punch his face, then threw all my luggage down the stairs of his six-story walk-up. Or when he screamed over me with his six-foot stature as I sank to the shower floor sobbing. And then there was the lying and the cheating (to the tune of posting online multiple times a day seeking Black women to fuck). And though I knew in my heart there was something off about a white guy who "only dates Black women," I didn't understand the sexual racism at play. That the hypersexualized stereotypes of Black folx leads non-Blacks to derive my appeal entirely from my race.[4]

All of it was violent and I was always to blame, often internalizing the problems as my own doing before he named me the culprit. None of his actions were cause enough to leave because they only affirmed what I'd always felt: I didn't deserve any better. I was just another Black woman he would use and abuse. Since my role as a Black woman is to help everyone before myself, I figured all of this was fixable. That The Ex just needed me to love him the right way and then, voilà, he would be okay. For a while, I think he believed it too. One of the many ways the "strong Black woman" trope kicks Black women and femmes in the ass is the belief that we can handle anything, and thus ought to. We also internalize the societal notion that we are not in need of care, but of course, we are.

Four years after I first met The Ex, I sat with a drug and

alcohol specialist during his pre-intervention. The specialist told me he had very little chance of getting better given his family dynamic (they never proceeded with said intervention). She told me I needed to stop finding broken men to fix. To leave The Ex alone. That I couldn't help him, nor was it my job to. That I should focus on myself. It was the first time I had ever considered such a thing. Not my job to fix others? Focus on . . . myself? This was a radical request for a girl who had worked so hard for love and acceptance, with little luck, her whole life. The epiphany rocked me to my core, and I spent the next five years single so I could focus on healing my heart and remedying the beliefs and trauma that led me to not only enter but remain in such a rocky and riotous relationship. None of this was to release The Ex from his wrongs, but rather to support me in finding my light.

Despite the "I'm all that" act I'd been putting on for ages, I had to come to terms with the fact that I didn't like myself very much. And that I often picked men who I knew, at least on some level, were no good for me—evidence of my unconscious belief that I wasn't worth a damn. A belief that was instilled and affirmed by white supremacy. When you don't feel like you're worth much, you don't act like you're worth much, so I also had to be with the ways in which my insecurities had caused my romantic partners harm. I had cheated on every partner I had ever had, emotionally if not physically. I didn't believe I was lovable, so I did what I could to soften the inevitable blow. Not an excuse, because there isn't one, just #facts. Despite being an overtly open person, I learned that my openness was not the same as vulnerability. In a world made to stamp Black women+ out, being vulnerable not only felt like death, it could very well lead to it. My love was also replete with rage, fueled by a lifetime of racism, misogynoir, and feeling less than. Though my rage was, and is, justified, the emotional and mental violence I inflicted on lovers was not. I had to get real honest with the ways I'd caused myself and others harm and apologize to those I had hurt. I began to understand it was impossible to truly love others if I didn't love myself. So I began to right my wrongs and rewrite the oppressive scripts that had been stuffed down my throat. I decided on a new destiny. One where Black women+ win, both in life and in love. But shit ain't easy.

IN THE BEDROOM & BEYOND

The impacts of race, as with all of our identities, infiltrate our hearts as well as our homes. Irrespective of who we are or whom we love, white supremacist heteropatriarchy plays a role. A white, cis, heterosexual couple will find themselves mired in heteropatriarchy—showing up, at a minimum, as binary and misogynist gender roles, identities, and expressions—but they are not forced to navigate the additional harms caused by racism, homophobia, and transphobia as queer and trans Black and Indigenous folx do. This freedom from further oppression both within and outside the relationship is an often unnoticed privilege held by white, cis, and heterosexual folx. Greater access to wealth, employment, health care, and other resources are privileges not only for individuals but for families and partnerships. BI&PoC, and particularly queer and trans Black and Indigenous women+, must endure an onslaught of extra stress caused by white supremacy in addition to the standard trials and tribulations inherent in dating and sustaining romantic relationships. This has shown up for me in many ways, including:

> being fetishized and assumed to be promiscuous or
>   sexually deviant because of misogynoir, like when my

sixteen-year-old white boyfriend's friends asked him how kinky I was in bed
> only dating cis white men for most of my life because my internalized oppression led me to believe whiteness and cis men were most desirable
> my Blackness being viewed by all men+ and women+ (including other Black folx) as aggressive, intimidating, and "masculine" and therefore not feminine enough—an experience often aggravated for Black trans women
> the conversations my white and Filipinx* husband and I are forced to have regarding raising multiracial Black kids and the oppression we know they will face from all races as a result

The extra harms BI&PoC must navigate when it comes to intimate relationships come in all shapes and sizes, including the mental, physical, spiritual, and emotional toll of enduring oppression every day; the impact of ancestral trauma from enslavement, colonization, genocide, and other violent forms of oppression; and the financial pressures caused by earning less income than our white counterparts while often being forced to provide for other family members. For Black communities, the criminalization of our men, particularly as created through the prison-industrial complex and school-to-prison pipeline, has had a distinctly deleterious impact on our intimate relationships.[5]

For queer and trans Black and Indigenous women+, these additional stressors are all the more aggravated. Black trans women have to navigate dating more cautiously, knowing that they constitute three out of every five LGBTTQIA+ homicide victims. Similarly, queer BI&PoC experience some of the highest rates of rape, physical violence, and stalking by intimate partners.[6] A consequence of the intersecting oppression caused by white supremacist cisheteropatriarchy.

In interracial partnerships, the impact of white supremacy is rarely addressed but always present. For example, less than 46 percent of white Americans will date outside their race,[7] but there are tons of white women who love sucking Black dick without any interest in Black liberation.[8] Who have magical thinking about being "non-racist" because they're fucking Blackness, while refusing to acknowledge the ways their white privilege causes their partner (and all BI&PoC) harm on the daily. In my own partnership, anti-Blackness has shown up when it was assumed I needed less care or support in hard situations because "I can handle it." It has also shown up in terms of succumbing to traditional gender identity roles, especially around the home, despite mutually strong intentions otherwise.

White supremacy is present in all of our love lives whether we are aware of it or not. But a lack of awareness causes even greater damage.

MY INNER QUEER-Y

From as far back as I can recall, I held a fear of being queer. When I was seven, I used to dance around my room naked, and when I saw the dark, muscular, "masculine" body in my mirror's reflection, I got shook. I was also totally terrified of being a lesbian. Stereotypes of the status quo were lodged deep within my young, impressionable mind. I even thought my mother, who never expressed any interest in men after leaving my father and always rocked a cropped coif, must be gay herself. Homophobia and transphobia were certainly part of the social fabric in the early '90s, and all the more in Jamaica where my mother was born and raised. By eight years old I was praying to the heavens that I wasn't gay. In part because I sensed that it wouldn't be acceptable to my family, and in part because I knew how much harder my life would become. Being a Black woman in a mostly white world was challenging enough—I didn't need to add queer to the mix.

I can't tell you exactly when these fears started, but I suspect they came shortly after my mother walked in on me and my female BFF in the midst of our seven-year-old playtime glory, which at that moment included orally pleasuring each other. I can't remember the specifics, but I know we were seriously scolded. It was impressed upon me, in action if not words, that sex was wrong. And sex with another woman was absolutely vile. This experience left an indelible mark. An act of pleasure, intimacy, and connection left me feeling guilty, shameful, and perverted. As a teenager, I struggled to claim my sexual identity and instead perceived sex as something to be taken from me rather than an act of mutual pleasure. I didn't trust or claim my own body and allowed men to take advantage of my despondency. As a teen I used to ridicule my mom's friends who came out in their forties or fifties, perpetuating the status quo stories that it was some kind of phase or cry for attention. I believed those who identified as bisexual were on the "bi-way to gay," as the homophobic saying goes. When I first met my husband, I thought he may be queer simply because of the strong emotional bonds he has with his close male friends (and likely the racist effeminization of Asian men). My homophobia was alive and well for most of my life. Minimizing the oppressive harm I've caused myself and others took a lot of work. And I have much more to do. Sadly, I didn't feel safe enough to explore my true sexual identity until I was in a supportive and loving relationship with my husband. All of which was also very much supported by the Black LGBTTQIA+ activists and the decades they've spent fighting for our acceptance. The deeper I dove into my own healing, the more I was able to claim the fullness of my identity. I am now clear, and proud to declare, that I am queer AF. Gender binaries are bullshit, and I love souls, no matter their genitalia. Though I'm happily married, I wonder how much confusion and heartache I could have been spared had my mom reacted differently that day. Had my queerness been accepted, understood, and normalized by society as it ought to have been. Part of the beauty of the current collective awakening is that more folx are freeing themselves from the gender identities and sexuality binaries forced upon us by white supremacy. We are returning to the remembering of a nonbinary* world, just as many Indigenous, African, and other BI&PoC communities lived before colonization.⁹ As we continue to do so, we help create more opportunities for queer folx, especially queer and trans Black and Indigenous women+, to be happy, safe, and free.

> >   < <

All of us, every single one of us, feel the impact of white supremacy in our relationships, either as additional pressures or triggers rooted in personal and interpersonal oppression or as the privilege that inherently comes from being free from them. It is on us to identify the oppressions we perpetuate in our bedrooms and beyond, and both do and demand better. Our love can be a form of resistance against the ills of domination, or it can be a tool for domination itself. Let us work to create the love that liberates, ourselves as well as one another.

Race-y Relations Exercise

Below are some questions to get you thinking about the ways in which race, gender identity, and sexual orientation impact your intimate relationships, however they may manifest. You can answer these alone, or, if you have an intimate partner (or partners) and it feels aligned, you can ask them to review these questions with you. If so, I suggest making sure they have some prior exposure to racial justice work as led by a Black or Indigenous woman+. Consider the following:

> Am I attracted to a specific race, color, or ethnicity? Why? Is this preference racist, anti-Black, and/or anti-Indigenous? Is it born from internalized oppression? How has white supremacy influenced what/who I do and do not find attractive?

> Who holds more racial and/or gender identity privilege (if anyone) in my relationship(s)? Why?

> How does race or gender identity privilege impact my relationship(s)?

> Has my partner(s) ever discussed the role of race or gender identity in our relationship(s)? Why or why not? How can I better acknowledge and honor race or gender identity, and any differences, within my relationship(s)?

> If my partner(s) and I are of different gender identities, ethnicities, races, and/or hues, have we acknowledged the power/privilege imbalance in our relationship(s)? If so, how?

> How might I better address and balance the race, gender identity, or other privileges in my relationship(s)?

> > > > > >

SEVENTEEN

Pay Us What You Owe Us

> Capitalism was built on slavery. And
> throughout the history of capitalism,
> we see the extent to which racism is
> intertwined with economic oppression.
>
> **—ANGELA DAVIS**

M ost of us spend the majority of our days, and thus lives, at work. Who our colleagues are, how clients and managers treat us, and what our work environment is like have a huge impact on our well-being, particularly as Black women+ in white supremacist spaces. I have a long list of personal experiences navigating different white- and men+-dominated workplaces, where I had to dim my light for half the pay. White supremacy, fueled by colonial capitalism, has led to a state of burnout for all humxns, but particularly for queer and trans Black and Indigenous women+, who are forced to balance not only the demands of career but also spearhead solutions for the deleterious impact of white supremacy on our families and communities as a whole. These burdens are only growing as the global pandemic and economic recession play out, both of which disproportionately harm communities of color.

TO BE YOUNG, GIFTED . . . AND BLACK

From as far back as I can recall, I had dreamed of becoming an attorney. I believe deeply in fairness, equity, and justice—elements I felt were often missing in my life and the ways my mother and I were treated, be it in doctors' offices, friends' homes, or grocery stores. When I received my admissions letter to one of Canada's most prestigious law schools, I was elated to say the least. But my three years at Allard School of Law were some of my worst. Turns out trying to juggle an all-encompassing (and colonial) course load and care for my disabled and chronically ill mother while searching for funding to stay in school was a wee bit of a shitshow. Who knew?! Life in private practice wasn't much better. The day before starting at a corporate law firm, I recall being consumed by fear. I knew I would be expected to put on an "attorney" mask to hide my true Black woman self from colleagues and clients. And I did. I swallowed my Blackness, because I felt I had to compartmentalize my humxnity in order to survive the racist, heteropatriarchal, capitalist, and downright violent work world I occupied.

In addition to the incredulous learning curve, unreasonable hours, and malevolent office politics, I was drowning in misogynoir. I was frequently assumed to be an assistant rather than an attorney by clients and other attorneys alike. Both would stare back at me in awe once corrected and then drill me on the legitimacy of my law degree. My contributions were often ignored or undermined, and my superiors treated me with a disrespect I never witnessed waged upon my white or male peers. One of my white male bosses routinely had me do his clerical work because he was too afraid of his own assistant (wtf!). The white women partners were even worse—one such woman screamed profanities at me when I asked for clarity on a file, and when I reported her behavior, I was told not to take it personally. Right!

I was hired at my dream firm only to find myself working around the clock to make rich white men richer. Men like a certain Trumplethinskin. Yes, at the height of my disillusionment, I am nauseated to say I worked with Captain Cheeto's corporation. Shit was bad! But I had massive student debt from putting myself through college and law school and a chronically ill mother to care for. I didn't think leaving was an option. Just leaving the office was hard enough.

My days were grueling, often eighteen to twenty hours long. One of the only people I saw outside of "regular" office hours was the firm's custodial engineer, Marie, and she didn't get to my floor until nine p.m. Everyone else was gone, but I always had more work to do. Marie had no qualms telling me how worried she was about me given that I always was wasting myself away in my office. I didn't disagree. When I met my closest coworker's baby, Jane, she took to me right away, as though we were already acquainted. Obviously I assumed it's because I'm awesome (duh), but my mom reminded me that given the hours my coworker and I spent working together while she was pregnant, baby Jane had likely heard *my* voice more than her dad's. The realization of how omnipresent our jobs had become made my friend and me cringe. When I started daydreaming about being hit by a bus so I could take a day off, I knew things were bad. After four years as a big-firm corporate attorney, I walked away. What I walked into wasn't much better.

NOT YOUR MULE OR MAMMY

I attempted to take some time off to rest and better tend to my mother, but my identity was so attached to working and doing, rather than being, that I found myself working—for free. I was terrified of being deemed a lazy Black woman. It wasn't until Spirit intervened in the form of a car crash that I finally laid my ass down. But soon I took on a role at a footwear company, only to find myself once again in a toxic work environment run by an abusive white man struggling with mental health issues. I quit after six months. After that, I had perhaps my worst ever experience working for an entitled, ego-driven, young white male film producer. Despite my law degree and countless other professional accomplishments, I was relegated to coffee runs and personal assistant tasks (all for white men). All of which was in addition to the all-consuming producer and business affairs role I was hired for. Though acts of monetary kindness were bestowed, they were also held over my head. I was perpetually made to feel less than, incapable, and unworthy. "No" was not an acceptable response to this dude, unless you were a white dude yourself. Still, I stayed way longer than I should have because I was socialized to believe that working too much, for little pay and no respect, to make rich white men richer, was my duty. I, like many Black women+, operated under a "mule mentality" passed down from my enslaved ancestors, who worked literally to death for white folx' wealth and welfare.

None of my experiences are uncommon. While all women+ face oppression at work, it is especially egregious for Black women and femmes (and of course more so for those living at additionally oppressed intersections). The retention rate for Black women attorneys is the lowest in America, with 17 percent of Black women leaving practice in 2015.[1] Black women in other professional positions are also exiting stage left on the oppressive office settings composing the status quo; and Black women constitute the fastest-growing group of entrepreneurs, with businesses owned by Black women increasing at a rate of 518 percent between 1997 and 2016.[2] Why? Let's just say I have a few fucking ideas!

#1—Dolla Billz

Black women and femmes work our asses off while enduring regular racial harms, and we get paid less to do it. On average, Black women earn 61 cents to every dollar a white man earns and to every 80 cents a white woman earns (and the disparity is worst in high-salary positions). It takes us until August 22 of the following year to earn what white men earned the year prior.[3] Latinx women (who may be of any race) also earn less than their non-Latinx or male counterparts, with Native American women earning 58 cents to every white man dollar and Latinx women earning just 53 cents.[4] A 2017 survey also held that cis queer women earn less than cis straight women, meaning queer and trans Black and Indigenous women and femmes likely earn less than everyone.[5]

As Erika Stallings pointed out in her *O, The Oprah Magazine* article, Black American women accrue an average debt of $30,366 upon graduating college, but white women accrue $21,993 (and white men only $19,486).[6] A married Black woman with a bachelor's degree in her thirties has a median wealth of $20,500, whereas the wealth of a married white women is a staggering $97,000. Single white women without a degree on average have $3,000 more in median wealth than a single Black woman *with* a degree.[7] For all the shit we're forced to endure, our paychecks don't come close to compensating (and some harms can never be rectified via remuneration). Add to this the fact that many Black women and femmes are also financially responsible for, if not a primary contributor to, other family members. Sending money to our parents is something 45 percent of college-educated Black American households do, as well as those of Latinx ethnicity—and naturally, all the worse for Afro-Latinx households.[8] I had left behind my aspirations of working in international humxn rights law because of compassion fatigue from navigating misogynoir in law school and, more important, the need to earn a sufficient salary to pay off my debts and care for my mom. Forty-two percent of Black American families rely on credit cards to cover basic living expenses,[9] and this only increases during global catastrophes. I have several family members who may not be alive today had I not been able to help them financially. Black women and femmes earn less and keep less of what we earn because white supremacy has ensured our family members require our financial care.

#2—More Work

What is even more wild about how little Black women and femmes earn compared with our white and/or male counterparts is that we are forced to do *more* work than everyone for lesser pay. Research shows that BI&WoC are asked to do the majority of "office housework," ranging from taking notes to ordering lunch to shutting the door at meetings.[10] Work that not only takes us away from the jobs we are paid to do but reestablishes a demeaning white supremacist heteropatriarchal status quo. I remember how I took notes at every meeting, organized all client events, and was the contact for support staff needing assistance. None of which I was compensated for, nor was it taken into account for job advancement. But when BI&WoC say no, we are labeled angry, aggressive, or emotional and face being penalized. Statistics show that BI&WoC who raise issues of discrimination are often pushed out of our jobs altogether. Especially Black women and femmes. And it's not just office housework we do. Many professional BI&WoC, particularly Black women and femmes, are forced into white-washed "diversity and inclusion" initiatives, which is exhausting work requiring emotional as well as mental and physical labor with zero fiscal rewards or accolades for achievement.[11] As Adia Harvey Wingfield shares in her book *Flatlining: Race, Work, and Health Care in the New Economy*, "Black workers are having to navigate environments where companies say they want more diversity but aren't putting resources or support into achieving that."[12] Racial justice, like so much else, is instead put on us.

#3—Less Care

BI&WoC get paid less to do more work, and to top it all off, we receive less support from colleagues, clients, and managers alike. A 2006 survey found that BI&WoC are the most likely to experience harassment at work comprised of both sexual harassment and racial or ethnic discrimination.[13] In the UK, 18 percent of LGBTTQIA+ folx have reported verbal abuse or misconduct at work, and 35 percent do not disclose their sexual orientation at work for fear of repercussion.[14] Added together, queer BI&WoC are subject to a hell of a lot of violence while trying to do our jobs. And it's worse for trans women, who are frequently laughed out of job interviews and constantly misgendered at work.

According to the *Harvard Business Review*, BI&WoC, especially Black women, also receive less care in the form of managerial support, such as socializing outside of the office, advocating for us and our work to executives, or help maneuvering office politics.[15] This lack of care, combined with the additional unpaid and unrecognized work forced on us, impacts our opportunities for advancement. Despite 64 percent of Black professional women declaring they want to advance in their job (double the number of non-Hispanic white women), we aren't given the opportunities. In 2018, BI&WoC represented only 4 percent of C-level executives compared with white women (19 percent) and white men (68 percent). Black women graduates from Harvard Business School reached the highest-level executive positions in 13 percent of cases, compared with 40 percent of their white women classmates. In the legal profession, only 1 percent of America's partners are Black women.[16] One of the many reasons I left law is because I never saw a single BI&WoC partner, let alone a Black woman or femme, who had a career or life I wanted for myself. When there are fewer BI&WoC in positions of power to help turn the tides and create safer spaces for the next generation, the cycle continues. So, we leave.

➤ ➤ ◄ ◄

The white supremacist work environments that BI&WoC, especially queer and trans Black women and femmes, must endure are very violent. This is true across the board no matter if we're professionals or gig workers. Whether I was a waitress, spin instructor, or attorney, every workplace I've ever entered has treated me with some level of disregard. Less pay, less care, and more work set BI&WoC up to fail, though we do our damndest to overcome (amen!). White supremacy leads to an exhaustion unparalleled. It leads to burnout, especially for queer and trans Black women and femmes, though none of us are immune.

BATTLING BURNOUT

Working in a colonial capitalist system, upholding and perpetuating white supremacy on the daily, left me tired. I don't mean I needed a nap. I mean my bones ached and my soul was exhausted. Exhausted from overworking, caretaking, navigating violence in white spaces, witnessing Black folx murdered by police and keeping my rage contained, all while trying to be a good friend, daughter, coworker, and humxn and trying to find time just for me. I was burned out.

I define burnout as physical, mental, and/or emotional exhaustion or loss of motivation usually caused by prolonged stress or frustration from work or otherwise. The white supremacist capitalist systems we live and work under have created a burnout epidemic. We have become addicted to work, as well as our phones, and technology ensures we are constantly online and available. Recent studies show that workers age thirty-four and under are the most overtaxed group of all: 74 percent of millennial women report feeling overwhelmed at work daily (compared with 64 percent of men),[17] and this is all the worse for Black women and femmes, who have a long legacy of exhaustion at the hands of white supremacist heteropatriarchy. As Tiana Clark shared in her article "This Is What Black Burnout Feels Like," "No matter the movement or era, being burned out has been the steady state of [B]lack people in [America] for hundreds of years."[18] Worldwide, we are tired not only from overdoing and attempting to rectify hundreds of years of our ancestors' exploited labor, but having to constantly explain racism and anti-Blackness while doing it.

Burnout is both a manifestation of grief and creates more grief in and of itself. For many Black women+, this grief comes from a lifetime of labor at the hands of systemic oppression resulting in little, if any, intergenerational wealth. I started working at thirteen to help my mom make rent, and I've held a job ever since. Through high school, to supplement my mom's income, and through college and law school, to pay for tuition. Even still, I fell short. There were many times we had only $5 between us. Times I considered working as an escort to help us get by. Had it not been for financial aid and a white college roommate who floated me funds, I would have been evicted from my college residence. I started law school without sufficient funds to finish first year, hoping it would work itself out in the end. It did, but it easily might not have. Like many Black women and femmes, I also had to mentally, emotionally, and physically care for a family member, my mom, which included becoming manager of our household at sixteen and all the emotional labor and mental load* that requires. By the time I quit law, I had serious adrenal burnout and two hernias. The impacts of chronic toxic stress and overworking still greatly affect my health today. It is no surprise that Black women and femme professionals are leaving toxic white work environments when our capacity and desire to stay on the hamster wheel is totally taxed from a lifetime of simply trying to survive. Still let me be clear, being a queer Black woman is a blessing. It is white supremacy that tries to wear us down.

Capitalism and white supremacy thrive on burnout as a tool to defeat racial justice. As therapist and advocate Dr. Jennifer Mullan says, "Our exhaustion is completely & utterly about the inequities in this systemic slaughterhouse. They keep us sick, tired & distracted from the bigger issue at hand."[19] Capitalism cannot exist without white supremacy and anti-Blackness to justify subjugating a certain subset of people, primarily queer and trans Black and Indigenous women and femmes. No matter your identity, when you are overworked and exhausted, your ability to rise up, to revolt, and to hold these abusive systems to account is diminished. When we conflate scrolling on Instagram and binge-watching Netflix with emotional or spiritual rest, only the most powerful and privileged (and, ultimately, white) prevail.

REENVISIONING WORK

The white supremacist capitalist model of work causes all of us harm, especially queer and trans Black women+ and other WoC. As proponents of a feminist economy explain, this model is based in individualism, ego, unaccountability, profit worship, scarcity, competition, and domination over people and nature.[20] The emotional labor (which is just labor) and mental load demanded from all women and femmes, and particularly Black and Indigenous ones, both at work and at home, remain invisible and go unrewarded under this model. It has resulted in disconnection and duress regarding child-rearing and more, as well as the expectation that women and femmes should not only spearhead household management but do so while holding executive office or running a business. It often demands the women and femmes who acquire or inherently possess power and privilege, based on race, class, or otherwise, to exploit poor BI&WoC as nannies or housekeepers in order to meet an oppressive workload. It is entirely untenable.

As Kundan Chhabra shares, there are seven forms of labor, and all need to be acknowledged so we can better understand how much work we are doing and asking of others, especially queer and trans Black and Indigenous women and femmes. These are:

> emotional
> intellectual
> mental
> spiritual
> environmental
> relational
> mitochondrial[21]

For example, asking Black women+ to educate you on anti-oppression is asking for emotional, intellectual, spiritual, mental, and relational labor (and sometimes all seven forms). Labor is labor, and asking others to work for free, without some form of energy exchange, perpetuates white supremacy, the systemic oppression of Black women+, and our ability to thrive financially and otherwise. The status quo expectation is that it is my duty to share my labor at zero cost, and because of internalized oppression, many Black women+ buy into this bullshit too. I am routinely asked by white folx to work for free, including by multimillion-dollar corporations. But Black women+ also frequently expect me to provide unremunerated time, energy, and labor. When we are conditioned to undervalue ourselves and give away our gifts for free, we expect the same in return. Well, I'm not here for it. I do not engage in the exploitation of time, energy, or labor (emotional or otherwise) of Black folx, especially Black women or femmes. An energy exchange does not require capital. In a feminine economy we can equitably exchange more and in more ways. Valuing myself is a counter-capitalist, pro-Black act of resistance.

A recent report found the global unpaid labor provided by women equated to $10.9 trillion in 2019, exceeding the combined revenue of the fifty largest companies on the Fortune

Global 500 list.[22] American women spend an average of 4 hours per day on unpaid labor like caring for children or the elderly, while American men spend only 2.5 hours daily.[23] In order to achieve equity for all, we need to reenvision work and success from the inside out.

The feminine economy suggests focusing on integrity, honesty, care, generosity, collaboration, sustainability, mindfulness, and abundance. This should also include and prioritize equity (i.e., anti-oppression).[24] Operating from the divine feminine, rather than the toxic masculinity required to uphold white supremacy, would mean prioritizing people over profits, honoring our interconnectedness with nature as well as one another, and fostering communal over individual welfare. We would work less and recognize and remunerate the unpaid labor of all women and femmes. Working less means consuming less and caring for the planet more. It also means we are more equipped to withstand economic crises and global pandemics. All of this would create a more connected, leisurely, and equitable workforce and world for everyone, especially queer and trans Black women and femmes who bear the bulk of the burden of additional and unpaid labor. Change is needed, and it is needed now. Queer and trans Black and Indigenous women and femmes are owed our pay. Pay us money, pay us respect. Pay us, period!

Waking Up the Workplace

Review the below checklist of suggested ways for you to actively create more inclusive spaces and opportunities for queer and trans Black and Indigenous women and femmes at work. As always, most of these suggestions can also be applied to folx of other or additional marginalized identities as well. If you do not have queer or trans Black and Indigenous women or femmes in your workplace, question why that is and use the below as offerings for improving your workplace. When you're done, write out a personal action plan for incorporating at least two to three applicable suggestions for you to commit to at work, ideally in the next ninety days (and if you have sufficient power or privilege in your workplace, share and implement recommendations with your colleagues and managers). Many thanks to McKensie Mack and Raquel Willis for sharing and/or inspiring some of these offerings:[25]

> Help ensure all queer and trans Black and Indigenous women+ are adequately remunerated for our time and energy/emotional labor expended at work, whether work-related or not. Whether it's a podcast interview, workshop, article, or piece of art. At a minimum, offer an honorarium. Remuneration need not be fiscal, but it must be aligned and sufficiently supportive for the people in question. "Exposure" doesn't count.

> Apportion a percentage of *all* profits to queer and trans Black and Indigenous folx as an ongoing rule (without using it as a marketing ploy).

> If your businesses is based on practices or wisdom from a BI&PoC community/culture (like yoga), apportion a large

percentage of *all* profits to that community (again, without using it as a marketing ploy).

> Hire and recommend us, especially for leadership and managerial positions (ensure you have at least two trans or queer Black or Indigenous folx in your executive).

> Team up with reputable organizations to support workplace training for us within your business or company.

> Research businesses owned and operated by us and request your workplace support them as much as possible (hire Black- or Indigenous-owned suppliers, affiliates, designers, caterers, tech support, engineers, etc.).

> Learn how to properly pronounce everyone's names and learn their pronouns (and always share your own). Check in to confirm you have them correct.

> Eliminate the use of Black American music in the workplace if the workplace, and everyone in it, is not actively and regularly countering anti-Blackness. In any event, do not permit the use of songs containing the N-word.

> Ensure your workplace and work platforms are accessible for all abilities.

> Take time to get to know us as people and don't confuse us with one another.

> If we accuse you of being discriminatory at work, listen. Express gratitude for our bravery in telling you and take time to process what was shared. Then apologize and put together an action plan to rectify the harm you've caused and prevent harm moving forward. Do not ask for additional unpaid labor from us to assist you.

> Check if we are tasked with the majority of "office housework" and take necessary action to reassign those tasks wherever possible.

> Hold accountable any colleague, manager, etc. who openly or covertly oppresses anyone for any reason.

> Demand a clear and inclusive anti-discrimination and anti-harassment work policy with tangible and actionable steps and full accountability if/when oppression arises.

> Act in allyship with us both inside and outside of work.

> Acknowledge and value our work, giving credit whenever it's due.

> Implement gender-neutral bathrooms.

> Provide generous health insurance for all staff and contractors, specifically ensuring trans Black and Indigenous folx have access to the health care they need.

> Demand an action plan for hiring, retaining, and promoting us, including an action plan for getting the workplace and everyone in it to partake in intersectional anti-oppression training led by a queer or trans Black or Indigenous racial justice educator.

NOW, WRITE DOWN TWO TO THREE ADDITIONAL ACTIONS YOU WILL TAKE TO CREATE MORE INCLUSIVITY FOR QUEER AND TRANS BLACK AND INDIGENOUS WOMEN+ (AND/OR OTHER OPPRESSED IDENTITIES) SPECIFIC TO YOU AND/OR YOUR WORKPLACE (REMOTE AND/OR IRL):

1. _____

_____

_____.

2. _____

_____

_____.

3. _____

_____

_____.

TO MY QUEER AND TRANS BLACK AND INDIGENOUS PEOPLES AND OTHERWISE OPPRESSED FOLX, BELOW ARE SOME TOOLS TO CONSIDER HOW TO MOVE FORWARD IF, BUT MORE LIKE WHEN, YOU ENCOUNTER EMOTIONAL OR OTHER VIOLENCE AT WORK:

> Identify if there is someone you trust to act in allyship with you regarding this issue and, if so, discuss it with them.

> To the extent possible, prioritize your comfort (and not the oppressor's comfort) regarding how and when to address the issue. Proceed however is going to feel best and right for *you* (with the understanding that you may not be able to, given that we rely on work to pay our bills).

> If it feels sufficiently safe (and/or you're done giving fucks), make a clear request. For example: *This is what happened, this is why it is not okay, and this is what I require from you/ management in order to fix it.*

> Shower yourself in compassion no matter what. Whether you speak up is mostly about what power and privilege you possess (or do not) and whether you work in a sufficiently safe environment (which most oppressed folx don't!). You deserve to feel safe and valued in all spaces, work included.

> Lean into your community for support. If you are currently without Earthly community, lean into energetic community (like communing with your ancestors, guides, or Spirit).

> >> > > >

EIGHTEEN

Becoming Unfuckwithable

> Sometimes people try to destroy you
> precisely because they recognize
> your power—not because they don't
> see it, but because they see it and
> they don't want it to exist.
>
> **—BELL HOOKS, *REEL TO REAL: RACE,***
> ***CLASS AND SEX AT THE MOVIES***

As a Black woman, prioritizing my joy and well-being in a world made by and for whiteness is a deeply political and revolutionary act. Honoring my anger, connecting with Spirit, and practicing culturally informed spiritual offerings have helped me affirm my power and speak truth to the atrocities of this world to help change them. Becoming unfuckwithable* means showing yourself compassion, while refusing to take shit from people resigned to the status quo. It is neither your job nor your business to change others. But it *is* your and our collective responsibility to call others in. To provide them with the invitation to change, grow, and evolve as you do the inner work to change, grow, and evolve yourself. And it is absolutely on us to set firm boundaries for what we will and will not accept (and therefore whom) in the quest for racial justice. We can have compassion for who and where people are and still call them in to do and be better. In fact, holding people accountable to do the work required to overcome oppression and call themselves in to their highest self is the purest form of compassion.

We are all needed in this fight to dismantle white supremacy. *You* are needed. Becoming unfuckwithable by leaning into your power, expressing your loving anger, and spending your privilege is how we can help extinguish the hot global mess we currently live in.

GIVING UP WHITE COMFORT

After all the years of racialized harm, of feeling ostracized, internalizing my own oppression, and believing *I* was problematic rather than the white supremacist systems around me (and those upholding them), I finally had space and capacity to address the harms head-on after the death of my mom. I stopped prioritizing white comfort and instead centered myself and Black and Indigenous women+. The audacity! Folx did *not* like it. It was and continues to be an incredibly painful and liberating process of releasing the people, places, and things that do not serve my highest good or prioritize the comfort, truth, and experiences of Black and Indigenous women+. Fighting to dismantle white supremacy can be a lonely path, but it is my deepest belief that we are all being beckoned to use our personal privileges and to claim our power to dismantle all systems of oppression, everywhere, forever. And that takes courage. And strength. And resillience. It requires an air of unfuckwithableness. This doesn't mean you don't care or won't feel. On the contrary, your unfuckwithableness is sourced from a deep and omnipotent care, particularly for the most marginalized. It is born from feeling deeply, and that is why you are so committed to doing what needs to be done to help heal the collective.

Becoming unfuckwithable compels us to address all the ways we get stuck (remember those?). The need to be good and right, centering the white gaze, people pleasing, refusing to face our shadow, etc. Below I set out the key elements to your becoming unfuckwithable so you can best champion racial justice both in your personal life and out in the world.

#1—Practice Wise Compassion & Discernment

The first element to becoming unfuckwithable is wise compassion. Both for ourselves as well as others, ideally at the same time. Wise compassion allows us to explore, identify, and hold space for our needs while also honoring the needs of others. Your needs for justice, acceptance, peace, love, and liberation deserve to be honored, *and* they will absolutely come up against other people's needs. Recognizing and asking for what we need is some of the hardest shit we can ever do! I struggle with this in a big way, but I have come to learn how declaring my needs is a compassionate act that honors my highest self, tends to my wounded inner child, and allows those in my life to fully show up, which is a gift to us all. The more I claim my needs, the more I allow others to claim theirs, and the more I am capable of meeting both. Including my need to forgive myself for the harms I have caused and those I permitted to be caused against me.

Wise compassion necessitates discernment, which is less of a mental practice and more of a remembering and reacquainting with our deepest source of knowledge: our intuition. Your truth/intuition/gut feeling, and a critical analysis of any biases or traumas that may be present within it, can create the foundations for discerning how and when is best to act in a manner that shows compassion for you as well as others, particularly the oppressed. Practicing wise compassion and discernment in the name of racial justice is also a practice of disconnecting from collective fear and releasing the need to people please. Others *will be* disappointed, if not downright outraged, by what it is you need and your choice to affirm what you believe in, and you will compassionately discern if, how, and when to continue engaging with such folx moving forward. Which brings us to the next element of becoming unfuckwithable—boundaries!

#2—Set Boundaries & Embrace Loving Anger

Setting clear boundaries for both yourself as well as others is a nonnegotiable when it comes to embracing unfuckwithableness and affirming your acts of allyship in the name of racial justice. The deeper I dove into my own racial justice journey the more I found had to change. I was evolving on every level, and the people, places, and things surrounding me needed to evolve as well or they would continue causing myself and others harm. And that was no longer acceptable. When I began setting my boundaries, I was scared shitless. My entire life had been about prioritizing the needs of others before my own and doing my best to find acceptance despite my differences. As family therapist Silvy Khoucasian says, "Not having boundaries is a way of enabling people to do us harm because we are afraid of conflict or disconnection."[1] When I began embracing my loving anger, voicing my truth, and allowing others to meet me, or not, it didn't go so hot. White people abandoned me for declaring my needs and refusing to tolerate oppressive behaviors. When I told my father that I needed him to speak to me with kindness and acknowledge his role as my parent in order for our relationship to continue, he called me a "fucking bully" (ironic, really, given my ask).

These responses were partly a result of having gone so long without having set any boundaries for the people in my life, and also in part because of the people I allowed in my life as a result of having not set them. Those who get the most upset by your boundaries are usually the ones who most benefited from you not having any. The responses from my friends and family were also because, after a lifetime of not speaking my truth, finally doing so was *very* charged. I am the first to admit I have communicated violently, and I've done my best to rectify harms caused and do better moving forward. A big piece of this is claiming my needs, expressing my loving anger, and setting boundaries early on and without apology. This way I am less in my own feelings when I do so, and it allows me to move from a place of more compassion for myself and others, as well as my needs (whether someone can meet them or not).

Real talk: setting boundaries means some folx will no longer wanna fuck with you. Maybe a lot of folx. We live in a culture that perpetuates conflict avoidance, fitting in over belonging, and inauthenticity. But you will like yourself more, and the connections and acts of allyship you will be able to undertake will be deeper and more meaningful. Setting boundaries for yourself means you can be with the truth that you aren't too much. That you are worthy of your needs. That there are many who won't be able to meet them and that changes nothing about who you are, so you feel empowered to get clear with folx however and whenever necessary. If people in your life are causing harm and refuse to stop, it is on you to take action. Especially when we hold power and privilege to do so. How others respond is more about their commitment to oppressive systems than it is about you. As entrepreneur and editor Doreen Caven says, "Prepare to be called a bully for interrupting societally approved behavior that is oppressive to others"[2] (sometimes by your own dad). Still, we can compassionately release people, things, and situations in a proactive, authentic way communicated nonviolently, rather than a reactive (often charged and potentially violent) one. Setting boundaries does not require making anyone bad or wrong, yourself included. There is a difference between reacting and moving away. Practice saying no. Without apology, without justification. Say *no* to oppressive others in order to say *yes* to you.

Boundaries allow us to stop carrying burdens for or trying to fix others. I haven't spoken to my father in six years, and though I wish we could have a loving relationship, I am affirmed in knowing I was clear in sharing my needs and refusing to be abused any longer. Same goes for the violent and anti-Black folx I once called friends. Sometimes moving forward with racial justice is impossible because we are trying to bring along those who cannot be part of the journey. Boundaries protect us, they help educate and call in others, and they help us to create more relationships and opportunities that serve our deepest needs, including those aligned with racial justice.

#3—Accountable Action

Becoming unfuckwithable also requires accountable action. Meaning we take action to hold others accountable and, perhaps more important, to ensure we hold ourselves accountable as well. Acting in allyship and committing to ending oppression mean we must act, and taking action means we will at some point or another fuck it up. Owning our mistakes, knowing it doesn't make us wrong or bad, is key. We have no right to call others into this work or demand their accountability if we are not doing the same ourselves. That would be an act of oppression, and we ain't here for it!

What is of particular importance is not succumbing to the tactics of the oppressor. We cannot dismantle the master's house using the master's tool, as Audre Lorde so wisely proclaimed.[3] We must work to stay vigilant of how and when we act, or intentionally refrain from action, and do our best to dismantle systems of oppression with the deep understanding that we are deeply immersed in them. We must remain teachable and humble and know that being unfuckwithable doesn't make us better than anyone else, just further along in a journey with no destination. We will always have further to go.

Owning our power and privilege is also crucial. Continuously doing our work to expose and enlighten where we most need to grow and appreciating that our evolution is a lifelong journey. Your work is to not only call in others, but call in *yourself*. Especially those with the most power and privilege (hi, white folx!). With every choice and every breath. And to have gratitude for those who help hold you accountable.

#4—Protect Your Energy

The final key element in your becoming unfuckwithable is protecting your energy. Boundaries play a major role, but they are not enough. You cannot rise to your highest being or help dismantle all systems of oppression if you are exhausted or burned out. Trust me, I've tried! Wasn't cute. Part of dismantling all systems of oppression is to rage against the capitalist machine keeping us oppressed. As Tricia Hersey of the Nap Ministry says, "Rest is resistance."[4]

Particularly for queer and trans Black and Indigenous women+, who have been socialized to overdo and over-accommodate in order to carry an unequal share of the collective's mental, emotional, physical, and spiritual labor. The capitalist powers that fund and fuel white supremacy want us distracted, sick, and tired. Your rest and your healing are the revolution. Black women+ more than anyone. Ask for help, and learn how to receive it. In addition to rest, we need to practice managing how and where we expend our energy. The urgent, entitled demands of white supremacy are violent in and of themselves. Time and energy are some of the most valuable resources we have. They are also a privilege to possess. Choose how you expend them with care.

THE ACT OF BECOMING

I didn't wake up unfuckwithable one morning. It was, and remains, a process. A journey. An ongoing and never-ending one at that. I get so many messages from BI&WoC asking me how. Who observe me telling it like it is while declaring fierce boundaries and think, *I could never*, but let me tell you: Yes, you absolutely can. I wasn't always so outspoken. Okay, maybe a little! But not too long ago, the mere thought of saying "white supremacy" to white folx, let alone schooling them on it, would have had my tummy in a twist. For me, the act of remaining silent became more painful than speaking up. And the deeper I dove into my inner work, the more I was able to heal my own heart and share my truth, because my truth is inextricably linked to the truth of who *you* are, who we are, and who we can be as a collective. My pain is a reflection of the pain of the planet.

I am also acutely aware that my privilege has granted me the ability to cut ties with whiteness in a way many BI&WoC

cannot. We have no choice but to navigate white folx and white supremacy, so we have a lot of healing to do. When I began calling out white supremacy, some BI&WoC found they couldn't relate to me anymore. They abandoned me in favor of whiteness because they didn't want to deal with the pain that comes from facing how oppression harms us. I was there too, once upon a time. Still, I would like to encourage us to prioritize *our* peace above that of our oppressors wherever and whenever possible. Black women and femmes more than anyone.

For white women+, becoming unfuckwithable means holding other white people accountable and taking intentional action to ensure there are consequences when they refuse to do so. Unfuckwithableness is giving up your allegiance to your "innocence," rolling up your sleeves, and getting in the damn ring. It means canceling white solidarity, supporting BI&WoC, especially Black and Indigenous women+, with your body as well as your words, and giving few fucks about the ways white supremacy will label you problematic for doing so.

No matter your race or identity, the act of becoming unfuckwithable defies white supremacy through an embodied appreciation for every element of who you are, be it your thick thighs, bold opinions, or unique talents. And that shit will ruffle feathers. Many, especially other women+, will be angered by your ability to embody your truth and freedom because they feel they've been given no opportunities to express their own. In many cases, they're right. They haven't. But becoming unfuckwithable demands we take it. That we reclaim our power, our truth, and our liberty so we can help ensure equitable power and liberty for *all*. Let me remind you that you are not difficult or hard to love. You aren't too much. You are *worthy*, you are *loved*. You *are* enough. You are UNFUCKWITHABLE.

Rest & Respite

We cannot become unfuckwithable if we're too tired to give a fuck.

We need to lean into our need for rest, whatever that means for us. Rest, which is not always the same as sleep, is part of how we take our power back. As Dr. Saundra Dalton-Smith explains, some forms of rest include:

> *Mental*—a need to quiet the inner chatter or critic and clear away mental baggage
> *Emotional*—a need to both feel and express your emotions, and stop prioritizing others first
> *Social*—a need for connection and to spend time with folx who energize and support you and eliminate/reduce interactions with those who don't
> *Creative*—the need to be inspired, find stillness, and experience serendipity
> *Spiritual*—the need to connect and align with Spirit and find inner peace
> *Sensory*—the need to reduce ceaseless audible or other noise, like the light pollution from screens or notifications from your phone
> *Physical*—the need for mind and body restoration from sleep, reduced effort, etc.[5]

SOME WAYS TO GET REST, AS INSPIRED BY TRICIA HERSEY, INCLUDE:

> saying no
> quiet time alone (which could be a nap, meditating, sitting in stillness)
> not rushing to respond to emails, texts, or DMs (or deleting those not deserving of a response)
> releasing the need to be helpful
> doing something for the sake of it (not to make money)
> a long shower or bath
> taking a break from social media[6]

My call to action is for you to take no action at all. Practice giving yourself permission to rest and try at least one of the forms of rest above this week. I also invite you to check in with your state of rest. Do you feel rested when you get up in the morning? Do you feel tired throughout the day? Are there certain people or places that make you feel more tired? Observe. Reflect. Set boundaries as and how necessary. You are worthy of your needs and you cannot become unfuckwithable from an empty cup.

If, or when, you feel sufficiently rested—find a way to create more rest and ease for Black women and femmes (particularly queer and trans and/or otherwise additionally oppressed).

> > > > > >

NINETEEN

Rise Up

> It's not about supplication, it's about
> power. It's not about asking, it's about
> demanding. It's not about convincing those
> who are currently in power, it's about
> changing the very face of power itself.
>
> **—KIMBERLÉ WILLIAMS CRENSHAW**

Well, my loves, here we are. Our time together is nearly complete, and I hope you are feeling grounded, empowered, and unfuckwithable in your ability to move forward and take the actions necessary to dismantle oppression however and whenever it manifests. To do the inner work required for critical collective change. It may seem like shit is about as bad as it can get, but here's the real: things are going to get a hell of a lot worse before they get any better. On an energetic level, they have to. Because the people with the most power and privilege have not been motivated to truly change . . . yet. Despite the increasing global chaos, they feel sufficiently comfortable. They still have money in the bank. Their well-being isn't compromised, and they can more or less continue business as usual. There isn't sufficient collective pressure to incite them to change. Some of *you* are these people. Society is more abundant than ever before, and yet over half of the global population—4.2 billion people—lives in poverty, most of whom are BI&PoC.[1] And the top eight billionaires (all cis white men) own more than the poorest half of the planet's population combined.[2] But the tides are beginning to turn. At some future moment we will hit a collective point so low that the consequences will be borne by *all*. No one will suffer more from the deleterious impacts of world catastrophes driven by capitalist white supremacy than those most oppressed. As the U.S. barrels toward civil war with global consequence, many, mostly white, Americans have newfound fears and anxieties that over half of the global population have been battling for lifetimes. *Will we have enough food? How will our kids survive? Am I safe?* Black and Indigenous North Americans have been at war all our lives. While non-Black and non-Indigenous folx participated in our oppression. But the status quo can only last so long. The unprecedented impact of the COVID-19 global pandemic has changed the game, and the world along with it. We are in a collective healing crisis that requires collective crisis for our healing. Many believe crises—be they perceived or real—are the only ways in which we collectively produce real change. Now, more than ever, is the time to get shit done.

It is no surprise that a pandemic of the lungs broke out shortly after much of the Amazon and Australian bush burned to the ground. Energetically, the lungs are affiliated with grief, and we are in the midst of a global collective catastrophe. Humxn supremacy has led to violent oppression of our planet and all species in it. Mother Earth herself is massively mourning. It is on us, and no one more than wealthy cis straight non-disabled white folx, to change the status quo and pressure the powerful and privileged into action. But we are running out of time to overthrow these systems of oppression before they become grossly inflated. These inequities have already become exaggerated, as we can observe through various global trends like:

Epidemic inequities–With the increase in global health crises comes an increase in global health and economic disparities. For example, the COVID-19 pandemic led to crushing situations for the poor, LGBTTQIA+, Latinx ethnicities, and Black and Indigenous communities, who were disproportionately impacted. The CDC confirmed that due to long-standing social and health inequities, both non-Hispanic Blacks and non-Hispanic Native Americans contracted COVID-19 at five times the rate of non-Hispanic whites.[3]

Environmental racism–The impact of colonial capitalism is most heavily endured by BI&WoC and the poor. For example, oil pipelines are regularly placed through Indigenous territories against Indigenous people's will, impacting their water, soil, and way of life on a good day but decimating them upon a spill.[4] Corporate pollutants like toxic waste, oil smoke, and soot are more prevalent in communities of color,[5] and Black and Indigenous folx are the most adversely impacted by climate change, as we have witnessed with Hurricanes Katrina and Sandy in America, the Australian wildfires, and the desertification in Africa. Climate justice is absolutely part and parcel of racial justice.

Digital colonialism*–American multinational corporations like Facebook can control our data, what information we receive, and how we receive it. In many countries of color, this occurs without consent.[6] These organizations have also shared the data of protesters of color, especially Black Lives Matters members, with private companies that partner with U.S. law enforcement to track, target, and silence us.[7] Many Black activists, myself included, have had our accounts shadowbanned or deleted for denouncing white supremacy.

DNA discrimination—More than twenty-six million people have shared their DNA with multinational corporations for analysis, but our most private information, our genetic code, can be used to oppress as well as assess.[8] The Chinese government has partnered with an American company to analyze DNA samples in order to target and oppress Uighurs, a Muslim ethnic minority.[9] The DNA of the most marginalized could be used similarly by any oppressive institution, including health insurers.

Racial wealth divide—All of the foregoing contribute to a growing racial wealth divide in America and beyond. The capitalist divide of wealth by race, along with the unequal economy, based on enslavement and stolen land, was created by and for the white and wealthy, and this divide is only growing.[10]

> > < <

Inequities or not, the state of the world and the systems dominating it are not sustainable. For anyone. India and China are following the destructive development practices created by America's and Europe's capitalist white supremacist models,[11] perhaps the reason COVID-19 exists in the first place, and we are all on a path to devastation. Our systems prioritize wealth over well-being, leaving us ill-equipped to handle global pandemics or lead joyful lives. Climate experts have confirmed we need to halve climate emissions by 2030 in order to avoid massive global disruption from climate catastrophes.[12] As I write this, rogue federal troops have been unleashed in cities across the

United States to silence, harm, and incarcerate those who defy the status quo. As more civilians rise up, those in control will seek to further entrench their power. We must act while we still can. We all have much to lose if things do not change, including humxnity itself. I'm not saying this to scare you, though many should likely be more scared than you are. I say this to arm you with the information for inspired action. This is not the first time we've had opportunity to create critical collective change, but it will almost certainly be our last.

RISING IN RESISTANCE

It is nearly impossible to imagine a world outside of capitalist white supremacy because it has never existed. Not while any of us have been here. I can fantasize as to what an anti-oppressive, divinely feminine, and spiritually aligned planet may be, but I don't know of any tangible examples. And though I work night and day to help overthrow the systems as they currently exist, it is impossible for me to escape them. All of our anti-oppression and racial justice work is done inside of global capitalist white supremacy, and because of this, all of us are still very much mired in it. I often question whether it is possible to truly dismantle a system from the inside out, or if it all needs to burn down for us to have any chance. We can only get so far utilizing technology to fuel our activism when Instagram, Twitter, and all the other platforms we use are created by and for the toxic and tainted system. When I take in the vast state of worldly inequities, I frequently wonder whether we're too far gone to make the changes necessary for a just world. Whether it's better we all be taken by Spirit so Earth can begin again without us, as it has before. Super depressing shit, I know. But it's real. Oppression of this scale has been around for the last few centuries at least, and though we've made vast improvements in many ways, not much has changed in many others. Sojourner Truth and all that. As a queer Black woman, I know better than to expect white people to get their shit together, but I am nothing without hope. Hope that this time will be different because we will open our hearts as well as our minds. Hope about all that will be possible when we commit to collective healing, when we begin to seriously peel back the bullshit and have the audacity to not only hope, but unify and act. Hope is ours to take and cultivate. No one can give it to us, nor can anyone take it away.

One of my biggest concerns, shared by other Black activists, was that Trump would *not* win the 2020 U.S. presidential election and white "progressives," especially cis white women, would go back to sticking their heads in the sand in the false and convenient hope that all would be well. For *them*. A consequence of their white (and other) privileges. As MLK Jr. said, the biggest obstacle for Black liberation is likely "the white moderate, who is more devoted to 'order' than to justice."[13] What I know for sure is that irrespective of who is or is not the president of the United States, things will *not* be well for anyone other than the top 1 percent. For queer and trans Black and Indigenous women+ especially. Yes, we need to do what we can within the systems as they currently exist. But the entire system, rooted in white supremacy, heteropatriarchy, ableism, classism, and every other form of oppression that exists, is fundamentally fucked. There is no single person or political party that can change that. Though it is unquestionably helpful to have folx from oppressed identities with "radical" (i.e., equitable) policies in power, their participation still requires them to play the game, and the game is stacked. This is true in America as it is everywhere else, in many places even more so. What is needed is an entire overhaul of the global systems we operate in and abide by altogether. And we have hit a collective rock bottom as a means to help us get there. It didn't have to be this way. But now our divine and Earthly assignment is a collective uprising, as led by queer and trans Black and Indigenous women+, to help change the very face of power itself. But we cannot achieve our ends by any means necessary. To do so would have us quickly reverting to the oppressor's tactics. This does not mean we refrain from radical action, quite the contrary. But our action is led with as much love as it is rage. It means we never forget the interconnectedness of humxnity and refuse to oppress others as justification for overcoming our own oppression. Sadly, within the systems we currently operate, this oppression is all too common, even in racial justice circles.

As certain Black and Indigenous activists and educators amass followers, taking on the cult of celebrity, they also amass the often oppressive power and privileges that come with it. We are observing how media and money continue to corrupt the mission. White supremacy infects even those whose work claims or seeks to rail against it, resulting in greed, ego, abuse, anti-Blackness, and whitewashed discourse. This is no big surprise, given that most Black and Indigenous folx have never truly been listened to or validated by the white status quo. And many in the racial justice space have yet to do the inner work required to heal *their* racial traumas, which is precisely why it's vital we discern between those playing the system to elicit change and those who have been caught up in the system itself. Caught up in centering whiteness. Sadly, there are several folx claiming to be in this work to support Black women+ while simultaneously stealing from and silencing us, especially those of us with less privilege. I don't care what race you are or how many followers you have, if you knowingly cause harm to Black or

Indigenous women+, you're not about deliverance but domination. We will all need to be held accountable and welcome being held to account. Especially those of us in the spotlight leading the way. Myself included. Racial justice demands we engage critically not only with the work but with those from whom we are learning it. If collective liberation stands a chance, we will all need to unplug from the matrix to envision the world, and our roles in it, anew.

The world is rapidly changing, and we need to consciously steer its direction so we can demand more and better. It is impossible to fully integrate ourselves under capitalist white supremacy because it inherently requires a disconnection of the mind and body. Our hearts are kept far from our heads, and we are all commodified as material goods. We need a world where healing is the priority. A world where free and equitable health care is a humxn right, universal basic income is the norm, the police are defunded, the prison-industrial complex is eliminated, and child-rearing is a communal act. A universe where hundreds of millions are not allowed to starve so a select few can amass billions. Where communal care trumps individualistic success, and those who have been systemically oppressed are valued, celebrated, paid, and prioritized. What I most hope to see is a world where Black women and femmes can finally rest. We need a revolution rooted in radical compassion, and we need to come together to create collective change. Now.

THIS IS NOT A MOMENT, IT'S A MOVEMENT

Though these are terrifying times, it gives me hope to witness the magnitude of action we can take as a collective when we appreciate the risks involved. It *is* possible to put people before profits. To allocate billions to support those in need. To reenvision our daily lives and the world as we know it. In the wake of the COVID-19 pandemic, many governments unified across party lines. Countries swiftly mandated public health care, decarceration, public childcare programs, and forms of universal basic income to protect their citizens. Though these were temporary measures, they need not be. Think of what is possible when enough of us realize how the status quo is gravely harming humxnity and put our energy behind ending oppression, supporting those in need, rectifying the climate crisis, and creating a world where we can all thrive. We do not have to passively watch the powers that be attempt to regain business as usual or use this atrocity to further entrench their powers. There's no going back. We can, we must, command a new way forward.

We all play a part in creating global, systemic change. That begins with our inner healing, but that is certainly not where it ends. We must commit to being the change, both with our words and, most important, with our actions. Below I've set out some of the higher-level ways you can contribute in a lasting and meaningful manner to soulful social justice and the revolution to end everything that never worked right to begin with.

#1—Revillaging & Community Care

One of the many ways we can support dismantling the oppressive status quo is through community care. As my girl Rihanna once said, "If there's anything that I've learned, it's that we can only fix this world together. We can't do it divided. . . . We can't let the desensitivity seep in."[14] We heal in community, not in spite of it. We rejuvenate, learn, and grow through our relationships—with ourselves and with others. We are all mirrors, we are all teachers, and we are all students. For all the technology we have, we are more connected but more separate than ever before. Revillaging is the act of creating a village around us to support one another through our day-to-day lives. To aid in rearing children, caring for those in need, and contributing to one another's healing and well-being.[15] Especially those most marginalized. Revillaging means recognizing the failures of the global state and taking it upon ourselves to fill the gaps, recognizing the system was built to prioritize the white and wealthy and instead putting people before profit, creating alternatives to capitalism, and striving for solidarity with the queer and trans Black and Indigenous women+ and disabled communities that first created and cultivated community care.

Connection and belonging are our deepest humxn needs, but in our fast-paced world we are less united, and less compassionate, than ever. Community care demands our time, tenderness, patience, and prioritizing. It is an act of re-membering. Revillaging also means more meaningful interactions, which strengthen bonds, promote compassion, and help defuse conflict. We cannot end global systems of oppression on our own, just as they were not created on their own. We must lean into our interconnectedness and the way the oppression of some is the oppression of all. Community is at the core of how we bring about the change we most need. Both by tending to our community and calling on our community to support us in committing to the vital work required to overthrow the status quo. In the words of model Aaron Philip, the goal is to "love more, love unapologetically, love without stigma or overcompensation."[16]

This means we need to start with our inner circle and move outward. We need to take time to find and tend to our people, and take equal measure to be the kinds of people we wish to keep and call in. I call these folx our Dream Support Team, or DST. These are folx you can rely on through thick and thin, who keep you accountable and help you through the tough times—and this work is tough! The folx composing your DST have the distinct honor and privilege of being a source of support for you, and you for them. Think *Golden Girls* or Notorious B.I.G. and Diddy. They will call you on your shit and hold loving, compassionate space when shit hits the fan. They will have the privilege of being a source of support and receiving your support in return. Ideally, folx on your Dream Support Team should be:

Compassionate–They deeply care about you and the most oppressed and seek to support, understand, and assist you.

Principled–They are trustworthy, impeccable with their word, and do what they say they will do.

Accountable–They aren't afraid to call you out when you fuck up, nor to call themselves out when needed, and they take appropriate action to rectify harms when they cause them and change behavior.

Diverse–They are diverse folx from different races, ethnicities, religions, classes, gender identities, sexual orientations, ages, abilities, etc. who can offer you various perspectives and insights.

Anti-oppressive–They are actively anti-oppressive and share your values to dismantle white supremacy, including all forms of oppression.

Your DST can comprise friends, family, lovers, neighbors, healers, therapists, or anyone who can support you in supporting yourself through this vital work of healing personally and collectively. In our modern age, your DST can be your primary village. Finding these folx won't be easy, and you'll be lucky if you have more than a few, but with time, effort, and patience, you will likely begin to cultivate a community. You are worthy of care and support as you lean into healing your heart and activating the hearts of others. The truth is—we won't succeed without it.

#2—Feel Our Feelings . . . Including Joy

The world is on fire, literally and figuratively. And we are apt to be overwhelmed by it all. When we dive into racial justice, we begin to witness things as we never had before. The violence, oppression, sickness, and hurt. The inner work cracks our hearts open and we feel it all. Our own personal pain as well as the mass grief of the collective. If we are to have any chance of staying steadfast, healthy, and hopeful in our efforts to dismantle global oppression, we need to feel our feelings and allow others to do the same. We need to stop maintaining the oppressive status quo that wants us to numb out, to live in fear, and to do as we are told. You have a right to your rage, and you can still lean into joy. For those comprising oppressed identities, our joy is part of the revolution. Learning how to cultivate it, keep it, demand it, and own it. Without fear, without guilt, without shame. Joy is our birthright. Each and every one of us, especially those of us who have been conditioned to feel unworthy of it.

Dismantling oppression does not mean confining ourselves to misery. We must learn how to acknowledge the ways we cause harm, do everything in our power to rectify it, both personally and collectively, and still seek to bring about joy for ourselves as well as others. Especially for those whose joy has been eliminated at the hands of white supremacy. How and when to prioritize pleasure greatly depends on your power and privilege—the more you have, the more you must work to support the joy of others before (but not to the exclusion of) your own.

No matter who you are, going within isn't easy. We must un-learn the ways of white supremacy to lead with a strong spine while keeping a soft heart. We must withdraw from binary ways of thinking and learn to better tolerate our mixed emotions. Joy and grief. Love and rage. This requires balance. And discernment. Tending to our inner child, connecting with our ancestors, pro-tecting our energy, and grounding with our breath—all tools we've moved through together here and that you can return to whenever you wish—can be of great support in identifying and leaning into our emotions. Attuning to ourselves and each other is how we can attend to the most critical needs of the day and motivate ourselves to action. Staying connected to and sharing our inner states of being—including our love, joy, and rage—is one of the many ways we can keep consistently committed to overthrowing the powers that be. It is how we activate our humxnity, awaken our full po-tential, and live in and on purpose. What we choose to do with our pain will define if and how we all survive.

#3—Act Up

The last and most important way we can contribute to much-needed global change is actively dismantling the status quo every day. There is much out of our control, but we have power to con-trol our actions: our impact, our vote, our energy, our compas-sion, our healing, our love. We all need to center queer and trans Black and Indigenous women+, center the interconnectedness of beings, and prioritize protecting the planet. We need to start where we are, and start today. Perfection is the enemy of prog-ress. Our work must balance earnest efforts not to fuck up with the belief that simply trying will always be better or cause less harm. It won't. But we need to choose to act anyways. We need to check and recheck ourselves, call in others, and do the work. Let's reflect on some key ways we've discussed to actively counter oppression (and a few new ones):

> Center and prioritize queer and trans Black and Indigenous women+ or, at a minimum, Black and Indigenous people in all racial justice efforts.
> Follow, learn from, and support (financially and otherwise) intersectional queer and trans Black and Indigenous anti-oppression educators/activists.
> Engage critically. Follow those paving the way but think for yourself, do your own research, and identify ways you can support solutions.
> Identify and acknowledge the ways oppression intersects and compounds.
> Specifically address your anti-Blackness and anti-Indigeneity and why they must take priority in racial justice.
> Act in allyship with all oppressed identities however and whenever you can.
> Educate yourself, being mindful to fact-check what you learn and of how and where you receive your information.
> Work to understand your power and privilege, your role as an oppressed oppressor, and what you need to do to both counter the harms you cause and spend your privilege every single day.
> Become unfuckwithable. Own your specific gifts and talents and put them to work to support the resistance.
> Stay humble, teachable, and a lifelong learner. This work is a journey without any destination, and no matter who you are, you will never be an expert.

> Create a clear, tangible anti-oppressive vision backed by anti-oppressive values. Write it down. Post it up. Revisit and update it frequently. Work every damn day (internally and externally) to make that vision a reality.

> Hold yourself and others accountable. This work cannot be done sheepishly nor in a silo. Call folx out whenever sufficiently safe to do so. Set clear boundaries, make them known, and take no shit.

> Better tolerate your discomfort and acknowledge your fuckups. Thoroughly think before you act. Rectify the harms you have caused and will continue to cause. Learn from your mistakes. Try again. Do better.

> Engage with, listen to, and uplift our youth (especially queer and trans Black and Indigenous youth). They have far less unlearning to do, and trust me, they know shit.

> Unite. We cannot create a new world order on our own, we must come together to dismantle the systems as they currently exist and forge a new path. Find others who are in this fight, lean on them, learn from them, organize your efforts, and demand a new way.

Racial justice is a choice you make every single day for the rest of your life. Every hour, every minute, every breath—you have and will continue to make the choice. To fight for or against. Engaging in authentic anti-racism means you will lose friends, family, work, time, money, sleep; but oh, what you will *gain*. Integrity, healing, compassion, conscious community, and, when enough of us align, a new world order.

The truth is that white supremacy isn't really gonna change unless and until white and white-passing folx are also willing to do better. It is imperative that everyone, but especially white/white-passing people who created, perpetuate, and benefit from white supremacy, commit to actively dismantling it from the ground up. White women+ in particular need to commit to doing their daily inner racial justice work. And call men+ in too. White folx cannot love, donate, vote, volunteer, post, or read their way out of racism. Ending oppression, of any form, demands much more.

It takes intentional, lifelong internal work, and the majority of white/white-passing folx aren't coming close. It requires a tolerance for discomfort, processing the plethora of emotions including grief, guilt, shame, and anger, and learning to stop centering whiteness and white comfort all day every day. White folx and other oppressors need to get honest with themselves about who they are and why they undertake an action—even if it's one they believe to be anti-oppressive. I want to see a world where white/white-passing folx put their bodies and privilege on the front lines to dismantle the systems *they* created so I and other Black folx, especially queer and trans Black women and femmes, can rest. We can't focus solely on what we do not want, but must also envision the world and systems for what we *do*. And we can dream up a new way outside of the current oppressive constraints only if we are healed, rested, and sufficiently liberated. Black and Indigenous women and femmes have been fighting for centuries for precisely that. We've come a long way. It's time for those with the most power and privilege to seal the damn deal.

All of us need to be addressing our anti-Blackness, promoting decolonization, and owning our roles as oppressed oppressors. We need to identify the harms we cause against those with less power and privilege so we can commit to causing less. These are times of great uncertainty, and that uncertainty creates an opening. Our grief can be our greatest gateway to grace. And grit. And we'll need it all.

> >   < <

We've learned a lot here together. I'm grateful you're here and I hope you now have tools you can return to time and time again as you continue this critical and constant work. There will always be more—to do, to learn and unlearn. This is just the start, but it can always be the support. Come back to these pages however and whenever you need. Read it all again from beginning to end or dip in and out however feels most aligned. No matter what, know that the work *must* continue. Beyond all you've learned— what matters most is what you will *do*. How will you use what you've gleaned here to challenge the status quo? Where will you direct your time, energy, and resources? How will your racial justice efforts center the most oppressed, rather than educating the oppressor? What will you do to incorporate anti-oppression into your daily life? How will you hold yourself and others accountable? When will you invoke your righteous rage? Who will you unite with to organize your efforts into collective action? How will you prioritize the care and well-being of Black and Indigenous women+? How will you tend to your heart and the hearts of the most oppressed through it all?

Racial justice is daily, lifelong work. It is hard AF and it must be done. When it comes to ending white supremacy, either you are part of the problem or you're actively working to be part of the solution. There is little gray area in the matter of collective justice. Inaction is an action. Silence is violence. As a popular proverb says: "We don't inherit the earth from our ancestors, we borrow it from our children."[17] What earth do you want to leave behind? We are all needed, particularly those with the most power and privilege, and however you can play your part, your part needs to be played. You are ready. You are able. The only question that remains is . . . are you willing?

I hope what you have learned will crack you open from the inside out. I hope you will use the insights you have gleaned here, no matter who you may be, to light a fire sent straight from Spirit directly beneath your booty to Do. Better. *Especially* white folx.

The time to face your shadow and commit to collective healing is now! Your future, my future, and *our* future depend on it.

Breathwork for Embodied Release

For this, our final exercise, you will want at least twenty to thirty minutes of quiet solitude. We are going to partake in a transformational breathwork exercise that involves active, three-part breath. This yogic practice, a form of *pranayama* (basically meaning "control the breath" in Sanskrit), was created by communities in India. Oxygen has beautiful healing and cleansing benefits for the mind, body, and soul, but most of us do not get enough breath, especially when we are stressed. This exercise will help you flush out what no longer serves and allow all the work we've done together to settle into your cells. If breathwork is inaccessible or overly uncomfortable for you, you can read below and simply take long breaths in and out, and/or imagine yourself actively breathing (the mind is a powerful thing!).

You may wish to have a blanket or socks nearby, and you can light candles or incense to help you get into the vibe if that feels aligned. Lastly, if available to you, you'll want a smartphone, tablet, or computer. I have curated a special guided breathwork audio track for this exercise (with a playlist!), which you can find online at www.rachelricketts.com /do-better. Alternatively, you can listen to the playlist alone by searching "Do Better Breathwork" on Spotify or play your own playlist of inspiring, heart-stirring songs for fifteen to twenty minutes (think Solange's *A Seat at the Table* album).

Once you are set up, you will want to lie on the floor if that is accessible to you. If not, you can lean against a wall or otherwise find a supported posture where you cannot fall down. If you have the guided track accessible, turn it on now, and I will guide you through. If not, read on.

PLACE ONE HAND ON YOUR LOW BELLY AND ONE HAND OVER YOUR HEART. BEGIN TO BREATHE DEEPLY THROUGH YOUR MOUTH AND FOLLOW THIS THREE-BREATH PATTERN:

1) Inhale long and slow into the bottom of your belly and into your diaphragm so you feel your stomach rise to meet the hand over your belly as it fills up with air. Breathe deeply, fully filling up your lungs, including the back of your ribs.

2) Next, inhale into your chest area where your hand is over your heart so you feel your chest rise to meet your hand. Again breathing fully into the chest area, including the back of the heart.

3) Finally, exhale long, slow, and controlled to release all the air from your belly and chest. Do not force or rush the exhale, it should be soft and slow.

If you're pregnant or on your moon cycle, just breathe long, connected breaths instead of the more active three-part breath. Practice your breath cycle for two to three rounds as you get used to the pattern and sensation. Ensure the breath is all happening through the mouth. Then hit "play" on your playlist and keep breathing for as long as you can through that time. You will be challenged, you will feel uncomfortable, and that is why it's called breath*work*. This is a beautiful opportunity to expand your capacity to tolerate your own discomfort. That said, you know your body better than anyone, so pay close attention and return to normal breath when needed.

Try to stay as still as you can; the only things moving should be your belly and chest. If your hands or feet cramp up, that is a frequent experience. Practice a softer exhale, and if that doesn't relieve the cramping, return to normal breath. If you need to cry, cry. This is your opportunity to really tap into yourself and allow whatever needs to move through you to move. Breathe, relax, and feel it so you can heal it.

Reflect on all we've learned together, breathe into the spaces that need more support, and breathe out all that no longer serves. When your playlist finishes, scream as loud as you can. Let it all out. Then seal your lips, return to regular breathing, and lie still to allow all that juicy energy to reverberate through your body. You got this! As always, let us honor and give thanks to Indian communities for cultivating this powerful practice and give back to them in whatever ways we are able.

Reflection Questions

When you finish your breathwork, journal on the following questions:

> How did this breathwork make me feel? What was most challenging? How did I get through?

> What did I most need to release? Did the breath help it move?

> How does my body feel? My heart?

> What are three ongoing anti-oppressive calls to action I will commit to today (lasting six months or more)?

This is an exercise you can return to on your own whenever you need support in the fight for racial justice. You are never alone in this work—we are in this together. At a minimum, you can always call on Spirit, your ancestors, and your breath!

WHAT NOW?

> > >> >> > >

Congrats—you've finished the book and are now anti-racist! KIDDING! Though we're at the end of our time together, you are nowhere near the end of your work. Take time to be with everything you have learned, then revisit all the calls to action set out in this book and keep going. I suggest starting with Owning My Impact (p. 182), Setting Your Racial Justice Values (p. 215), You Betta Act in Allyship (p. 232), Rest & Respite (p. 292), and Chapter 6's Getting Spiritually Activated prompts. Review, rereview, ask informed questions to appropriate people, and be critical and mindful of all you ingest here and out in the world. This sounds counterintuitive, but do not take anything I've said as fact simply because I (or anyone else) said it. The goal is to be constantly learning and unlearning. Do your own research (but #followBlackwomen+), critically engage with the concepts presented while being mindful of how white supremacy plays out in your learning, questioning, and critiquing. Revisit the soulcare prompts on a regular basis to support you in caring for yourself and better tolerating the discomfort that arises as you lean into radical racial justice. And actively take up the work of dismantling white supremacy as though your life depends on it. Because it does.

To continue this vital work, join me over at www.rachel ricketts.com/do-better for more info including discussion topics, my racial justice webinars, and a list of racial justice resources (with other Black and Indigenous educators to support and learn from).

You are a wise, worthy, intuitive, and capable humxn and you *can* do better. I hope you will.

With love and anger,
xo Rachel

ACKNOWLEDGMENTS

I did not write this on my own and especially want to thank the Black queer, trans, dark-skinned, fat, disabled, poor, elder American women and femmes who paved the way. This work truly takes a village, and I want to thank everyone who has played a role in my learning and unlearning, including those who have caused me the most harm (often serving as my greatest teachers).

To my mom for always being my greatest champion (I know I did you proud!). To my husband, Tyler, for nourishing, loving, and encouraging me—thank you for being my best friend.

To Auntie Donna for your daily prayers and helping me fill in the gaps my mom isn't here to. To my cousin Safiya for being a beacon of bright blackity Black light.

To my incredible agents, Wendy Sherman and Cherise Fisher (you're a goddamn goddess, Cherise!), and my team at Atria for helping birth my first book baby into the world (especially Michelle, Libby, Shida, Dana, Morgan, Melanie, and Maudee). To McKensie Mack and Vita E. at Radical Copy, and to Nikki Fraser, for helping me and this book be more inclusive. To Nancy Tan for copyediting, Melissa Medwyk for guiding the book cover design, and my publicist Kathleen Carter for spreading the gospel. Linday Keele—thank you for your unwavering support and for being my first reader!

To Team RR—Tianna Grey, J. Chavae, and Karlene Graham—for helping hold shit (and me) down. I love and appreciate you more than I can say. To Chantaie, Tiffany, Sara, Natasha, Steph, Gen, Kait, KP, LB, Britt, Sarah, Sachi, Beth, Renee, Kari, Liz, Rachel, Randy, Meenadchi, Anita, Ken, Thansha, Dionne, ShiShi, and Maryam—I love y'all. To all the Black folx who inspire me—Harriet Tubman, Audre Lorde, Toni Morrison, Oprah Winfrey, Maya Angelou, James Baldwin, Malcolm X, Tupac Shakur, MLK Jr., Marsha P. Johnson, bell hooks, Angela Davis, Brittney Cooper, Janet Mock, Munroe Bergdorf, Janaya Khan, Patrisse Cullors, Solange, and so many more—I bow in deep gratitude.

To the Sami, Mississaugas of the Credit, Anishnabeg, Chippewa, Haudenosaunee, Wendat, Musqueam, Lumad, Bali Aga, and all Indigenous peoples of the lands upon which I wrote and dreamed this book.

I need to thank all my guides, spirits, and guardians for supporting, protecting, and empowering me to write and all the healers who supported me in my healing (Jen Maramba, Julie Third Eye Goddess, and Kim Boivin especially!).

I want to thank my ancestors for giving me the privilege of being their greatest legacy. I am simply the conduit of all they have manifested to fruition, and I am blessed to be their descendant. To my future ancestors, I hope reading this serves you even half as much as it served me writing it.

Lastly, I want to thank myself—for navigating mad oppressive trauma, working my ass off to help myself heal, and bravely defying the bullshit that is white supremacy. May we all rage against its existence.

GLOSSARY

anguage is confined and yet always changing. Since English is the colonizer's language, concepts outside of colonized ideology cannot be adequately captured, nor will we all agree on how to best capture such concepts. Below are definitions of the words and acronyms used in this book as I understood and agreed with at the time of writing, and I give thanks to the Black queer and trans activists and educators who paved the way for much of this language and my own understanding of it. I invite you to research further and update anything that no longer aligns as we all continue to learn, grow, and do better.

AAVE—Acronym for African American Vernacular English, a dialect of English created by Black Americans, most notably queer and trans Black Americans, including words like: "yo," "word," "slay," "preach," "girl," "queen," "werk," "mad," "dope," "bomb," etc. Given the status quo of anti-Blackness, and the fact that many Black folx are oppressed when *we* use it, the use of AAVE by non-Black folx is appropriative and harmful.

Ableism—The pervasive system of discrimination and exclusion that oppresses people who have mental, emotional, and/or physical disabilities.

Ally—A person who actively uses their privilege to advocate on behalf of someone else who doesn't hold that same privilege. One cannot *be* an ally (nor name themselves as such), but one can act in allyship.

Anti-Blackness—Race-based oppression against anyone from the Black-African diaspora as perpetuated by any race or ethnicity, including Black. Consequently, proximity to Blackness is something to be shamed, no matter your race or ethnicity.

Anti-racism—An active, daily, consistent, and continuous process of personal and collective change to eliminate individual, institutional, and systemic racism derived from white supremacy as well as the oppression and injustice racism and white supremacy cause.

Asexual—Defined by the UC Davis LGBTQIA Resource Center as sexual orientation generally characterized by not feeling sexual attraction or a desire for partnered sexuality.

Authentic anti-racism—Intersectional and comprehensive anti-racism synonymous with "racial justice" (see definition on page 332).

Bias—A conscious or unconscious prejudice against an individual or group based on their identity.

Bisexual—Being attracted to folx with the same gender identity as your own as well as to folx with other gender identities (which may be "male," "female," or otherwise). Can be synonymous with "pansexual."

BI&PoC—Acronym for Black, Indigenous, and People/Person of Color. Some spell this as "BIPoC," but I have added the ampersand to encourage us to read out the full term in order to help mitigate against depersonalizing BI&PoC and our experiences.

BI&WoC—Acronym for Black, Indigenous, and Woman+/Women+ of Color. Some spell this as "BIWoC," but I have added the ampersand to encourage us to read out the full term in order to help mitigate against depersonalizing BI&WoC and our experiences.

Call in/call out—"Call out" is generally described as challenging someone on their oppressive language or behavior, while "call in" is similar though intended to refer to doing so in a compassionate and/or patient way. I don't believe in policing people's responses, especially not the oppressed, so either is fine in my books (I do both), so long as neither is emotionally or otherwise violent.

Cisgender/cis—Defined by Trans Student Educational Resources as someone who exclusively identifies as their sex assigned at birth. Being cis is not indicative of gender expression, sexual orientation, hormonal makeup, physical anatomy, or how one is perceived in daily life.

Classism—The systematic oppression of subordinated class groups (i.e., the poor) to advantage and strengthen the dominant class groups (i.e., the rich).

Climate change—A change in global or regional climate patterns, in particular a change apparent from the mid- to late twentieth century onward and attributed largely to the increased levels of atmospheric carbon dioxide resulting from humxn-made behavior.

Colonialism—When a national or other collective power violently subjugates another by conquering and exploiting an area and/or its people, often while forcing its language and cultural values on the subjugated region and/or inhabitants. Mostly performed by white Europeans or Americans.

Cultural appreciation—Defined by Susanna Barkataki as seeking to connect with cultures different from one's own from "the inside out." It respects the codes, mores, values, and practices of the culture. Cultural appreciation can happen when one enjoys or respects the culture of origin and, instead of harming or taking, gives back and uplifts the source culture.

Cultural appropriation—A particular power dynamic in which members of a dominant culture steal intellectual, spiritual, cultural, and/or informational wealth from a culture of people who have been systematically oppressed by that dominant group (most notably by white or white-passing folx).

Decolonization—A long-term process involving the bureaucratic, cultural, linguistic, psychological, and spiritual divesting of colonial power and simultaneous promotion of Indigeneity. Includes an acknowledgment of settler privilege or proximity to it.

Digital colonialism—Defined by the World Wide Web Foundation as the new deployment of a quasi-imperial power over a vast number of people (often poor and/or communities of color) without their explicit consent, manifested in rules, designs, languages, cultures, and belief systems by a vastly dominant power.

Disabled—Refers to the experience of a functional and/or social disadvantage or restriction of an activity caused by contemporary social organization (as created by systemically oppressive forces). Disabilities are socially created by the status quo. Use "people with disabilities" or "disabled people." Do not use "the disabled," which implies disabled folx occupy a separate sect of society.

Emotional labor—A term created by sociologist Arlie Hochschild meaning to "induce or suppress feeling in order to sustain the outward [support] that produces the proper state of mind in others." Under white supremacy, this is unacknowledged labor most often expected from women and femmes.

Emotional violence—A range of psychological-based behaviors inflicted, intentionally or unintentionally, to manipulate, silence, hurt, coerce, control, belittle, isolate, intimidate, or otherwise psychologically, verbally, emotionally, or spiritually harm another, including gaslighting, spiritual bypassing, white silence, white entitlement, and others.

Equality—A discourse that focuses on same or equal treatment, as opposed to equitable impact. Often perpetuates discriminatory practices by the dominant culture due to a failure to consider the holistic and intersectional issues creating and perpetuating oppression. Focus on equity instead.

Equity—Defined by the Canadian Race Relations Foundation as "a condition or state of fair, inclusive, and respectful treatment of all people. Equity does not mean treating people the same without regard for individual differences." One of the goals of racial justice.

Ethnicity—A group of people who identify with one another based on common ancestral, social, cultural, or national experiences like Jewish, Latinx, Tamil, or African-American. Not the same as race.

Fat—A reclaimed, once pejorative, word for people considered outside of the Eurocentric ideals of beauty because of their body weight or size. Being fat is not a problem, but the negative stereotypes about fat folx are. Fat folx are oppressed as a result of their body size (see "fatphobia").

Fatphobia—The irrational fear of, aversion to, or discrimination against folx of larger body size (for example, naming all fat people unhealthy). Rooted in anti-Blackness, as Eurocentric ideals of feminine beauty were founded in opposition to Black women's bodies, specifically the body of Sarah Baartman.

Feminism—There are many definitions and critiques even within the feminist movement, but my favorite definition is based on scholar and author Chimamanda Ngozi Adichie's notion, which is "a [movement of people] who believe in the social, economic and political equality of all [gender identities]."

Femme—Historically used in the lesbian community but increasingly used by other LGBTTQIA+ folx to describe gender expressions that reclaim, claim, and/or disrupt traditional constructs of femininity inclusive of those who actively embody a femme identity or gender presentation irrespective of sex assigned at birth or sexual orientation.

Filipinx—Pronounced *Phil-i-PEEN-ex*, an inclusive, non-gender-specific way of referring to people who descend from the Philippines.

Folx—An alternate spelling of the noun "folks" that emphasizes inclusion and the existence of all gender identities.

F.Y.I.—Acronym for Fuck Your Intentions (and Feel Your Impact). A reminder to center impact over intention.

Gaslighting—A malicious, often hidden abusive technique causing mental and emotional harm that can occur in any sort of relationship. It causes the recipient to doubt themselves and/or their reality.

Gender—Shared by Shay-Akil McLean and D.A.T.T. as "the range of mental and behavioral characteristics pertaining to, and differentiating between and across, masculinity and femininity. In Western societies, the accepted cultural perspective on gender views women and men as naturally and unequivocally defined categories of being with distinctive psychological & behavioral propensities that can be predicted from their reproductive function" (as set out in Candace West and Don H. Zimmerman, "Doing Gender," *Gender & Society* 1, no. 2 [June 1987]: 126). It is a social construct fundamentally different from the sex one is assigned at birth.

Gender expression—Refers to how a person expresses their gender identity, usually in terms of dress, behaviors, etc., which may or may not correlate to traditional notions of "masculine, feminine," or otherwise.

Gender identity—Defined by the UC Davis LGBTQIA Resource Center as a *sense* of one's self as trans, genderqueer, woman, man, or other (socially constructed) identity, which may or may not correspond with the sex and gender one is assigned at birth. Due to the status quo observance of gender binaries, our gender identity may not align with how we experience power, privilege, or oppression. For example, if a nonbinary person is perceived as masculine in certain settings, then they benefit from patriarchy in those instances.

Gender non-conforming (GNC)—Refers to folx who have a gender identity and/or expression that exists beyond traditional gender "norms."

Genderqueer—Refers to individuals whose identities exist beyond the binary. It can be an umbrella term for anyone between or outside identities of "male" and "female."

Girl+—Refers to girls (cisgender or transgender), as well as any young person who may hold less assigned gender power. The "+" is derived from Bear Hebert to include all those who self-identify as oppressed by misogyny similarly to those who identify as girls, including femme, femme-passing, gender non-conforming, nonbinary, agender, genderqueer, intersex folx, and all those who live outside of identities that terms or language can describe now or in the future.

Grief—The normal and natural humxn emotional response to a loss, change, or lack of change of any kind, usually exhibited by overwhelming sadness and other conflicting feelings. Can be individual and/or collective.

H.A.R.M.—Acronym for Heartbreaking Acts of Racism (or other oppressive bullshit) formerly known as "microaggressions." Magnifies the harm caused by seemingly small bullshit acts of racism or similar violence.

Heteronormativity—Defined by the UC Davis LGBTQIA Resource Center as a set of lifestyle norms, practices, and institutions that promote binary alignment of "biological" sex, gender identity, and gender roles; assume heterosexuality as a fundamental and natural norm; and privilege monogamous, committed relationships and reproductive sex above all other sexual practices.

Heteropatriarchy—A dominant ideology whereby heterosexuality and patriarchy are centered as the social norm, with all other sexualities, gender identities, and sexual expressions deemed deviant and consequently oppressed.

Hispanic—An ethnic identifier to distinguish someone of Spanish descent (island of Hispaniola). Excludes Portuguese descent or language.

Humxn/humxnity—An alternative spelling to "human" removing the reference to "man" to specifically connote humxns and humxnity inclusive of all gender identities.

Institutional racism—Defined by Dismantling Racism Works as the ways in which global structures, systems, policies, and procedures of institutions are founded upon and then promote, reproduce, and perpetuate advantages for white people and the oppression of BI&PoC.

Internalized oppression—Defined by the University of Kansas's Community Tool Box as when people who are targeted, discriminated against, or oppressed over a period of time internalize—believe and make part of their own self-image and internal view of themselves—the myths and misinformation that society communicates to them about their group.

Intersectionality—A term created by law professor Kimberlé Williams Crenshaw, it is a metaphor for understanding the ways that multiple forms of inequity or disadvantage sometimes compound themselves and create obstacles that often are not understood within conventional ways of thinking about anti-racism, feminism, or whatever social justice advocacy structures we have. It's a prism for understanding certain kinds of problems.

Intersectional spirituality—A means to aid us in invoking a multifaceted approach to wellness that promotes culturally informed, racially sensitive, and nonappropriative spiritual teachings and practices as the path forward for healing the collective divide. It provides a framework for embracing spi̇̇ ual and wellness practices as a way to unpack our privileges, help heal our own hearts, and dismantle white supremacy, while also acknowledging the ways they have been and continue to be used to do the exact opposite.

Intersex—Folx born with variations in sex characteristics. Intersex people are as common as redheads and often forced into gender assignment surgery at very young ages without their consent.

Latinx—Pronounced *La-teen-ex*, is a non-gender-specific way of referring to people of Latin descent, including Portuguese. Latinx is an ethnicity, not a race (though both are social constructs).

LGBTTQIA+—An abbreviated acronym for LGBTTQQIAAP+ (defined below).

LGBTTQQIAAP+—The unabbreviated acronym that stands for Lesbian, Gay, Bisexual, Transgender, Two-Spirit, Queer, Questioning, Intersex, Androgynous, Asexual, Pansexual. The "+" is an all-encompassing representation of any other sexual or gender identities people may use or prefer as known now or in the future.

Men+—Refers to men (cisgender or transgender), as well as anyone else who may hold more assigned gender power. The "+" is derived from Bear Hebert to include all those who self-identify as benefiting from patriarchy similarly to those who identify as men, including masculine, masculine-passing, gender nonconforming, nonbinary, agender, genderqueer, intersex folx, and all those who live outside of identities that terms or language can describe now or in the future. This is set out as such because our gender identity may not align with how we experience power, privilege, or oppression (see "gender identity" for more) and that power can also change based on how others do or do not perceive us.

Mental load—An unpaid form of labor comprising all the mental work, organizing, planning, list-making, and mental space holding you do to manage your personal and professional life and those of the ones you love. Can be related to work, managing the household, caretaking responsibilities, etc. Under white supremacist/binary gender roles, women and femmes are expected to carry more mental load.

Microaggression—The everyday verbal, nonverbal, and environmental slights, snubs, or insults, whether intentional or unintentional, which communicate hostile, derogatory, or negative messages to target persons based solely upon their marginalized group membership. It is an act of violence and in no way "micro." See "H.A.R.M."

Misgendering—Defined by the UC Davis LGBTQIA Resource Center as attributing a gender to someone that is incorrect/does not align with their gender identity. It is an act of violence.

Misogynoir—A portmanteau that combines (1) "misogyny" (prejudice against women, girls, femmes, and femme-presenting folx) and (2) "noir" (the French word for "black") as coined by the queer Black feminist Moya Bailey to describe the specific intersection of anti-Blackness and sexism Black women+ face. Common iterations include the labels "angry," "sassy," "promiscuous" ("Jezebel"), or "strong."

Neurotypical—Having a style of neurocognitive functioning that falls within the dominant societal standards of what is deemed "normal." Folx with developmental or other cognitive challenges are deemed to fall outside of the dominant (i.e., "normal") neurotypical umbrella.

Nonbinary (enby)—Most commonly used to describe someone whose gender identity does not fall within the traditional binary gender categories of "male" or "female."

Non-Black Person/People of Color (non-Black PoC or NBPoC)—A person or people racialized as non-white and non-Black including non-Black Indigenous folx, East Asians, and South Asians.

Non-disabled—Folx who do not experience a functional and/or social disadvantage or restriction of an activity caused by contemporary social organization (as created by systemically oppressive forces).

Oppression—Defined by Dismantling Racism Works as the systematic subjugation of one social group by a more powerful social group for the social, economic, and political benefit of the more powerful social group.

Pansexual—A person attracted to people of all gender identities, whether "male, "female," or otherwise (*pan* is Greek for "all").

Patriarchy—Defined by the Canadian Race Relations Foundation as the norms, values, beliefs, structures, and systems that grant power, privilege, and superiority to those who identify or appear as "men" or masculine, and thereby marginalize and subordinate those who identify or appear as "women" or feminine.

Person/People of Color (PoC)—A highly diverse and grossly over-categorized grouping of people from a variety of socially constructed races including Black, Indigenous, South Asian, and

East Asian. Folx from marginalized ethnicities including Latinx and Jewish are sometimes included (which I disagree with), and it is often used to intentionally erase Black people (for example, referring to the "experiences of PoC," which erases anti-Blackness). Whenever possible, avoid this term and specifically identify the race or ethnicity you are referring to. Also see "BI&PoC."

Poor—A reclaimed, once pejorative, word to describe folx economically oppressed under white supremacist capitalist systems of inequity. A person is considered poor if their income, if any, falls below that required to meet their basic needs. Poverty is a systemic issue. In order for some people to amass wealth, there must be people who are poor.

Power—The legitimate and legal ability to access and directly control or influence all institutions sanctioned by the state often held solely by white or white-passing people.

Prejudice—A feeling or prejudgment toward a person or group member based solely on that person's group membership. Not always negative, but often is.

Privilege—A special right, advantage, or immunity (often unearned) granted or available only to a particular person or group of people often to the detriment of others. Privilege can be based on race, gender identity, ability, sexual orientation, class, immigration status, language, nationality, religion, ethnicity, beauty, and more.

Pronouns—Linguistic tools used to refer to someone in the third person that are often tied to gender in English and some other languages. Pronouns include: they/them/theirs, ze/hir/hirs, she/her/hers, he/him/his, and any others as folx identify now or in the future.

Queer—This term is a reclamation of a pejorative word. It is intentionally abstract in meaning but is often used as an umbrella term to encompass all non-heterosexual and/or non-cisgender identities.

Race—An ever-evolving, socially constructed, nonscientific grouping of humxns based on shared physical qualities created for political purposes to benefit the white and wealthy. There are traditionally five socially constructed "races": white, Black, Indigenous, East Asian, and South Asian, and folx can belong to more than one. Note: the classic five races are not exhaustive and do not adequately account for West Asian or North African folx, among others.

Racial justice—Defined by Race Forward as "the systematic fair treatment of people of all races resulting in equitable opportunities and outcomes for all." Racial justice—or racial equity—goes beyond "anti-racism." It is not just the absence of discrimination and inequities, but also the presence of deliberate systems and supports to achieve and sustain racial equity through proactive and preventative measures. It is the proactive reinforcement of policies, practices, attitudes, and actions that produce equitable power, access, opportunities, treatment, impacts, and outcomes for all. Racial justice requires dismantling white supremacy, which necessitates ending all forms of oppression and must center and prioritize those who are most oppressed, being queer and trans, poor, fat, disabled, old, undereducated, non–English speaking, and otherwise oppressed Black and Indigenous women+.

Racism—A global system of race-based oppression and discrimination of BI&PoC created by and for the benefit of white people. The culmination of prejudice, privilege, and power as only held by white or white-passing individuals.

Sex—A nonbiological, medically constructed categorization usually assigned at birth (or via ultrasound) based on socially agreed upon biological criteria, most commonly via the external appearance of genitalia.

Soulcare—The actions or inactions we undertake in order to best care for our souls and highest selves. It is part of communal care and understands that we must care for one another, as well as ourselves, in order for any of us to truly be well. It is about giving ourselves what we need in order to nourish our beings so that we can get into the world and demand a more equitable planet for *all*.

Spirit animal—An appropriated concept assigned to the sacred rituals of some Indigenous tribes by colonial forces. The tribes that do have a concept related to a "spirit animal" have specific traditions that go along with it, as the spirit serves a specific function in their belief system. Not to be used by anyone outside of such tribes. Try "animal friend" or "spirit guide."

Spiritual Activism—Daily, active, ongoing anti-oppressive thought, speech, and actions informed by a connection with a secular or non-secular spiritual power. It begins with deep inner work, which can be supported by culturally informed and culturally appreciative spiritual practices such as meditation, breathwork, energy healing, and yoga.

Spiritual bypassing—Defined by John Welwood as the tendency to use spiritual ideas and practices to sidestep or avoid facing unresolved emotional issues, psychological wounds, and unfinished developmental tasks.

Spirituality—Defined by Brené Brown as having to do with deep feelings and convictions, including a person's sense of peace, purpose, connection to others, and understanding of the meaning and value of life; may or may not be associated with a particular set of beliefs or practices.

Standpoint theory—A feminist theoretical perspective that argues that knowledge stems from social position such that the most marginalized have the best and most objective ability to assert knowledge.

Status quo—The existing state of affairs or way things are now, especially regarding social or political issues. To maintain the status quo is to be resistant to change.

Systemic racism—Includes the policies and practices entrenched in established institutions, which result in the exclusion or promotion of designated groups.

Transgender/trans—Defined by Trans Student Educational Resources as encompassing the many gender identities of those who do not identify or exclusively identify with their sex assigned at birth. Other terms that may be deemed trans include: "transsexual," "gender non-conforming," "gender nonbinary," "agender," "androgynous," "genderqueer," and "genderfluid," among many others. Being transgender is not indicative of gender expression, sexual orientation, hormonal makeup, physical anatomy, or how one is perceived in daily life.

Two-Spirit—An umbrella term originated by Indigenous North American tribes to honor the fluid and diverse nature of gender and attraction and its connection to community and spirituality. In most tribes, Two-Spirits were neither "men" nor "women"; they occupied a distinct, alternative gender status, but the distinct meaning is tribe specific.

Unfuckwithable—The state of leaning into your power, owning your privilege, using your voice, and prioritizing your needs so you can best serve the collective, particularly those most marginalized.

Weaponized kindness—Created by Leesa Renee Hall, this is using the quality of being friendly, gentle, tender, or considerate as a tool to guilt someone into abandoning their justified anger, loving boundaries, or much-needed self-care.

White centering—The common, status quo tendency to center whiteness and white people's feelings, comfort, well-being, and safety above those of BI&PoC, particularly in discussions about race and racism. An act of white supremacy.

White entitlement—The belief that BI&PoC, especially Black women and femmes, need to educate white folx about race, speak to white folx kindly and compassionately about race, and otherwise behave in a way that allows white people to remain coddled and comfortable about their power and privilege.

White exceptionalism—The false idea or belief held by a white person that they are a "good" white person and somehow exceptional and thus excluded from benefiting from and perpetuating systems of white supremacy and causing BI&PoC harm. Exceptionalism also means white folx believe they have acquired dominance as a racial group because they "worked harder," as opposed to having exploited Black and Indigenous communities for economic advancement. A form of violence.

White fragility—Coined by Robin DiAngelo, it is a state in which even a minimum amount of racial stress becomes intolerable, triggering a range of defensive moves, like silence, anger, guilt, or leaving the stress-inducing situation, that reinstate white racial equilibrium. This is a form of emotional violence and this term severely undermines the abusive harm these behaviors inflict, which is why I have renamed it "white wildness" (see definition on page 338).

White gaze—A term created by Toni Morrison to describe the pervasive cultural assumption that the reader of a work is white and the resulting impact it creates for all, especially Black folx. The white gaze exists beyond reading and writing and includes the inherently white supremacist perspective of all white people and the ways in which they view BI&PoC, which causes BI&PoC harm.

White innocence—The false belief held by a white person that they are not implicated in or perpetuating white supremacy and are therefore "innocent" in the global systems of racial oppression of BI&PoC. A form of violence.

Whiteness—The state of both being white and perpetuating white supremacy. Whiteness is a constantly shifting boundary separating those who are entitled to have certain race-based privileges from those whose exploitation and vulnerability to violence are justified by their not being deemed white.

White-passing—Light-skinned BI&PoC who are perceived as "white" in some or many contexts and therefore possess white privilege in those circumstances. Being white-passing can be fluid (can depend on your racial expression, who you are around, etc.), or it may be fixed, particularly when white-passing BI&PoC reject, avoid, or deny their BI&PoC ancestry. Being white-passing need not in any way invalidate your racial or cultural identity, but it does mean you possess power and privilege that darker-skinned BI&PoC do not.

White privilege—Refers to the unquestioned and unearned set of advantages, entitlements, benefits, and choices bestowed on people solely because they are white (as beneficiaries of historical conquests) or white-passing. Generally white people are unaware they hold this privilege.

White silence—When white or white-passing folx witness racism but refuse to say or do anything about it. A form of violence.

White supremacist culture—An ethos of values and characteristics that helps to perpetuate a paradigm of race-based and other oppression. Characteristics include: individualism, perfectionism, binary thinking, power hoarding, right to comfort, exploitation, extraction, and more.

White supremacist heteropatriarchy—A society or culture dominated by the superiority and dominance of white people and cisgender heterosexual men that results in the oppression of all others, particularly queer and trans Black and Indigenous women and femmes.

White supremacy—The common, status quo, globally held, and often unconscious belief that white people, and thus white ideas, beliefs, actions, and ideologies, are in some way superior to all other races (especially Black and Indigenous folx). White supremacy is behind many, if not all, forms of oppression, including capitalism, fatphobia, ableism, homophobia, transphobia, and others that originated with delineating "whiteness" from "Blackness" or "Native-ness."

White violence—All forms of emotional, mental, spiritual, and physical violence perpetuated by white folx, intentionally or otherwise, toward BI&PoC, including white entitlement, white solidarity, white silence, white wildness, etc.

White-washing—When white folx, as a group and as individuals, appropriate the practices, traditions, and teachings of communities of color and transform them into something more palatable or comfortable for them. BI&PoC can also white-wash their own or other BI&PoC traditions to make them more commercial or palatable to white people.

White wildness—The fragile and ferocious defensive response white folx commonly have in regard to race or racism.

Womanism—Created by Alice Walker, it is a social theory based on and centering the history and experiences of women+ of color, particularly Black women+. It acknowledges that Blackness is not a component of the feminism of Black women+, but instead the Blackness of a Black woman+ is the lens through which we understand our femininity.

Woman+/Women+ of Color (WoC)—A highly diverse and grossly over-categorized grouping of women+ (usually referring to cis women) from a variety of socially constructed races including Black, Indigenous, South Asian, and East Asian. Folx from marginalized ethnicities, including Latinx and Jewish, are sometimes included (which I disagree with), and it is often used to intentionally erase Black women+ (for example, referring to the "experiences of WoC," which erases misogynoir). Whenever possible, avoid this term and specifically identify the race or ethnicity you are referring to.

Women+—Refers to women (cisgender or transgender), as well as anyone else who may hold less assigned gender power. The "+" is derived from Bear Hebert to include all those who self-identify as being oppressed by misogyny similar to those who identify as women, including femme, femme-passing, gender non-conforming, nonbinary, agender, genderqueer, intersex folx, and all those who live outside of identities that terms or language can describe now or in the future. This is set out as such because our gender identity may not align with how we experience power, privilege, or oppression and that power can also change based on how others do or do not perceive us (see "gender identity" for more).

Womxn—An alternative spelling to "women" or "woman" that some (often cis women) believe is more inclusive and represents cis and trans women as well as other identities historically excluded from conversations and movements about women such as BI&WoC and LGBTTQIA+ women. Some also include those oppressed as women, such as femmes or femme-passing people, in this definition. Many trans activists argue this spelling is transphobic, as trans women are just women, and those who do not identify as women, such as femmes or nonbinary folx, should be separately named.

NOTES

Introduction

1 Mickey ScottBey Jones, *An Invitation to Brave Space*, accessed August 20, 2020, https://onbeing.org/wp-content/uploads/2019/10/An-Invitation-to-Brave-Space.pdf.

one—Me, Myself & I

1 Rebecca Epstein, Jamilia J. Blake, and Thalia González, *Girlhood Interrupted: The Erasure of Black Girls' Childhood*, Georgetown Law Center on Poverty and Inequality, 2017, https://www.law.georgetown.edu/poverty-inequality-center/wp-content/uploads/sites/14/2017/08/girlhood-interrupted.pdf, p. 1.

2 Ibid.

3 Mohan B. Kumar and Michael Tjepkema, *Suicide among First Nations People, Métis and Inuit (2011–2016): Findings from the 2011 Canadian Census Health and Environment Cohort (CanCHEC)*, Statistics Canada, June 28, 2019, https://www150.statcan.gc.ca/n1/pub/99-011-x/99-011-x2019001-eng.htm.

4 James Baldwin et al., "The Negro in American Culture," *CrossCurrents* 11, no. 3 (Summer 1961): 205. Available at https://www.jstor.org/stable/24456864?seq=1.

5 Jennifer Mullan (decolonizingtherapy), "We Are Fucking Exhausted," Instagram, April 23, 2019, https://www.instagram.com/p/BwnqwefA0WC/?utm_source=ig_web_copy_link.

6 News clip originally aired on Fox29.com (date unknown). Available at 4 Ben Media, "Black Protester in Charlotte Tells Reporter That White

Lives Don't Matter," YouTube, September 25, 2016, https://www.you tube.com/watch?v=DFxypvk0u88.

7 Ibid.

8 Dan Merica, "Trump Says Both Sides to Blame amid Charlottesville Backlash," CNN, August 16, 2017, https://www.cnn.com/2017/08/15 /politics/trump-charlottesville-delay/index.html.

9 Arlie Russell Hochschild, *The Managed Heart: Commercialization of Human Feeling* (Berkeley: University of California Press, 2012), p. 7.

10 Shereen Masoud, "When Non-Black PoC Hide behind Blatant White Supremacy to Ignore Their Own Complicity," Afropunk, November 17, 2017, https://afropunk.com/2017/11/non-black-poc-hide-behind-blatant -white-supremacy-ignore-complicity/.

two—Where We Get Stuck

1 Katty Kay and Claire Shipman, "The Confidence Gap," *Atlantic*, May 2014, https://www.theatlantic.com/magazine/archive/2014/05/the-confi dence-gap/359815/.

2 Ibid.

3 Judith E. Glaser, "Your Brain Is Hooked on Being Right," *Harvard Business Review*, February 28, 2013, https://hbr.org/2013/02/break-your -addiction-to-being.

4 Jalal al-Din Rumi, "A Great Wagon," in *The Essential Rumi Selections*, trans. Coleman Barks (Edison, NJ: Castle Books, 1995), p. 36.

5 Susan Kelley, "Morisson Speaks on Evil, Language and the 'White Gaze,'" *Cornell Chronicle*, March 11, 2013, https://news.cornell.edu /stories/2013/03/morrison-speaks-evil-language-and-white-gaze.

6 Toni Morrison, *Playing in the Dark: Whiteness and the Literary Imagina- tion* (New York: Vintage, 1992), p. 45.

7 Audre Lorde, "Poetry Is Not a Luxury," in *Sister Outsider* (Berkeley, CA: Crossing Press, 2007), p. 39.

three—White Supremacy Starts Within

1 "Study: White and Black Children Biased toward Lighter Skin," CNN, May 14, 2010, https://www.cnn.com/2010/US/05/13/doll.study/index .html.

2 "Personality Set for Life by 1st Grade, Study Suggests," Live Science, August 6, 2010, https://www.livescience.com/8432-personality-set-life -1st-grade-study-suggests.html.

3 Manda Mahoney, "The Subconscious Mind of the Consumer (and How

to Reach It)," *Working Knowledge*, January 13, 2003, https://hbswk
.hbs.edu/item/the-subconscious-mind-of-the-consumer-and-how-to
-reach-it.

4 Mary Elizabeth Dean, "Inner Child: What Is It, What Happened to
It, and How Can I Fix It?," BetterHelp, April 10, 2020, https://www
.betterhelp.com/advice/therapy/inner-child-what-is-it-what-happened
-to-it-and-how-can-i-fix-it/.

5 "C.G. Jung: 'One Does Not Become . . . ,'" *Jung Currents*, http://jung
currents.com/jung-shadow-darkness-conscious. (From Carl Jung, "The
Philosophical Tree," in *Alchemical Studies* 13, *Collected Works of C. G. Jung*
[London: Routledge, 1967].)

6 Vanissar Tarakali, "Surviving Oppression; Healing Oppression," *Tarakali Education* (blog), https://vanissarsomatics.com/surviving-oppression
-healing-oppression/.

7 Ibid.

8 Claudia Rankine, "The Condition of Black Life Is One of Mourning,"
New York Times, June 22, 2015, https://www.nytimes.com/2015/06/22
/magazine/the-condition-of-black-life-is-one-of-mourning.html.

9 Lorde, *Sister Outsider*, p. 62.

10 Mab Segrest, *Born to Belonging: Writings on Spirit and Justice* (New Bruns-
wick, NJ: Rutgers University Press, 2002), p. 247.

11 Adapted from Tarakali, "Surviving Oppression."

four—White Supremacy Runs the World

1 "Genetics vs. Genomics Fact Sheet," National Human Genome Research Institute, last updated September 7, 2018, https://www.genome
.gov/about-genomics/fact-sheets/Genetics-vs-Genomics.

2 Bridget Alex, "With Ancient Human DNA, Africa's Deep History Is
Coming to Light," *Discover*, February 8, 2019, https://www.discover
magazine.com/planet-earth/with-ancient-human-dna-africas-deep-his
tory-is-coming-to-light.

3 Janaya Future Khan, "Janaya Future Khan's Guide to Understanding
White Privilege," *Vogue*, June 3, 2020, https://www.vogue.co.uk/arts
-and-lifestyle/article/janaya-future-khan-privilege.

4 Ana Gonzalez-Barrera, "Hispanics with Darker Skin Are More Likely
to Experience Discrimination Than Those with Lighter Skin," Pew Research Center, July 2, 2019, https://www.pewresearch.org/fact-tank/2019
/07/02/hispanics-with-darker-skin-are-more-likely-to-experience-dis
crimination-than-those-with-lighter-skin/.

5 Equality Institute (theequalityinstitute), "The Pyramid of White Supremacy," Instagram, March 20, 2019, https://www.instagram.com/theequalityinstitute/p/BvQiQ5UFH3F/.

6 Ibid.

7 Preeti Varathan, "For One Year, All the South Asians in the US Were Considered 'White,'" Quartz India, September 2, 2017, https://qz.com/india/1066287/for-one-year-all-the-south-asians-in-the-us-were-considered-white/.

8 Sarah Parvini and Ellis Simani, "Are Arabs and Iranians White? Census Says Yes, but Many Disagree," *Los Angeles Times*, March 28, 2019, https://www.latimes.com/projects/la-me-census-middle-east-north-africa-race/.

9 Adapted from Nicki Lisa Cole, "The Definition of Whiteness in American Society," ThoughtCo., November 8, 2019, https://www.thoughtco.com/whiteness-definition-3026743.

10 Paula Rogo, "Amanda Seales Hilariously Explains the Difference between White People and People Who Happen to Be White," *Essence*, January 26, 2019, https://www.essence.com/celebrity/amanda-seales-white-people-yes-girl-podcast-hbo-comedy-special/.

11 Bernard Marr, "How Much Data Do We Create Every Day? The Mind-Blowing Stats Everyone Should Read," *Forbes*, May 21, 2018, https://www.forbes.com/sites/bernardmarr/2018/05/21/how-much-data-do-we-create-every-day-the-mind-blowing-stats-everyone-should-read/#78427b7460ba.

12 James Baldwin, *Nobody Knows My Name* (New York: Dial Press, 1961), p. 224.

13 Adapted from "White Supremacy Culture," Dismantling Racism Works, https://www.dismantlingracism.org/white-supremacy-culture.html (accessed July 15, 2020).

14 "2018 Hate Crime Statistics: Victims," Federal Bureau of Investigation, Department of Justice, https://ucr.fbi.gov/hate-crime/2018/topic-pages/victims.

15 Cleuci de Oliveira, "Brazil's New Problem with Blackness," *Foreign Policy*, April 5, 2017, https://foreignpolicy.com/2017/04/05/brazils-new-problem-with-blackness-affirmative-action/.

16 John Gramlich, "Black Imprisonment Rate in the U.S. Has Fallen by a Third since 2006," Pew Research Center, May 6, 2020, https://www.pewresearch.org/fact-tank/2020/05/06/black-imprisonment-rate-in-the-u-s-has-fallen-by-a-third-since-2006/.

17 Audra Williams, "Race and Food Insecurity in Canada," Centre for Social Innovation, November 27, 2019, https://socialinnovation.org/race
-and-food-insecurity-in-canada/.

18 "Black Caribbean Pupils Three Times More Likely to Be Excluded,"
Full Fact, October 5, 2016, https://fullfact.org/education/black-carib
bean-pupils-three-times-more-likely-be-excluded/.

19 Jasmine Cameron-Chileshe, "Black Mothers Are Five Times More
Likely to Die in Childbirth—So What's Being Done?" *Telegraph*,
September 22, 2019, https://www.telegraph.co.uk/health-fitness/body
/black-mothers-five-times-likely-die-childbirth-done/.

20 Roni Caryn Rabin, "Huge Racial Disparities Found in Deaths Linked
to Pregnancy," *New York Times*, May 7, 2019, https://www.nytimes.com
/2019/05/07/health/pregnancy-deaths-.html.

21 "Conversations with White People: Dialogues about Race," panel discuss-
sion led by IC Bailey, A Different Booklist, Toronto, December 5, 2019.

22 Alaina E. Roberts, "How Native Americans Adopted Slavery from
White Settlers," Al Jazeera, December 26, 2018, https://www.aljazeera
.com/indepth/opinion/native-americans-adopted-slavery-white-settlers
-181225180750948.html.

23 David M. Halbfinger and Isabel Kershner, "After a Police Shooting,
Ethiopian Israelis Seek a 'Black Lives Matter' Reckoning," *New York
Times*, July 13, 2019, https://www.nytimes.com/2019/07/13/world/mid
dleeast/ethiopian-israeli-protests-racism.html.

24 Faulty race science created the stereotype of "the big Black woman"
and associated fatness with being African. "Thinness became a form of
American exceptionalism," Sabrina Strings says (*Fearing the Black Body:
The Racial Origins of Fat Phobia* [New York: New York University Press,
2019], p. 11).

25 Combahee River Collective, "The Combahee River Collective Statement," https://americanstudies.yale.edu/sites/default/files/files/Keyword
%20Coalition_Readings.pdf (accessed July 15, 2020).

26 Kyle Powys Whyte, "White Allies, Let's Be Honest About Decolonization," *YES!*, April 3, 2018, https://www.yesmagazine.org/issue/decolo
nize/2018/04/03/white-allies-lets-be-honest-about-decolonization/.

27 Robert M. Poole, "What Became of the Taíno?" *Smithsonian Magazine*,
October 2011, https://www.smithsonianmag.com/travel/what-became
-of-the-taino-73824867/.

28 "Jesuit Reduction," Wikipedia, https://en.wikipedia.org/wiki/Jesuit_re
duction (accessed July 15, 2020).

29 Paul Spoonley, "Ethnic and Religious Intolerance: Intolerance towards Māori," Te Ara—The Encyclopedia of New Zealand, http://www.TeAra .govt.nz/en/ethnic-and-religious-intolerance/page-1 (accessed July 16, 2020).

30 J. R. Miller, "Residential Schools in Canada," The Canadian Encyclopedia, last edited June 25, 2020, https://www.thecanadianencyclopedia.ca /en/article/residential-schools (accessed July 15, 2020).

31 "A Brief Definition of Decolonization and Indigenization," Indigenous Corporate Training Inc., March 29, 2017, https://www.ictinc.ca/blog /a-brief-definition-of-decolonization-and-indigenization (accessed July 15, 2020).

32 Eve Tuck and K. Wayne Yang, "Decolonization Is Not a Metaphor," *Decolonization: Indigeneity, Education & Society* 1, no. 1 (2012): 3, https:// www.latrobe.edu.au/staff-profiles/data/docs/fjcollins.pdf.

33 National Association of Independent Schools (NAIS), "Kimberlé Crenshaw: What Is Intersectionality?" YouTube, June 22, 2018, https://www .youtube.com/watch?v=ViDtnfQ9FHc.

34 Chuck Collins et al., *Dreams Deferred: How Enriching the 1% Widens the Racial Wealth Divide*, Institute for Policy Studies, 2019, https:// ips-dc.org/wp-content/uploads/2019/01/IPS_RWD-Report_FINAL -1.15.19.pdf.

35 Dedrick Asante Muhammed, Rogelio Tec, and Kathy Ramirez, "Racial Wealth Snapshot: American Indians/Native Americans," National Community Reinvestment Coalition, November 18, 2019, https://ncrc .org/racial-wealth-snapshot-american-indians-native-americans/.

36 John Paul Tasker, "Inquiry into Missing and Murdered Indigenous Women Issues Final Report with Sweeping Calls for Change," CBC News, June 3, 2019, https://www.cbc.ca/news/politics/mmiwg-inquiry -deliver-final-report-justice-reforms-1.5158223.

37 Catherine Edwards, "The Little-Known Role Sweden Played in the Colonial Slave Trade," *Local* (Sweden), June 15, 2020, https://www.thelo cal.se/20200615/how-can-sweden-better-face-up-to-its-colonial-past.

38 Jo Becker, "The Global Machine behind the Rise of Far-Right Nationalism," *New York Times*, August 10, 2019, https://www.nytimes.com/2019 /08/10/world/europe/sweden-immigration-nationalism.html.

39 Mark Townsend, "Black People '40 Times More Likely' to Be Stopped and Searched in UK," *Guardian*, May 4, 2019, https://www.theguardian .com/law/2019/may/04/stop-and-search-new-row-racial-bias.

40 Minda Zetlin, "Racism Helped Drive Prince Harry and Meghan Markle Out of the U.K. and Away from the Royal Family," *Inc.*, January 11,

2020, https://www.inc.com/minda-zetlin/prince-harry-meghan-markle -leaving-uk-royal-family-racism-tabloids.html.

41 "Slavery in Brazil," Wikipedia, https://en.wikipedia.org/wiki/Slavery _in_Brazil (accessed July 20, 2020).

42 Maria Laura Canineu and Andrea Carvalho, "Bolsonaro's Plan to Legalize Crimes against Indigenous Peoples," Human Rights Watch, March 1, 2020, https://www.hrw.org/news/2020/03/01/bolsonaros-plan -legalize-crimes-against-indigenous-peoples#.

five—Inheriting Mama Trauma

1 *13th*, directed by Ava DuVernay, Netflix, 2016.

2 "The Effects of Stress on Your Body," WebMD, https://www.webmd .com/balance/stress-management/effects-of-stress-on-your-body (accessed July 15, 2020).

3 Iyanla Vanzant, *In the Meantime: Finding Yourself and the Love That You Want* (New York: Simon & Schuster, 1998).

4 Andrew Curry, "Parents' Emotional Trauma May Change Their Children's Biology. Studies in Mice Show How," *Science*, July 18, 2019, https://www.sciencemag.org/news/2019/07/parents-emotional-trauma -may-change-their-children-s-biology-studies-mice-show-how.

5 Mary Annette Pember, "Trauma May Be Woven into DNA of Native Americans," Indian Country Today, October 3, 2017, https://indian countrytoday.com/archive/trauma-may-be-woven-into-dna-of-native -americans-CbiAxpzar0WkMALhjrcGVQ.

6 "Bonnie Duran, Director of the Center for Indigenous Health Research," interview, Indigenous Wellness Research Institute National Center of Excellence, November 1, 2013, https://iwri.org/bonnie-duran -director-of-the-center-for-indigenous-health-research/.

7 Joy DeGruy, *Post Traumatic Slave Syndrome: America's Legacy of Enduring Injury and Healing* (Portland, OR: Joy DeGruy Publications, 2017).

8 Cindy George, "Do You Have Post-Traumatic Slave Syndrome?," *Ebony*, August 26, 2015, https://www.ebony.com/health/do-you-have-post-trau matic-slave-syndrome/.

9 Ibid.

10 Tarakali, "Surviving Oppression."

11 Maria Popova, "The Science of How Our Minds and Our Bodies Converge in the Healing of Trauma," *Brain Pickings*, https://www.brainpick ings.org/2016/06/20/the-body-keeps-the-score-van-der-kolk/ (accessed July 15, 2020).

12 "Preventing Adverse Childhood Experiences," Centers for Disease

Control and Prevention, last reviewed April 3, 2020, https://www.cdc
.gov/violenceprevention/aces/fastfact.html.

13 Aubrey Marcus, "How to Deal with Addiction with Dr. Gabor Maté,"
YouTube, September 15, 2017, https://www.youtube.com/watch?v=c59x
FqlO2cA.

14 Jennifer Weinberg, "Mind-Body Connection: Understanding the Psycho-
Emotional Roots of Disease," Chopra, April 26, 2019, https://chopra.com
/articles/mind-body-connection-understanding-the-psycho-emotion
al-roots-of-disease.

15 Martin Caparrotta, "Dr. Gabor Maté on Childhood Trauma, the Real
Cause of Anxiety and Our 'Insane' Culture," Human Window, July 1,
2020, https://humanwindow.com/dr-gabor-mate-interview-childhood
-trauma-anxiety-culture/.

16 "Easing the Dangers of Childbirth for Black Women," *New York Times*,
April 20, 2018, https://www.nytimes.com/2018/04/20/opinion/child
birth-black-women-mortality.html.

17 Jason Silverstein, "I Don't Feel Your Pain: A Failure of Empathy Perpetuates Racial Disparities," *Slate*, June 27, 2013, https://slate.com
/technology/2013/06/racial-empathy-gap-people-dont-perceive-pain
-in-other-races.html.

18 Patia Braithwaite, "Biological Weathering and Its Deadly Effect on
Black Mothers," *Self*, September 30, 2019, https://www.self.com/story
/weathering-and-its-deadly-effect-on-black-mothers.

19 Kwame McKenzie, "Toronto's Black Community Faces Far Greater
Risk of Having Serious Mental Health Problems," *Toronto Star*, January 27, 2020, https://www.thestar.com/opinion/contributors/2020/01/27
/torontos-black-community-faces-far-greater-risk-of-having-serious
-mental-health-problems.html.

20 *State of the World's Indigenous Peoples: Indigenous Peoples' Access to Health
Services*, United Nations, https://www.un.org/esa/socdev/unpfii/docu
ments/2016/Docs-updates/SOWIP_Health.pdf, p. 97.

21 Tracey Bignall et al., *Racial Disparities in Mental Health: Literature and
Evidence Review*, Race Equality Foundation, 2019, https://raceequality
foundation.org.uk/wp-content/uploads/2020/03/mental-health-report
-v5-2.pdf.

22 "Coronavirus Disease 2019 (COVID-19): Health Equity Considerations and Racial and Ethnic Minority Groups," Centers for Disease
Control and Prevention, last updated July 24, 2020, https://www.cdc
.gov/coronavirus/2019-ncov/need-extra-precautions/racial-ethnic-mi
norities.html.

six—Getting Spiritually Activated

1 Dan Schwabel, "Brené Brown: How Vulnerability Can Make Our Lives Better," *Forbes*, April 21, 2013, https://www.forbes.com/sites/dan schawbel/2013/04/21/brene-brown-how-vulnerability-can-make-our -lives-better/#6a4dc60b36c7.

seven—Unearthing Our Internalized Oppression

1 Marya Axner, "Section 3. Healing from the Effects of Internalized Oppression," Community Tool Box, Center for Community Health and Development, University of Kansas, https://ctb.ku.edu/en/table-of-con tents/culture/cultural-competence/healing-from-interalized-oppression /main.

2 "Quotes by Steve Biko," South African History Online, https://www .sahistory.org.za/archive/quotes-steve-biko (accessed July 16, 2020).

3 Adapted from "Internalizations," Dismantling Racism Works, https:// www.dismantlingracism.org/internalizations.html.

4 Adapted from Tarakali, "Surviving Oppression."

5 Lorde, *Sister Outsider*, p. 41.

eight—Spiritual Bypassing & Emotional Violence

1 John Welwood, "Human Nature, Buddha Nature: On Spiritual Bypassing, Relationship, and the Dharma," interview by Tina Fossella, *Tricycle Magazine*, Spring 2011, http://www.johnwelwood.com/articles/TRIC _interview_uncut.pdf, p. 1.

2 Corinna Rosella (riseupgoodwitch), "Maybe You Manifested It . . . ," Instagram, November 20, 2018, https://www.instagram.com/p/Bqa4o NaHYwb/?utm_source=ig_web_copy_link.

3 "Publications—Books: *White Fragility: Why It's So Hard for White People to Talk About Race*," Robin DiAngelo, PhD, https://robindiangelo.com /publications/.

4 Leesa Renee Hall (leesareneehall), "Weaponized Kindess," Instagram, November 17, 2019, https://www.instagram.com/p/B4-OML0n9Bh.

5 Soraya Chemaly, *Rage Becomes Her: The Power of Women's Anger* (New York: Atria, 2018), p. 18.

6 Liz Plank, *For the Love of Men: A New Vision for Mindful Masculinity* (New York: St. Martin's Press, 2019), p. 106.

7 Meenadchi, *Decolonizing Non-Violent Communication* (Los Angeles: CO-Conspirator Press with the Women's Center for Creative Work, 2019).

nine—Spirituality, Anger & Activism

1 Brené Brown, "Defining Spirituality," Brené Brown.com, March 27, 2018, https://brenebrown.com/blog/2018/03/27/defining-spirituality/.

2 Jamila Osman, "Colonialism, Explained," *Teen Vogue*, November 22, 2017, https://www.teenvogue.com/story/colonialism-explained.

3 "White Supremacy Culture," Showing Up for Racial Justice, https://www.showingupforracialjustice.org/white-supremacy-culture.html (accessed July 16, 2020).

4 Mary Hynes, "'It Was Devastating': Queer Evangelical Survives Gay Conversion Therapy and Helps Others Heal," *Tapestry*, CBC Radio, February 14, 2020, https://www.cbc.ca/radio/tapestry/life-changing-moments-1.5464890/it-was-devastating-queer-evangelical-survives-gay-conversion-therapy-and-helps-others-heal-1.5464893.

5 McKensie Mack (mckensiemack), "That Rage Is Not about Control . . ." Instagram, June 30, 2020, https://www.instagram.com/p/CCEHIhLjSQe/.

6 Solange, "Mad," *A Seat at the Table*, Saint Records/Columbia Records, 2016.

ten—Intersectional Spirituality

1 Brand Minds, "The Health & Wellness Industry Is Now Worth $4.2 Trillion," Medium, April 25, 2019, https://medium.com/manager-mint/the-health-wellness-industry-is-now-worth-4-2-trillion-866bf4703b3c.

2 Nicole Cardoza, "From Magazine Controversy to $1M Raise," Medium, September 12, 2019, https://medium.com/@nicolecardoza/from-magazine-controversy-to-1m-raise-9e57927762da.

3 Susanna Barkataki, "The Unbearable Whiteness of Being *Yoga Journal*: Roots, Reverence, Representation and Reparations," Susanna Barkataki.com, June 26, 2019, https://www.susannabarkataki.com/post/the-unbearable-whiteness-of-being-yoga-journal-roots-reverence-representation-and-reparations.

4 Gaia Staff, "Kemetic Yoga: Resurrection of an African Legacy," Gaia, October 26, 2016, https://www.gaia.com/article/kemetic-yoga.

5 Susanna Barkataki, "What Is the Difference between Cultural Appropriation and Cultural Appreciation?," Susanna Barkataki.com, August 27, 2019, https://www.susannabarkataki.com/post/what-is-the-difference-between-cultural-appropriation-and-cultural-appreciation.

6 Brittney C. Cooper, *Eloquent Rage: A Black Feminist Discovers Her Superpower* (New York: St. Martin's Press, 2018), p. 47.

7 Susanna Barkataki, "How to Decolonize Your Yoga Practice," *HuffPost*, March 2, 2015, https://www.huffpost.com/entry/how-to-decolonize -your-yo_b_6776896.

8 Haley Lewis, "Indigenous People Want Brands to Stop Selling Sage and Smudge Kits," *HuffPost*, November 30, 2018, https://www.huffingtonpost .ca/2018/11/29/indigenous-people-sage-and-smudge-kits_a_23602571/.

9 Tess McClure, "Dark Crystals: The Brutal Reality behind a Booming Wellness Craze," *Guardian*, September 17, 2019, https://www.theguard ian.com/lifeandstyle/2019/sep/17/healing-crystals-wellness-mining -madagascar.

10 Lewis, "Indigenous People Want Brands to Stop Selling Sage and Smudge Kits."

11 "New Study Reveals Wellness Tourism Now a $639 Billion Market— to Reach $919 Billion by 2022," Global Wellness Institute, November 6, 2018, https://globalwellnessinstitute.org/press-room/press-releases /new-study-reveals-wellness-tourism-now-a-639-billion-market/.

12 Chris Lowe, "The Trouble with Tribe," *Teaching Tolerance*, Spring 2001, https://www.tolerance.org/magazine/spring-2001/the-trouble-with -tribe.

13 La Sarmiento, "Forgiveness from the Heart," Liberate: Black Medita- tion App (Zen Compass, 2020).

twelve—Magnifying "Microaggressions"

1 Derald Wing Sue, "Microaggressions: More Than Just Race," *Psychol- ogy Today*, November 17, 2010, https://www.psychologytoday.com/ca /blog/microaggressions-in-everyday-life/201011/microaggressions-more -just-race.

2 Ibid.

3 Alia E. Dastagir, "Microaggressions Don't Just 'Hurt Your Feelings,'" *USA Today*, February 28, 2018, https://www.usatoday.com/story/news /2018/02/28/what-microaggressions-small-slights-serious-consequences /362754002/.

4 Cooper, *Eloquent Rage*, p. 204.

5 Ericka Hart (ihartericka), "Call Outs Are Love . . . ," Instagram, June 30, 2020, https://www.instagram.com/p/CCEWUlMgdLV/?utm_source= ig_web_copy_link.

6 Jamie Samhan, "Michelle Obama Talks About Overcoming Being Labelled an 'Angry Black Woman,'" *ET Canada*, July 7, 2019, https://etcanada.com /news/472066/michelle-obama-talks-about-overcoming-being-labelled -an-angry-black-woman/.

7 Sydette Harry (@Blackamazon), "Why Do I Have . . . ," Twitter, June 16, 2017, https://twitter.com/Blackamazon/status/875817415862562816.

8 Tarana J. Burke (@TaranaBurke), "Apologies Are Not Work . . . ," Twitter, April 11, 2018, https://twitter.com/TaranaBurke/status/9839497805 84984576.

9 Leesa Renee Hall (leesareneehall), "Money Is the Cheapest Investment," Instagram, December 9, 2018, https://www.instagram.com/p /BrLN3vLn-AD/?utm_source=ig_web_copy_link.

10 Ibid.

11 Robby Soave, "UConn Will Pay White Fragility Author Robin DiAngelo $20,000 to Train School Administrators," *Reason*, August 14, 2020, https://reason.com/2020/08/14/uconn-will-pay-white-fragility-author -robin-diangelo-20000-to-train-school-administrators/.

12 Text message from ShiShi Rose to the author, July 20, 2020.

13 Glennon Doyle, *Untamed* (New York: Dial Press, 2020), p. 210.

14 Ibid., p. 219.

15 Text conversation between ShiShi Rose and the author, July 20, 2020.

fourteen—Acting in Allyship

1 Ericka Hart (ihartericka), Instagram, February 19, 2019, https://www .instagram.com/p/BuEgstLgA1K/?utm_source=ig_web_copy_link.

2 Kénta Xiadani Ch'umil, "Redefining Activism," Momotaro Apotheca, June 4, 2020, https://momotaroapotheca.com/blogs/vaginal-wellness /redefining-activism.

3 Jacobs Institute, "Respecting Our Relations: Dori Tunstall on Decolonizing Design," Medium, January 31, 2019, https://medium.com/@Jacobs DesignCal/respecting-our-relations-dori-tunstall-on-decolonizing-de sign-d894df4c2ed2.

4 Pro-Intersectional Feminism (iwritefeminism), "As Yourself," Instagram, April 28, 2020.

5 Jaya Saxena, "The Safety Pin Symbol for Solidarity Is Being Co-opted by White Supremacists," *Daily Dot*, November 14, 2016, https://www .dailydot.com/irl/white-supremacists-safety-pin/.

6 Florence Given, *Women Don't Owe You Pretty* (London: Cassell, 2020), p. 211.

fifteen—Better Befriending Black Women+?

1 Cooper, *Eloquent Rage*, p. 171.

2 Lorde, *Sister Outsider*, p. 66.

3 Destiny Turner-Vanlear (@thadalaimama), "I Don't Expect . . . ," Twit-

ter, August 8, 2018, https://twitter.com/ThaDalaiMama/status/102731
0259046637568.

sixteen—What's Love Got to Do with It?

1 Ashley Brown, "'Least Desirable'? How Racial Discrimination Plays Out in Online Dating," NPR, January 9, 2018, https://www.npr.org /2018/01/09/575352051/least-desirable-how-racial-discrimination-plays -out-in-online-dating.

2 "Black Women & Domestic Violence," Blackburn Center, February 25, 2020, https://www.blackburncenter.org/post/2020/02/26/black-women -domestic-violence.

3 Cooper, *Eloquent Rage*, p. 195.

4 "Sexual Racism," Wikipedia, https://en.wikipedia.org/wiki/Sexual_rac ism (accessed August 13, 2020).

5 Margaret Goff, "Three Ways Mass Incarceration Affects Women of Color," Urban Institute, March 30, 2018, https://www.urban.org/ur ban-wire/three-ways-mass-incarceration-affects-women-color.

6 "The Problem: DV in LGBTQ Communities & Barriers to Safety," VAWnet.org, https://vawnet.org/sc/rates-and-prevalence-dv-lgbtq-com munities (accessed August 13, 2020).

7 George Yancey, "Crossracial Differences in the Racial Preferences of Potential Dating Partners: A Test of the Alienation of African Americans and Social Dominance Orientation," *Sociological Quarterly* 50, no. 1 (Winter 2009): 121–43, https://doi.org/10.1111/j.1533-8525.2008 .01135.x.

8 Jasmine and Mikey (keyztolili and american_mikey), Instagram, June 3, 2020, https://www.instagram.com/p/CA-IipFFB61/.

9 Shay-Akil McLean, "Patriarchy & Gender," Decolonize ALL the Things, December 30, 2014, https://decolonizeallthethings.com/learning-tools /patriarchy-gender-lesson-plan/.

seventeen—Pay Us What You Owe Us

1 Stephanie Russell-Kraft, "Law Firms Struggle to Hire and Keep Black Women," Bloomberg Law, January 6, 2017, https://news.bloomberglaw .com/business-and-practice/law-firms-struggle-to-hire-and-keep-black -women.

2 Michelle Cheng, "Why Minority Women Now Control Nearly Half of All Women-Run Businesses," *Inc.*, November 2018, https://www .inc.com/magazine/201811/michelle-cheng/minority-women-entrepre neur-founder-womenable.html.

3 Sarah O'Brien, "Here's How the Wage Gap Affects Black Women," CNBC, August 22, 2019, https://www.cnbc.com/2019/08/22/heres -how-the-gender-wage-gap-affects-this-minority-group.html.

4 Ibid.

5 John Schneider and David Auten, "Prudential LGBT Survey Reveals Sexual Orientation Pay Gap," *Forbes*, November 30, 2017, https://www .forbes.com/sites/debtfreeguys/2017/11/30/prudential-lgbt-survey-re veals-sexual-orientation-pay-gap/#67154c751916.

6 Erika Stallings, "The Color of Money," *O, The Oprah Magazine*, September 2019, p. 115.

7 Ibid., p. 116.

8 Ibid.

9 Catherine Ruetschlin and Dedrick Asante-Muhammad, *The Challenge of Credit Card Debt for the African American Middle Class*, NAACP/ Dēmos, December 2013, https://naacp.org/wp-content/uploads/2016 /04/CreditCardDebt-Demos_NAACP.pdf.

10 Ruchika Tulshyan, "Women of Color Get Asked to Do More 'Office Housework.' Here's How They Can Say No," *Harvard Business Review*, April 6, 2018, https://hbr.org/2018/04/women-of-color-get-asked-to-do -more-office-housework-heres-how-they-can-say-no.

11 Ibid.

12 Adia Harvey Wingfield, *Flatlining: Race, Work, and Health Care in the New Economy* (Oakland: University of California Press, 2019), p. 18.

13 Zuhairah Washington and Laura Morgan Roberts, "Women of Color Get Less Support at Work. Here's How Managers Can Change That," *Harvard Business Review*, March 4, 2019, https://hbr.org/2019/03/women -of-color-get-less-support-at-work-heres-how-managers-can-change -that.

14 Chaka L. Bachmann and Becca Gooch, *LGBT in Britain—Work Report*, Stonewall/YouGov, April 2018, https://www.stonewall.org.uk/system /files/lgbt_in_britain_work_report.pdf.

15 Washington and Roberts, "Women of Color Get Less Support."

16 Ibid.

17 Anne Helen Petersen, "How Millenials Became the Burnout Generation," *BuzzFeed*, January 5, 2019, https://www.buzzfeednews.com /article/annehelenpetersen/millennials-burnout-generation-debt-work.

18 Tiana Clark, "This Is What Black Burnout Feels Like," *BuzzFeed*, January 11, 2019, https://www.buzzfeednews.com/article/tianaclarkpoet /millennial-burnout-black-women-self-care-anxiety-depression.

19 Mullan (decolonizingtherapy), "We Are Fucking Exhausted."

20 Jennifer Armbrust, "Proposals for the Feminine Economy," Sister, https://sister.is/proposals-for-the-feminine-economy (accessed July 19, 2020).

21 Kundan Chhabra, "Art as Alchemy and Activism," Medium, March 21, 2018, https://medium.com/@kundanchhabra/art-as-alchemy-and-activism-5e84b6c63004.

22 Gus Wezerek and Kristen R. Ghodsee, "Women's Unpaid Labor Is Worth $10,900,000,000,000," *New York Times*, March 5, 2020, https://www.nytimes.com/interactive/2020/03/04/opinion/women-unpaid-labor.html.

23 Ibid.

24 Armbrust, "Proposals for the Feminine Economy."

25 McKensie Mack (mckensiemack), "Put Trans People in Positions of Leadership . . . ," Instagram, October 29, 2019, https://www.instagram.com/p/B4NCj0GFN8D/?utm_source=ig_web_copy_link.

eighteen—Becoming Unfuckwithable

1 Silvy Khoucasian (silvykhoucasian), "Not Having Boundaries . . . ," Instagram, August 16, 2019, https://www.instagram.com/p/B1PDkiUBfQN/?utm_source=ig_web_copy_link.

2 Quoted in Jee Hei Park (jeeheipark), "Prepare to Be Called a Bully . . . ," Instagram, March 8, 2019, https://www.instagram.com/p/BuwX7S9BeME/?utm_source=ig_web_copy_link.

3 Audre Lorde, "The Master's Tools Will Never Dismantle the Master's House," in Lorde, *Sister Outsider*, pp. 110–14.

4 The Nap Ministry (thenapministry), "Rest Is Resistance," Instagram, July 9, 2020, https://www.instagram.com/p/CCbO_IbpTkU/?utm_source=ig_web_copy_link.

5 Adapted from Molly Shea, "The 7 Types of Rest You Need to Actually Feel Recharged," Shine, July 20, 2020, https://advice.shinetext.com/articles/the-7-types-of-rest-you-need-to-actually-feel-recharged/.

6 Adapted from The Nap Ministry (thenapministry), "Resting Can Look Like . . . ," Instagram, July 14, 2020, https://www.instagram.com/p/CCpbxP5Jx6q/?utm_source=ig_web_copy_link.

nineteen—Rise Up

1 "World's Billionaires Have More Wealth Than 4.6 Billion People," Oxfam International, January 20, 2020, https://www.oxfam.org/en/press-releases/worlds-billionaires-have-more-wealth-46-billion-people.

2 "The World's 8 Richest Men Are Now as Wealthy as Half the World's Population," Reuters, January 16, 2017, https://fortune.com/2017/01/16/world-richest-men-income-equality/.

3 "Coronavirus Disease 2019 (COVID-19)," Centers for Disease Control and Prevention.

4 "A Pipeline through Historically Native Land Has Sparked Protests in Canada," *Economist*, February 20, 2020, https://www.economist.com/the-americas/2020/02/20/a-pipeline-through-historically-native-land-has-sparked-protests-in-canada.

5 Vann R. Newkirk II, "Trump's EPA Concludes Environmental Racism Is Real," *Atlantic*, February 28, 2018, https://www.theatlantic.com/politics/archive/2018/02/the-trump-administration-finds-that-environmental-racism-is-real/554315/.

6 "Resisting Digital Colonialism," Internet Health Report 2018, April 2018, https://internethealthreport.org/2018/resisting-digital-colonialism/.

7 Sam Biddle, "Police Surveilled George Floyd Protests with Help from Twitter-Affiliated Startup Dataminr," *Intercept*, July 9, 2020, https://theintercept.com/2020/07/09/twitter-dataminr-police-spy-surveillance-black-lives-matter-protests/.

8 Jessica Bursztynsky, "More Than 26 Million People Shared Their DNA with Ancestry Firms, Allowing Researchers to Trace Relationships between Virtually All Americans: MIT," CNBC, February 12, 2019, https://www.cnbc.com/2019/02/12/privacy-concerns-rise-as-26-million-share-dna-with-ancestry-firms.html.

9 Bob Fredericks, "China Allegedly Collecting DNA Samples for Surveillance Using US Tech," *New York Post*, June 17, 2020, https://nypost.com/2020/06/17/china-gathering-dna-samples-for-surveillance-using-us-tech-report/.

10 Collins et al., *Dreams Deferred*.

11 "Future Skills: A Conversation with President Barack Obama," Economic Club of Canada & the Global Institute for Conscious Economics, Metro Toronto Convention Centre, Toronto, January 23, 2020.

12 Roger Pielke, "The World Is Not Going to Halve Carbon Emissions by 2030, So Now What?" *Forbes*, October 27, 2019, https://www.forbes.com/sites/rogerpielke/2019/10/27/the-world-is-not-going-to-reduce-carbon-dioxide-emissions-by-50-by-2030-now-what/#40091cdf3794.

13 DeNeen L. Brown, "Martin Luther King Jr.'s Scorn for 'White Moderates' in His Birmingham Jail Letter," *Washington Post*, January 15, 2018,

https://www.washingtonpost.com/news/retropolis/wp/2018/01/15/martin-luther-king-jr-s-scathing-critique-of-white-moderates-from-the-birmingham-jail/.

14 Alaa Elassar, "Rihanna Calls on Friends and Allies to 'Pull Up' during Powerful Speech at 2020 NAACP Image Awards," CNN, February 23, 2020, https://www.cnn.com/2020/02/23/us/rihanna-naacp-presidents-award-speech-trnd/index.html.

15 Beth Berry, "In the Absence of the Village, Mothers Struggle Most," Revolution from Home, April 26, 2016, https://revolutionfromhome.com/2016/04/absence-village-mothers-struggle/.

16 Aaron Philip (aaron__philip), "On This #TDoV," Instagram, March 31, 2020, https://www.instagram.com/p/B-Zug38lWun/.

17 Quoted in Kevin E. Trenberth, "Are We Good Stewards of the Planet Earth?," graduation address, Bridge School, Boulder, CO, May 30, 2008. Available at http://www.cgd.ucar.edu/cas/Trenberth/website-archive/gradSp2-moved.pdf (accessed July 20, 2020).

ABOUT THE AUTHOR

RACHEL RICKETTS is a queer, multiracial Black woman. As a global thought leader, racial justice educator, healer, speaker, and writer, she hosts intersectional racial justice workshops worldwide, including her renowned Spiritual Activism series. Rachel cultivates change by fusing her experiences as an attorney, a trained anti-racism educator, and a grief coach with her spiritual certifications in breathwork, yoga, mindfulness, and Reiki. She has helped numerous global brands with anti-racism efforts, including Google, WeWork, and Lululemon. Rachel was named one of Well+Good's 2020 Changemakers and has been featured in international media such as *The New York Times*, *Cosmopolitan*, *Goop*, and *The Atlantic*. She loves donuts, dancing, disruption, and all things metaphysical (ideally at the same time). Learn more about Rachel at **rachelricketts.com** and on Instagram **@iamrachelricketts**.